WHAT
YOU
STILL
DON'T
KNOW
ABOUT
MALE SEXUALITY

WHAT YOU **STILL** DON'T KNOW ABOUT MALE SEXUALITY

Dr. Barry McCarthy

Thomas Y. Crowell Company   Established 1834   New York

Designed by Joy Chu

Manufactured in the United States of America

Library of Congress Cataloging in Publication Data

McCarthy, Barry W   1943-
What you still don't know about male sexuality.

Bibliography: p.
Includes index.
1. Men—Sexual behavior.   2.   Masculinity.   I.   Title.
HQ28.M3   301.41'76'32   77-4239
ISBN 0-690-01443-0

10 9 8 7 6 5 4 3 2 1

ACKNOWLEDGMENTS

MOST BOOKS, and especially one on a topic like male sexuality, reflect the present state of knowledge and attitudes in the culture. The material presented here is strongly influenced by the writing and research of four people—Alfred Kinsey, William Masters and Virginia Johnson, and James McCary—all of whom have contributed greatly to the field.

The book itself began as a joint process with three other psychologists who were in a sense my coauthors: Dr. Sally Kugler, Mr. Blake Chaffee, and Dr. Fred Johnson. I very much appreciate their work on earlier drafts and revisions, and their valued criticism and continued support. One of the things I've learned in doing this book is that I'm a better psychologist and sex therapist than writer, and I have very much appreciated and enjoyed working on the final draft with an excellent writer, Ken Gewertz. It has been a real pleasure to see my dull writing changed to an interesting and readable form with little or no loss of content.

Many others have contributed to bringing this book to fruition, including my agent, Ann Buchwald, whose support and knowledge were critical; Crowell's editor-in-chief, Paul Fargis, who saw promise in the book; and Beverly Bush, who had to decipher my horrible handwriting. My editor, Arnold Dolin, deserves a great deal of credit and admiration for guiding the book through innumerable revisions.

Another source of information and support came from my students and clients, who allowed me to better understand their lives and feelings.

This book is dedicated to my wife and children. To Emily, who has helped me tremendously, and to Mark, Kara, and Paul, who have taught me to be a father. Hopefully, we will be able to live out the attitudes and guidelines expressed in this book.

CONTENTS

WHAT
YOU
STILL
DON'T
KNOW
ABOUT
MALE SEXUALITY

1
The Myth of the Male Machine, or Keeping up Appearances

IF YOU ARE READING THIS, it is probably because you think there might be something about male sexuality that you still don't know. If you happen to be in a bookstore or have found this book on a friend's coffee table, and there are people present who may be watching you as you read, chances are that you are feeling self-conscious. After all, men aren't supposed to have to read about sex. They are supposed to know all about it already. Acknowledging that there is still something left to learn is a sign of weakness, an admission that you are not the man you ought to be.

It is pity that so many men feel this way because the present era is unparalleled in the amount of information that has come to light on human sexuality. Surveys and laboratory studies have provided definitive answers to questions about human sexual functioning and behavior that for years were matters of conjecture. The herculean investigations of Dr. Alfred Kinsey, for example (*Sexual Behavior in the Human Male*, 1948, and *Sexual Behavior in the Human Female*, 1953), demonstrated that the sexual activity of most of us was neither excessive nor unusual, but fit comfortably into a wide spectrum of variation. After Kinsey, it became plain that everyone had a sex life, a fact that had often been cast in doubt during the long sexual cover-up of the Victorian age. Another great milestone came with the publication in 1966 of *Human Sexual Response* by Dr. William H. Masters and Virginia E. Johnson. Using an array of medical testing instruments as well as a movie camera, these pioneering sex researchers studied the physiological responses of volunteers engaging in sexual intercourse and masturbation in the laboratory. From this innovative and controversial method of investigation came a wealth of fresh data on the ways in which humans actually respond to sexual stimulation. With the publication of Masters and Johnson's *Human Sexual Inadequacy* in 1970, we gained an understanding not only of sexual response but also of how to deal with sexual dysfunction and promote better functioning and more pleasurable sexual experiences.

"But what does that have to do with me?" you may ask. The answer is that the findings of sex researchers are important to all of us. Although sexuality is a natural, physiological function, our sexual attitudes and behavior are learned. Our sexuality can be a source of great pleasure, a means of intimate communication, an expression of affection—or it can be a cause of pain and unhappiness. Whether sex has a positive or negative effect on our lives depends at least in part on whether our sexual attitudes are based on ignorance and misinformation or on fact. Obtaining accurate information about sex is often the first step in making a good sexual adjustment.

Unfortunately, few of us are really well informed about sex. In fact, it has been estimated that only about one out of four men in our society has received an adequate sex education. Despite the fact that the subject of sex seems to permeate the contemporary media, sexual myths and misconceptions continue to be prevalent. Many generally well-informed and sophisticated men unquestioningly accept certain beliefs about sex that are in fact completely untrue. If you doubt that you are one of these, you might find it instructive to take the following test. Simply read each statement and indicate whether it is true or false.

1. The size of a man's penis is an indication of the strength of his sex drive.
2. The larger the penis, the greater the stimulation for the woman during intercourse.
3. A man's sexuality peaks during adolescence. After the age of twenty, his sexual ability, his interest, and his enjoyment of sex all decline.
4. It is natural for a man to be interested chiefly in intercourse and orgasm. Foreplay and affectionate touching appeal mostly to women.
5. The ability to ejaculate rapidly is a sign of masculinity.

6. If you have experienced impotence once, it is likely that you will have a major sex problem.
7. The extent of a man's success in his first intercourse experience is usually an indication of how successful he will be during the rest of his sexual life.
8. On the average, black men have larger penises than white men and also have a stronger sex drive.
9. Masturbation is detrimental to a man's sexual ability.
10. A liking for oral-genital sex is a sign of latent homosexuality.
11. Male and female sexual responses are essentially different from one another.
12. Having homosexual fantasies or feeling attraction for other men is usually a sign of latent homosexuality.
13. Homosexuality is generally considered a form of mental illness.
14. The most natural position for sexual intercourse is the male superior.
15. A healthy, well-adjusted man should have no trouble performing sexually in any situation.
16. Since conception takes place in the woman's body, it is her responsibility to prevent an unwanted pregnancy.
17. Erection is always a sign of sexual excitement and indicates a need for intercourse on the part of the male.
18. A good lover is able to give his partner an orgasm each time they have intercourse.
19. Some men are just naturally better lovers than others. While you may be able to learn certain sexual skills, you will never be able to match the performance of someone who has more inborn ability than you do.
20. Simultaneous orgasm is the most fulfilling sexual goal for a couple.
21. The normal frequency of intercourse for a couple in their twenties or thirties is four times a week. Having intercourse less often indicates that you have a low sex drive.
22. Sexual intercourse should be avoided during menstruation and pregnancy.
23. People who have suffered a heart attack or a stroke had better avoid intercourse.
24. Women respond to sexual stimulation much more slowly than men and must be "worked on" by their partners to get them ready for intercourse.

25. When a man reaches adulthood, he naturally loses interest in fantasy and masturbation and concentrates exclusively on intercourse.

If you answered true for any of the above statements, then there are things you can learn about sexuality because *every one of the twenty-five statements is false*. They are all common sex myths which are widely accepted to this day despite overwhelming scientific evidence to the contrary. Moreover, they have led to incalculable dissatisfaction, frustration, insecurity, and misunderstanding for both men and women.

But while inaccurate information about sex is detrimental to men and women, it is men who are more likely to perpetuate and cling to the old sex myths. Because men are expected to be sexually knowledgeable, it is difficult for them to admit that they may be ignorant or misinformed. Because they cannot admit their ignorance, they will not allow themselves to ask questions and to be receptive to sexual information. And in the absence of accurate information, the old and damaging sex myths are perpetuated *ad infinitum*.

The situation brings to mind the story of Socrates and the Delphic Oracle. In Plato's dialogue *The Apology*, Plato's master, Socrates, is defending himself against a charge of corrupting the minds of Athenian youth. He has been accused of setting himself up as an authority on all things, of believing himself wiser than all other men. In defending himself, Socrates explains to the court how the charge came to be made. He says that in the past a student of his went to the Delphic Oracle to inquire whether there was anyone else in the world wiser than Socrates. The Greeks put their faith in the Delphic Oracle much as we put our faith today in the Gallup or Roper polls. In answer to the student's question, the oracle replied that no, there was no one wiser than Socrates.

Hearing of the answer the oracle had given, Socrates was perplexed, for he himself knew that his wisdom was not very great. Yet he knew that the oracle could not tell a lie. So he decided to try to understand what the oracle had said by testing it. He went to all the men with the greatest reputations and questioned them, seeking to learn how wise they were. He found that while many of these men had great knowledge within their own fields, all of them made the mistake of assuming that their knowledge extended to other fields as well, about which they really knew very little. Finally, Socrates came to understand the meaning of the oracle's answer: He is the wisest of men who, like Socrates, *knows that he does not know.*

When it comes to sex, it is apparent that the wisest of men aren't men at all, but women. For women are far more receptive than we are to information and advice on sexuality. They are far more willing to admit their lack of knowledge and expertise, while we tend to be smug sexual know-it-alls convinced that what we don't already know isn't worth learning. Women, on the other hand, seem to be more capable of recognizing that there is room for improvement.

Walk into any bookstore or library and look at the books on sexuality. You will see many volumes for, by, and about women, but hardly any devoted to the subject of male sexuality. The receptivity of women to advice on sexuality is well known. With us the case is different. Publishers assume (and not without reason) that we will turn away from such books with a shrug of "Who needs it? I know it already."

It is not only in bookstores that one sees evidence of the male know-it-all attitude toward sex. I have encountered it many times myself in my work as a college teacher. For eight years I have taught a course in human sexual behavior in the psychology department at a large metropolitan university. Not only do roughly twice as many female students enroll in the course but males tend to ask fewer questions and rarely take part in class discussions. Generally speaking, the female students are no more embarrassed to reveal their incomplete knowledge of human sexual behavior than they would be to confess their ignorance of organic chemistry or symbolic logic. As a result, they seem to derive far greater benefit from the course.

This reluctance on the part of most men to learn about sex from books or in classroom situations extends to an uneasiness about exchanging sexual information on a personal basis as well. Few fathers are able to communicate freely with their sons about human sexuality. Far too often, sex is a taboo subject in the home until the father finally decides that it is time for him to inform his son about the "facts of life," or to give him a package of rubbers and tell him to stay out of trouble. This father-son confrontation often takes the form of a brief, awkward lecture that answers only such basic questions as who puts what where, if even that. Since the father himself probably harbors many misconceptions about sex, he is likely to pass these on to his son. Moreover, since the son has been discouraged from thinking of his parents as sexual beings all his life, and because he senses his father's discomfort, he is usually unwilling to ask questions in order to clarify the points he does not understand.

The reluctance to discuss sex frankly and openly affects other male relationships besides that between father and son. It is very rare to find young males who are truthful with each other about their first sex experiences. The best available statistics show that about 20 percent of all males are unsuccessful in their first intercourse, generally because they fail to achieve or maintain an erection or because they ejaculate before the penis enters the vagina. One out of five is a substantial proportion, enough to make the experience a rather common one. And yet, can you imagine the following dialogue taking place?

"Hey, Jimmy, how'd it go with Harriet last night?"
"Not too good, Fred. I couldn't get a hard on."
"Well, don't worry about it, Jim You'll do better next time."

It is far more likely that Jimmy would claim that he had performed like a prize bull, even if his experience with Harriet had been the greatest fiasco of his young life. Or, if Jimmy were so foolish as to admit that he had been impotent, it is probable that Fred would never let him hear the end of it. We are not kind to each other where sex is concerned. People who harbor anxieties and insecurities rarely are.

Thus, most of us end up cheating ourselves out of a great deal of sexual pleasure. Not only are we expected to be sexually knowledgeable without having received adequate instruction but we are also expected to perform flawlessly at every sexual opportunity. Trying to live up to these impossible demands is likely to cause anxiety and insecurity. For many men, sex is a bluff, a desperate struggle to maintain the image of the infallible "male machine." When sex becomes so competitive, so performance-oriented, there is little room left for pleasure.

The size of our equipment, the number of times we can come— these are the things that concern us, not how much enjoyment we derive from the sexual experience. Most destructive of all is the notion that we must never default, never fail to perform. According to the commonly accepted standard, a "real man" is able and willing to have sex anytime, anywhere, with any available female. It rarely occurs to us that the ability to meet such demands is simply not human. Absolute reliability is a standard that is applied to machines, not people. And yet, this is precisely what we appear to be demanding of ourselves.

The time has come for us to escape from the rigid and oppressive male image that has for so long prevented us from fully enjoying our sexuality. Women have already begun sloughing off their socially imposed image, and we may be able to learn a great deal from their example. The object of the feminist movement is not to put down men, but to defeat the confining and inhuman conventions that frustrate both men and women. As a result of this effort, there has been an awakening of women's sense of themselves as autonomous beings, in control of and responsible for their own sexuality. It is a shame that many men feel threatened by women who insist on being equal both as people and as sex partners. As we shall see later in this book, the most enjoyable sexual experiences result when both the man and woman are able to understand and express their own sexual needs as well as respond to those of their partner.

The object of this book is not to transform the reader into a superlover whose performances will leave his partners panting for more. Understanding a woman's anatomy and pattern of response and knowing the kinds of stimulation that are most effective in producing arousal and orgasm are necessary aspects of being a good lover, but they are not the most important. A good lover is not just a technician; he is someone who can enjoy and be involved in the feelings of tenderness, intimacy, and erotic response that occur during sexual interaction. In addition to knowing how to give pleasure, he is able to accept it as well. He sees himself as deserving of pleasure, and he understands that lovemaking is not just a skill to be practiced within the confines of the bedroom, but rather is one expression of a general feeling of comfort, affection, and communication between partners.

Thus, the purpose of this book is twofold. It is, on the one hand, to present the most accurate, reliable information presently available on male sexuality and on topics related to male sexual functioning. On the other hand, it is to help the male reader integrate his sexuality with the rest of his life in a way that will bring him greater fulfillment and satisfaction. The book is addressed to men, but women are encouraged to read it as well. Indeed, since sex is the most intimate form of human communication, it can be extremely beneficial to a couple's relationship for a woman to gain some insight into the needs and conflicts that affect her man.

This book covers all the aspects of sex which I have found to be of interest or importance to most men. You can read the chapters consecutively as a survey of male sexuality, or use the book as a reference source to be consulted about specific questions and problems. In certain instances, where there is a question of sexual attitudes and values, I have committed myself to a particular position on the basis of my personal and professional experience. However, you need to take into account your own unique background, experiences, and values in deciding how relevant my recommendations are to your own life. In my opinion, the range of normal sexual behavior takes in any private activity between consenting individuals which provides a sense of sharing and pleasure, is not coercive, does not involve children, and is not physically or psychologically destructive. The choice is yours and depends on what you and your partner find satisfying and pleasurable.

My preparation for writing about male sexuality has included not only formal training and study in the field of psychology but also many of the experiences, both negative and positive, that form the typical background of the majority of males in our society. As a boy in Chicago, I received no real sex education from family, church, or school. What knowledge I had came largely from my peers, and if, as a young man, I had taken the sex-myth quiz presented earlier in this chapter, I would have done very poorly. Like most of my friends, I thought of sex primarily in terms of conquest. Although I managed to "score" with a fair number of sex partners, my achievements never seemed quite up to par, and I invariably exaggerated them. I took little responsibility in these early encounters, usually leaving contraception up to the woman. Nor did it occur to me to care about or even notice my partners' responses. When I was twenty-one, I began an affair which lasted for about a year and a half, and this was the first time I began to relate to a sex partner on a person-to-person basis—an important learning experience for me.

At the age of twenty-three, I started graduate work in psychology at Southern Illinois University. It was there that I met Emily, and we were married less than a year later. But despite the closeness and affection we felt for each other, I carried with me into the marriage many of the erroneous and destructive assumptions about sex and sex roles which I had picked up earlier in my life. This led to problems and conflicts that had to be worked out between us. Although we never had a sexual dysfunction problem, our sexual relations were only mediocre at first, and it took us well over a year before we became comfortable with sex and were able to communicate, experiment, and be spontaneous. Today, after eleven years of marriage and three children (two biological, one adopted), sex continues to improve for Emily and me. I attribute this not only to the fact that we care deeply about each other but also to the accurate sexual information and positive attitudes gained through my work in psychology, first as a psychology intern in a hospital and later as a therapist, college teacher, and counselor.

My decision to go into the field of sex therapy came about, as such decisions so often do, quite accidentally. I happened to choose a research project in sexual dysfunction and found, to my surprise, that there had been very little work done in that field. This aroused my interest and eventually led me to enter sex therapy professionally. I feel that my work as a professional has given me a rather practical viewpoint on sexuality. It seems to me that most sexual unhappiness is a result of poor learning experiences. In many cases, sexual functioning and sexual satisfaction can be improved tremendously, as it was for me, just by retracing those early steps to gain a better understanding of one's sexuality and then setting off again with a positive and open attitude.

I do not believe that being male is something that one should be ashamed of or apologetic about. Nor do I think that men, either individually or as a group, have to atone for the sins of male chauvinism. No amount of breast-beating can cause relations between a man and woman to become more pleasurable or rewarding. What is needed is not guilt, but communication, understanding, sensitivity. When these are achieved, there is no limit to the pleasure that can be derived from a sexual relationship.

In the following chapters I will be dealing with various topics relating to the male sexual life cycle, with specific sexual problems encountered by men, with methods of enhancing your self-concept and ability to function sexually, and with certain decisions and responsibilities that are a necessary part of your sexuality. Throughout, I will draw on case studies of clients that I have treated as a sex therapist (their identities have been disguised), as well as my own personal experiences, to provide relevant illustrations of the points being discussed.

This is basically a book of ideas and information, not a book of do-it-yourself sex therapy or a treatise on sexual techniques. If, by presenting an integrated and positive view of male sexuality, my book can help readers reexamine their attitudes toward sexuality and regain some of the pleasure and fulfillment which their traditional preconceptions have robbed them of, it will have amply served its purpose.

2
The World's Greatest Pleasure Apparatus — Your Body

ALMOST FROM THE MOMENT we are born, we are fascinated by our bodies. At first it is the mere sensation of having limbs that can extend and contract and thrash about, which is an endless source of exhilaration and delight. Later we learn to coordinate our movements with what we see and discover the distinction between ourselves and the outside world. Within the first year of our development, we find that we can produce enjoyable sensations by rubbing and stroking our genitals: sexual awareness is born. This awareness grows as we mature. Not only is it quite natural for young children to stimulate themselves but it is also natural for them to be intensely curious about their own sex organs—and those of others around them. Examining and comparing genitals, mutual genital touching, playing "doctor"—these activities are all a normal part of the process of growing up and are engaged in by the vast majority of children of both sexes. These early experiences of looking, touching, and exploring are important in developing a positive attitude toward oneself, one's body, and sexuality.

Unfortunately, as children, most of us have received strong messages of disapproval which discourage us from pursuing these exploratory practices. We learn that our bodies, and especially our genitals, are something to be hidden, to be ashamed of. Very conservative parents often go as far as to teach their children that they should even avoid looking at their own bodies. As a result of this negative learning, the natural curiosity we once had about our bodies is blunted. We tell ourselves that the time for self-exploration is over, that we have outgrown such childish pursuits, that there is nothing left to learn. Actually, the average adult knows surprisingly little about his body generally and his genitals specifically. Obeying the dictates laid down by his parents, he imagines that he is acting virtuously by paying as little attention to them as possible, by maintaining a state of detached ignorance. Needless to say, such an attitude detracts from a person's capacity to enjoy and feel comfortable with his sexuality.

Why not give way to that long-suppressed childhood curiosity and become reacquainted with your body? Find a time when you have fifteen or twenty minutes of privacy—it could be the next time you take a bath or shower—and set it aside for sexual self-exploration. Take off your clothes and sit down on the bed or on the floor. A full-length mirror will be helpful because it gives you total view. You may also want to use a hand mirror to look at hard-to-see areas. Relax and, above all, put aside any gnawing thoughts that you are doing something wicked or unhealthy. You are only taking a good look at your body, and who has a better right to look at it than you?

Start with the testicles (or balls, if you prefer—there's really no reason to favor medical or "polite" terms over common usage). Hold them in your hand, using your hand mirror to examine them from all sides. Let yourself become conscious of their weight and shape. You needn't be afraid of hurting them. All of us know from experience how painful a low blow can be, but under normal circumstances, the testicles are surprisingly resilient. Even our dependence on athletic supporters for strenuous activities is largely a learned need. Male animals, whose testicles are no less vulnerable than ours, engage in physical activities that make human athletics seem tame and yet suffer no ill effects. Among primitive peoples, males often run, dance, and fight without wearing supporters, and they experience no genital injury.

The testicles are the principal male sex glands. Inside the two egg-shaped bodies, there are one to two feet of fine tubing, packed in like spaghetti into a mold. These are called the seminiferous tubules, and it is within them that the sperm are manufactured. The testicles also manufacture the male sex hormone, testosterone, which is responsible for triggering the development of male physical characteristics. In combination with psychological factors, testosterone also contributes to regulating the sex drive. So efficient are the testicles in maintaining a satisfactory testosterone level that if one of them is removed in surgery, the remaining testicle is quite capable of carrying on by itself without any decrease in sexual functioning. If you do suspect that your testicles or any other part of your sexual system is not functioning properly, the person to see is a urologist. A physician specializing in complaints of the genito-urinary tract, the urologist is the closest thing, for men, to a gynecologist.

Sperm are created by the millions in the testicles. Once they are mature, they leave the testicles by way of the vas deferens, two soft, thin tubes which you can feel going up into the body cavity. The vas leads into the seminal vesicles, storage chambers for the sperm, and thence into the prostate. It is in the prostate that the sperm are mixed with seminal fluid, the whitish, alkaline liquid that spurts from the penis during ejaculation. Sperm are extremely tiny, con-tributing only slightly to the total volume of the ejaculate, the major portion of which consists of seminal fluid, or semen. Thus, when the vas deferens is severed in the vasectomy operation, only sperm are left out of the picture. A sterilized male continues to ejaculate sem-inal fluid as before, with no noticeable decrease in force, amount, or enjoyment.

The testicles are housed in a bag of loose, wrinkled skin called the scrotum. In most cases, one testicle, usually the left, hangs lower than the other. As every male knows, the scrotum can contract or relax, at times allowing the testicles to dangle freely against the thighs, at other times drawing them up into a neat, tight package. These changes are brought about by tiny muscles in the scrotum, largely in response to a rise or fall in temperature. In order to manufacture sperm, the testicles must be a few degrees cooler than body temperature. The scrotum's ability to tighten and loosen is a device for regulating this temperature. When it is cold, the muscles contract, warming the testicles by bringing them in close contact with the body. When the outside temperature rises, the opposite occurs, and the testicles are given an airing to cool them off.

The scrotal muscles also come into play during sexual excitement. When a man is very aroused, his testicles rise in the scrotum and also increase in size. If his arousal does not culminate in ejaculation, the swelling remains, causing an uncomfortable condition popularly known as "blue balls." This is temporary, however, and causes no permanent damage.

Emerging just above the scrotum is the base of the penis. It is unlikely that there are many men who have not handled and looked at their penis. It is the focus of such intense emotional feelings for most men that probably few are able to regard it dispassionately. You may be proud of it, ashamed of it, anxious about it, afraid of it, or have mixed feelings about it, but it is unlikely that you think of it with quite the same attitude as you have, for example, toward your ear. Yet the penis is, after all, an organ like any other, adapted for specific purposes.

So it should be an interesting experience for you at this point to try to clear your mind of all preconceived notions and to look at your penis as if you have never seen it before. The penis is composed chiefly of spongy erectile tissue. There are, in fact, three distinct cylindrical bodies, two on top and one underneath, which are bound together by sheets of thin membrane. The three cylindrical bodies are what give the penis its somewhat triangular cross section when it is erect. Erection occurs when blood enters the penis through arteries running through the erectile tissue. Simultaneously, muscles near the base of the penis contract, preventing the blood from leaving the penis through the veins. Erection is triggered by nerve centers in the lower spinal column. The actual stimulus that causes erection may come from the brain in the form of erotic thoughts or impressions, or it may come from direct tactile contact. The first kind of erection, sometimes called "spontaneous erection," is more common in younger men. As men become older, they usually find that they need more stroking and rubbing of the penis and the genital area in order to obtain an erection. This is not an indication that they are becoming impotent—impotence is not one of the normal symptoms of aging in men—it just means that their pattern of sexual response is changing.

Erection is a natural physiological response. A newborn male baby usually has his first erection within a few minutes of delivery. Every night while sleeping, whether he is dreaming or not, or whether he is currently sexually active or not, the typical male has an erection about every 90 minutes, thus having four or five erections during his night's sleep. Laboratory studies have been done with ninety-year-old men in good health who have been able to get erections and function sexually.

The head of the penis is called the glans, Latin for "acorn." For the majority of males, the glans is the most sensitive part of the penis, having an extremely high concentration of nerve endings. Usually, the most sensitive area of the glans is the ridge at its base called the corona. On the underside of the penis, where the corona divides into a sort of swallowtail shape, there is a small flange of skin joining the glans to the shaft. This is known as the frenum, and it too is frequently highly sensitive. These areas of greatest sensitivity vary according to the individual. Some men, for example, may find that the shaft of their penis is more sensitive than the glans. Some enjoy having their anal area stimulated, while others may find this not at all pleasurable.

In uncircumcised men, the foreskin, or prepuce, extends over the glans but retracts when the penis becomes erect. Jews, Muslims, and many other ethnic and religious groups remove the foreskin in an operation known as circumcision. During the last few decades, circumcision has become a common practice in many advanced nations, but for health reasons rather than religious or cultural ones. The oily substance emitted by the Tyson's glands, located just behind the corona, collects under the uncircumcised foreskin to form a smelly deposit called smegma. Smegma can be eliminated by regular cleanings, but when it is not, it may become a source of infection and, possibly, of penile cancer. Opponents of circumcision have maintained that removal of the foreskin renders a man less sensitive to sexual stimulation and reduces his enjoyment of the sex act. But since it is in the glans and not the foreskin that the concentration of nerve endings is highest, this seems rather unlikely. In any case, there is not the least shred of evidence to back up this assertion, so anyone who feels that his capacity for arousal is not what it should be is wasting time if he tries to pin the blame on his obstetrician.

One reason it is particularly important to get our facts straight about the male sexual anatomy and physiology is that this area of knowledge is one which has always been obscured by myth, superstition, and misinformation. Perhaps this is because the subject of the sex organs is such an emotionally charged one for the majority of men. Thus, men who readily accept scientific findings in other fields will often stubbornly perpetuate myths about the sex organs as though a loyalty to unsubstantiated sexual folklore was one of the prerequisites of being truly male. One myth that continues to exert a powerful influence in the face of scientifically established fact concerns penis size. Therefore, in the interest of eliminating the baleful effects of such sexual myths, I think it might be beneficial to discuss this particular subject in some detail.

Penis size differences (or imagined differences) have been the basis for an enormous amount of male anxiety. Perhaps the sense of inadequacy has its roots in the childhood experience of a young boy comparing his father's penis with his own. To a child, an adult penis may seem so large and formidable that he can hardly imagine his own organ ever growing to that size. Once such a feeling of inadequacy takes root, it is very easily reinforced. One way this commonly occurs is through the practice of making comparisons between one's own penis and those of other males, often in the steamy underworld of the locker room. What male has not found himself glancing (surreptitiously, of course, so as not to be mistaken for a homosexual) at the genitals of other men as they change into their swimsuits or gym shorts and finding, to his dismay, that nearly all of them seem larger than his own?

Actually, such a comparison is misleading for two reasons. First, as the result of perspective, a penis of the same size may look larger when it is seen from a distance as part of someone else's body than when it is seen from above as part of one's own. Second, it is very misleading to judge the size of a penis when it is in the flaccid state. Studies have shown that, generally speaking, the larger a man's penis when limp, the less it will increase in size when erect. In other words, penises that are smaller in the flaccid state have a greater erective potential. Thus, there tends to be an equalizing factor in the matter of penis size, and the variations in size among erect penises are much less than one might suspect.

There are individual variations, of course, just as there are variations in body size. (Penis length varies much less than body height, however; nor are height and penis size at all related.) The average penis is from 2 1/2 to 4 inches long in the flaccid state and from 5 1/2 to 6 1/2 inches long when erect, with a diameter of about 1 inch when limp and about 1 1/2 inches when erect. But these are only averages, and, like most averages, they do not mean much, except perhaps that someone, somewhere, has been very busy with a measuring tape. I think it would be far more accurate to say that a normal penis is one that is of proper size to function in intercourse. This definition, as we will soon see, is one that takes in just about all of us.

The idea that men with larger penises have a stronger sex drive and are capable of greater sexual performance would appear to be a matter of common sense. After all, the larger a man's muscles are, the stronger he usually is. However, as anyone who has taken a course in elementary logic knows, the analogy can be a highly misleading form of reasoning. And the speciousness of this particular idea becomes clear when we examine the results of controlled, scientific testing. Masters and Johnson have spent years observing the sexual functioning of hundreds of subjects under laboratory conditions, and they have found no relationship whatever between penis size and sexual ability.

The related idea that a large penis is capable of giving a woman more pleasure than a small one may be based on the mistaken notion that it is the vagina which is the source of a woman's sexual pleasure. Actually, a woman's most sensitive genital area is the clitoris—a small, cylindrical organ located at the top of the vestibule at the joining of the labia minora. The clitoris has, in fact, fully as many nerve endings as the penis, concentrated into a much smaller area. It is the focal point of sexual pleasure in the female, just as the penis is the focal point for the male. During intercourse, the clitoris is stimulated by the pulling and rubbing action caused by the couple's pelvic thrusts—a stimulation that is in no way dependent on the penis size. The vagina, on the other hand, which is in direct contact with the penis itself, has few nerve endings and is not particularly sensitive to sexual stimulation. Moreover, the vagina is an extremely elastic organ that adjusts to the penis almost immediately, whether it is large or small. The idea of sexual incompatibility based on the size of a couple's sexual organs is, perhaps with extremely rare exceptions, a myth. Because of the distensible nature of the vagina, virtually any man and woman should be well suited, at least physically, to give each other pleasure.

It must be admitted, of course, that some women may be attracted to men with large penises in much the same way that some men are attracted to women with large breasts. Pornographic films, magazines, and books—with their emphasis on physical endowments—are probably at least partially to blame for encouraging a female obsession with men who are "hung," just as they encourage a male obsession with women who are "stacked." Similarly, they probably reinforce feelings of inadequacy among men and women who think they are not well endowed. But, as we have seen, a woman who imagines that a large organ automatically makes a man an excellent lover is just as naive as a man who believes that all large-breasted women are necessarily good in bed. A passion for size, on the part of either a man or a woman, may be seen, essentially, as a preference and, as such, it is that individual's personal concern. Why should you let someone else's taste serve as a criterion for passing judgment on your own anatomy?

In the last analysis, whatever nature has given us is ours to make the most of. Nor do we have much cause to accuse nature of favoring some men over others. With extremely rare exceptions, we are all about equally suited physically to both give and receive sexual pleasure. Great lovers are made, not born. The ability to enjoy sex and to make sex enjoyable for your partner is primarily dependent on the extent of your knowledge, skill, sensitivity, imagination, and ability to communicate—all of which are a matter of learning and experience, not natural endowment. Once a man becomes aware of his real potential as a lover, once he learns how truly satisfying his sex life can be if he gives up performance-oriented sex for pleasure-oriented sex, the question of size can be forgotten.

3
Masturbation: No Fun for the Fastest Gun

Father to son, upon finding him masturbating: "Stop that!
   Don't you know masturbation can make you go blind?"
Son to father: "Aw, Dad. Can't I just keep it up until I get
   nearsighted?"

THERE IS MUCH that this little dialogue can tell us about the significance of masturbation in the lives of most men. The father's warning
typifies an older, repressive attitude that saw blindness as only one of
a number of ills that were the inevitable result of "self-abuse." The
son's reply, however, expresses an opposing point of view, based not
on pseudomedical theory, but on the truth of experience. Masturbation is fun, he is saying. Masturbation is a *lot* of fun—perhaps not
worth losing your eyesight over, but certainly worth having to wear
glasses.

While most of us would privately agree with the boy that masturbation is fun, few would admit to such an unabashed enthusiasm for
it. Adolescents do often compare notes on their masturbatory experiences and may at times masturbate together—either in pairs or
in larger groups. But once heterosexual relations become a reality,
or even a possibility, masturbation is often pushed into the closet. "I
don't need it anymore," a young man might say, which is essentially a
way of bragging that his sex life is so full that there is simply nothing
left over for autoeroticism. But it is only in rare cases that such a
boast comes anywhere near the truth. The average young, middle-

class, unmarried male has intercourse relatively infrequently. Petting to orgasm may account for another, probably somewhat larger, share of his sexual activity. By far the largest portion of his sexual outlet occurs in the form of masturbation; yet it is only with the utmost reluctance and shame that he is likely to admit to this. Married men have an even tougher time confessing the truth. Surveys show that a large percentage of men continue to masturbate occasionally after marriage. Yet most men seem to consider masturbation within the marital situation an "abnormality," an indulgence for which there is no justification.

Such an attitude is difficult to understand. Few of us believe anymore that masturbation is physically harmful. Nor would many of us deny that it is pleasurable. Is it not strange then that a harmless pleasure should generate such strong disapproval and guilt feelings?

Actually, it is not strange at all when one considers the prevailing male attitude toward sexuality. For the average male, sex is a goal-oriented activity. The ultimate object is heterosexual intercourse culminating in orgasm; if the man "gives" his partner an orgasm, too, so much the better. Anything else is considered a failure or, at best, merely a step on the road to success. Thus, adolescent boys will confront a peer returning from a date with the question, "What did you get off her?" "I got tit" is pretty good. "I got two fingers in" is better. But the greatest achievement is, of course, to have had intercourse—to have "scored". The male who has scored the most frequently is apt to be envied the most by his friends. Clearly, where heterosexual relations are concerned, particularly among young males, quantity is everything, quality practically nothing. The young man who reports to his friends that he and his girl friend merely caressed each other's face for an hour but that it was a "fantastic experience" would probably be ridiculed since he failed to acquire any of the recognized "trophies."

Since intercourse is the male's ultimate sexual goal, it follows that masturbation, which does not contribute directly to the achievement of that goal, serves no practical purpose and is therefore unjustified. All that it produces is pleasure, and pleasure, from the male point of view, is not acceptable as an end in itself.

Because of the warnings we have been given as children, and because of its reputation as "a poor substitute for intercourse," most of us feel guilty when we do engage in masturbation. This does not stop us from doing it, however. Studies show that about 95 percent of men, including married men, do masturbate. The unfortunate aspect of this situation is not that we are so lacking in self-control, but that our guilt feelings can prevent us from enjoying masturbation to the fullest, and can prevent us from making masturbation the liberating and satisfying experience it can be. When we do masturbate, most of us remain stubbornly goal-oriented. We insist on telling ourselves that these occasional lapses serve only one purpose—to relieve sexual tension. Consequently, we generally get the act over with as quickly as possible—the sooner orgasm is reached the better. Seldom do we give ourselves the chance to realize that masturbation, far from being a shameful necessity, is actually one of the best possible ways of learning about our sexual responses and of increasing our sensitivity to sexual stimulation—lessons that can then be applied with enormous profit to partner sex.

It may come as a shock to many males for masturbation to be recommended as a positive good. I can almost hear a reader exclaiming, "You're actually telling guys that it's good for them to whack off?" I am saying just that, but the sort of masturbation I am advocating has little in common with the hurried, goal-oriented, tension-relieving experience so aptly described by terms such as "whacking off," "jerking off," or "beating your meat."

Most males who masturbate bring themselves to orgasm in an average of two to three minutes—often in as little as one minute. The desire to achieve rapid ejaculation originates in early adolescence, probably in a situation very similar to the one faced by the boy in our opening joke. Most adolescent boys, aware that their parents disapprove strongly of masturbation, develop an understandable reluctance to linger over the experience. Get through with it quickly and dispose of the evidence before mom or dad barges in. This pattern is usually reinforced in the college dormitory situation where, even though nearly every young man masturbates, none wants the others to know about it. Later on, when a man gains greater privacy, the need for such secrecy disappears, but the habit remains. He takes for his own the negative views of his parents and peers. The male may no longer fear discovery, but he does fear his own loss of self-respect. Hence, he may strive to keep the act of masturbation a secret from his conscious mind, cut off from his mature, respectable, day-to-day life.

In a literal sense, he follows the biblical injunction, "Let not thy right hand know what thy left hand doeth." Also, by confining the pleasure to be derived from masturbation to the brief moments of ejaculation, he minimizes his enjoyment of the act, thus, to an extent, appeasing his sense of guilt. My own adolescent masturbatory experience was the usual one of the hurried and clandestine act, followed by guilt when I saw semen stains on my sheets. As a married man, when I masturbate now, my focus is on making it a leisurely and sensual act.

There is a sense too in which the exclusive practice of rapid, ejaculation-oriented masturbation can be seen as yet another aspect of the male-machine concept. The male who stimulates his penis with the sole intent of "shooting off" as quickly as possible is, in effect, treating himself like a machine, a kind of sexual mechanism. What he is doing is much like the action of the motorcyclist who, stopped at a red light, twists the grip of his bike in order to hear the reassuring sound of his motor accelerating. But the penis is not primarily a mechanism. It is an integral part of yourself, a part of the enormously complex pattern of interacting physical and psychological components that make you a human being.

Nor is the penis the only part of you that is sexual. It does have a very high concentration of nerve endings. But then so do other parts of your body like your hands, thighs, and face. And as anyone knows who has ever had a massage, even parts of the body whose nerve count is relatively low, like the back, can be extremely susceptible to pleasurable sensations. What I am saying is that, in a very real sense, your whole body is a sex organ. Masturbation need not be only a way of triggering brief, intense sensations localized in the penis. It can be a method of awakening the sexual potential of the entire body. As such, it can serve to vastly increase a man's capacity for sexual response with a partner.

The sort of slowed-down, sensuous, whole-body masturbation that I am recommending and which I will describe in detail may be somewhat threatening to many men. In order to assuage their guilt feelings, men tell themselves that they don't masturbate to experience erotic sensations, but rather to relieve tension. There can be no doubt, though, that when you masturbate more slowly, concentrating on the pleasure you are experiencing, what you are doing is erotic. This may be disturbing at first. You may be afraid that thoughts and feelings which you believe should remain buried will emerge and take control. Such fears are quite natural and understandable. In fact, nongoal-oriented masturbation can show you parts of yourself of which you were unaware. But you needn't fear such revelations. Just as it is a truism that in order to accept love from others you must learn to respect and value yourself, it is also true that in order to accept and feel comfortable with sexual stimulation from a partner you must learn to experience the desirability and responsiveness of your own body.

The concept that most of us have of our own sexuality is unnecessarily rigid. The fact that you can respond to and become turned on by your body does not make you a narcissist. Quite to the contrary, a man's failure to be a responsive, imaginative lover can often be ascribed chiefly to the fact that he is not in touch with his own body. By developing the capacity to experience a greater range of pleasure and sensuality, we are likely to derive considerably more pleasure from our bodies and our sexuality than we thought possible. Equally important, our heightened self-awareness will make us more conscious of our partners' sexual needs and responses. Before we can guide and direct our partners in the kind of touching and pleasuring that are most arousing for us, it is useful to discover and accept this sort of stimulation for ourselves. Thus, in the sense that a "real man" is one who is knowledgeable about and responsible for his own sexuality, who can respond and interact sensitively with a partner, masturbation can serve to enhance your masculinity.

Arthur, a client of mine, provides a good example of how different orgasm-oriented masturbation and sensuous masturbation can be in their effect on a man's sex life. A reporter for a large city newspaper, thirty-seven, and divorced, Arthur had a twenty-year history of premature ejaculation, a fact that was related to his general anxiety about sex. Ever since adolescence, Arthur had masturbated rapidly and furtively. His only remembrance of his father telling him anything about sex was when he said to him, "If I ever catch you jerking off, I'll beat you silly!" That didn't stop Arthur from masturbating, but it did increase his sense of guilt and anxiety, as well as the rapidity of his response. Later, in his heterosexual experiences, Arthur ejaculated rapidly, and had no understanding or appreciation of affectionate touching or foreplay. He came to me for help in overcoming his rapid ejaculation problem. As part of his therapy, I had him engage in prolonged sensuous touching and self-exploration, but without going to orgasm. He was uncomfortable doing this the first time and said he felt silly stopping before he ejaculated. But the second time was better and the third better still. Soon he was able to stimulate himself and reach a high level of arousal without feeling the need to ejaculate. He learned that the process of getting there was enjoyable, as well as the orgasm itself.

He was able to stimulate himself for at least ten minutes before coming to orgasm, and in fact found the orgasm more pleasurable than before. This experience proved important to him in overcoming his rapid ejaculation problem with a partner.

Before discussing some specific masturbation exercises, I would like to spell out a few general points:

First, although it is usual for masturbation to end with orgasm, try to rid yourself of the preconception that each masturbation experience *must* end in orgasm. Remember, we are trying to get away from the male-machine concept of the body. Try not to think of your genitals as a mechanism that must be forced to react in a certain predictable way. Concentrate rather on stimulating your genitals, as well as the rest of your body, in various ways and observing your feelings and responses. Resist the temptation to judge a particular response as either bad or good according to whether it produces a strong erection or hastens ejaculation. There is no disputing the fact that, in terms of the intensity of the pleasure, ejaculation is the high point of any sexual experience. However, in order to broaden and deepen our capacity for erotic response, we should be able to forgo an occasional high point for the sake of exploring the range of our middles and lows. Above all, try not to become anxious if a particular stimulus does not seem to be bringing you closer to orgasm. To a certain extent, we are all ejaculation addicts, and there is a tendency, when slow, whole-body stimulation is not producing a strong response, to say, "Forget this nonsense. Let's get down to business with some good old-fashioned pumping." If you do fall prey to this syndrome, don't worry. There's always a next time. But remember, just because you are not responding strongly at the moment does not mean that you have lost your capacity to respond. The ejaculation is there when you want it. So relax and enjoy yourself.

Secondly, most of us, even those who consider themselves liberal or radical in other areas, are arch-conservatives when it comes to masturbation techniques. A man who orders roast beef and baked potato every time he eats in a restaurant would be considered pretty unadventurous. But this is exactly what most of us do when we masturbate. The average male works out a certain technique for masturbation during early adolescence, and thereafter he sticks to that technique until the day when his penis and hand finally part company, convinced all the while that his is the only technique possible. It may surprise such diehards to learn that there are virtually as many masturbation techniques as there are masturbators. Masters and Johnson, who studied masturbation in a laboratory setting, found that no two of their test subjects used precisely the same method. And yet it rarely occurs to most of us to vary the technique we've become accustomed to. Again, we seem determined not to try to increase the pleasure we derive from masturbation. As long as a method is not physically harmful or compulsive, there is really nothing that can be said against it. Just as experimentation is to be encouraged in lovemaking, it is to be encouraged also in masturbation.

Finally, a few words about how to deal with anxiety produced by going too far too fast. You may find that some of the exercises cause you to feel uncomfortable. This is quite natural. After all, the habits of a lifetime are not broken easily. The important thing to remember is that if you feel anxious or uncomfortable as a result of touching yourself in a particular place or in a particular way, don't stop, but go back to an earlier movement, one that caused you no anxiety. Or perhaps stop for a while—but with the intention to return to the exercise when the anxiety dissipates. In this way, you will be able to carry out your self-exploration in slow, easy stages. Your goal is not to reach orgasm, but rather to explore new territory. Remember, you are doing this for yourself. You deserve to be treated gently and with respect.

The Exercises

As adolescents we masturbate in response to sexual tension, usually without much thought about how we do it. The hand moves to the penis without conscious thought, the movements follow the well-worn tracks of a habitual pattern. There is nothing wrong with masturbation of this sort, but it serves no purpose other than providing simple, uncomplicated pleasure or easing mental or physical anxiety. Like most habits, it moves only in a tight, unvarying circle of desire and reward, going nowhere. In fact, for many men, masturbation is a response to anxiety, rather than simply being a pleasure outlet. I encourage such men to masturbate only when they are "horny" or want a sex outlet, and not to masturbate when they feel anxious.

Exercise 1. In order to make masturbation a learning experience, we must vary the pattern. Relaxation of the body and mind is essential in setting the stage for such an experience. A leisurely bath or shower is often a good way to begin. As you wash yourself, using scented soap if you like, massage your arms, shoulders, back, and legs, relaxing your muscles as much as possible. You probably have an inner timing device that goes off in your head when you think your allotted time in the tub has expired. Ignore it. Get out when you feel clean, relaxed, and refreshed and ready for the next phase. Be conscious of your sensations as you move from a wet environment to a dry one—the dripping of water from your body, the slight chill if it is cool, the breaking out of tiny, clean beads of sweat if it is hot. Dry yourself vigorously, concentrating on the feel of the rough towel on your skin.

Without putting on your clothes, go into the bedroom and make whatever preparations you need to feel comfortable. This may include turning down the lights, putting on music, turning on the airconditioner. Lie down on the bed in a relaxed, unrestrained position. Luxuriate. Enjoy your sense of physical freedom. Remember, there is no one watching you or judging how you look. You can achieve a deep state of relaxation by tensing the muscles in each part of your body in succession, then focusing on the feeling of relaxation as you release the tension. Breathe deeply and evenly, repeating a word like "relax" or "calm" over and over to yourself in rhythm with your breathing.

When you are completely relaxed, roll over on your side, focusing on the way your body feels as you move. Touch yourself slowly and gently, avoiding the genital areas at this point. You might try closing your eyes at first, so you can focus better on your sensations. Move from feet to head, noticing how each part of your body feels when you touch it. Vary the pressure of your touching from light to heavy, noticing your response in each case.

After you feel you have explored your body sufficiently through touch, you may want to turn to visual exploration. Look at yourself in a full-length mirror. Try to see your body objectively, the way you might look at a piece of sculpture. Instead of making judgments about yourself like, "I'm too fat," or "My chest is too flabby," concentrate on the curves and masses of the different parts of your body, noticing the way they fit together. Use a second mirror to view your body from the rear. Look at yourself in a way you have never done before, like standing with your back to the mirror, bending over and looking at your reflection through your legs.

Now concentrate on your genitals. Examine your penis, looking at and touching its various parts, including the glans, frenum, corona, and shaft. Examine your scrotum and testicles. Notice how your genitals look when you stand up, sit down, and lie down. The idea of this exploration should be to help you to feel comfortable and relaxed with your body. When you feel that you have achieved this objective—and this may take several sessions—you may end the exercise.

Exercise 2. Prepare for the second exercise as you did the first, with a leisurely shower or bath, followed by a few minutes of deep breathing and muscle relaxation. This time, concentrate more on specifically erotic sensations. Touch yourself in whatever way you find most sensually pleasing. Try stimulating your nipples, which are highly sensitive in many men, just as they are in women. Notice how they become erect after stroking or massage.

Taking your time and remaining relaxed, begin stroking the insides of your thighs. Run your fingers through your pubic hair, noticing the sensations that occur when you do so. Finally, move your hand to your genitals. Experiment with different types of touching and stroking to discover the method you find most arousing. Try a technique of penile stimulation that you do not ordinarily use. If you usually use hard strokes, try gentle ones. If you are accustomed to stimulating only the shaft of your penis, concentrate on the glans. Experiment with stroking and holding the testicles as well. You may continue this stimulation until you reach orgasm, but do not feel under any pressure to do so. The object of this exercise is to help you to acquire new knowledge of and comfort with genital stimulation.

Exercise 3. This time omit or include the preliminary shower, whichever you prefer. Bathing is a sensual and relaxing experience, but there is no need to make a ritual of it. Concentrate again on nongenital and genital touching and caressing, noticing which sort of stimulation is most arousing for you. You may wish to experiment with erotic literature or pictures as a device for enhancing arousal. Fantasy is also an effective method of intensifying sexual stimulation (and I'll have more to say about sex fantasies in the following chapter). Do not fall into the trap of opting for rapid, genital-oriented stimulation to orgasm, but be aware, as your arousal slowly mounts, of the complete cycle of sexual stimulation. Notice how your penis becomes larger and harder as ejaculation approaches, how the glans swells and becomes suffused with blood. Be aware of the increasing tension in your body.

When you do ejaculate, concentrate on those moments of intense sensation. Feel the contractions of the ejaculatory ducts within the penis, look at the semen as it spurts from the meatus. After ejaculation has ended, notice how your penis slowly loses its erectness. Also notice how your breathing and heartbeat have speeded up during arousal and are now returning to normal levels. Do you feel relaxed, sleepy, or energetic after an orgasm? Examine your semen, noticing the way it feels, smells. Try to become accustomed to it and comfortable with it. You may even want to put a drop on your tongue to see how it tastes. The object of this exercise is to help you accept and appreciate the natural and total functioning of your body during sexual arousal.

Exercise 4. In this last exercise, continue your experimentation to find the type of stimulation that is most arousing for you. Explore the possibilities of nongenital touching as well as genital stimulation. Introduce one or more elements into this exercise which you have never tried before. You may, for example, wish to experiment with some lubricant such as a lotion, oil, or cream. Or try masturbating by lying facedown and rubbing your penis against the sheet or a towel. You might also try rolling a towel into a cylinder and inserting your penis inside to simulate a vagina. Or try placing a pillow under your pelvis and rubbing your penis against it. Feel free to use any type of fantasy or erotic art as a focus for your stimulation. Pull out all the stops and fully enjoy the process of slowly and sensuously bringing yourself to orgasm. Explore the full extent of your capacity for arousal.

After completing these exercises, it should be clear to you that masturbation, far from being a "poor excuse for the real thing," can be an extremely rewarding sexual experience in its own right. Learning to use masturbation to gain pleasure and self-knowledge rather than just as a penis-oriented sexual safety valve can be an excellent way of becoming comfortable with your body and its natural and healthy responsiveness to stimulation. It is amazing how, once you begin to try sensuous, whole-body self-stimulation, the pleasure of the experience—no longer confined to the brief 3 to 10 seconds of orgasm—expands into a whole new world of erotic sensations. Not only is this very pleasurable in itself, but it can help you in a very real way to respond more sensitively and to communicate more effectively with a partner.

4

Sexual Fantasies: Your Private X-Rated Cinema

THE WONDERFUL THING about sexual fantasies is that you can have them any way you like. You and you alone have the last word on casting, plotting, directing, editing, camera angles, and special effects. And since you are also the only person who ever will or can see your fantasies, you need never be concerned with bad reviews or censorship. As an accompaniment to masturbation, sexual fantasies can be marvelously effective for increasing arousal. A sexual fantasy can provide a pleasant interlude in the middle of a tedious day. During intercouse, fantasy can transform a familiar sex partner into someone exotic, unattainable. In short, everything sexual that you have ever wanted or wondered about can be yours, through the magic of fantasy.

But then why do we suffer so much anxiety, guilt, and confusion because of our sexual fantasies? Why do we often worry that our fantasies may be used as evidence to prove us "abnormal" or "perverse"? Why do we believe that our sexual fantasies will someday get out of control, that instead of being mere entertainment, they will begin to exert a sinister influence over our actions in the real world? If there is no such thing as censorship where fantasy is concerned, why do we often feel as though a strike force from the Anti-Smut League were standing outside our head, ready to march in and close the theater down?

In order to answer these questions, we must explore some of the attitudes our society has held regarding fantasy in general and sexual fantasy in particular.

The major portion of our lives is rational and predictable, proceeding smoothly according to certain agreed-upon rules and conventions. We wake up at the same time each morning, take the same drive or train ride to work, interact with our friends and associates using the same well-worn conversational formulas. Even when something unexpected happens—a sudden promotion or a traffic accident—it is a predictable sort of surprise, and there are generally certain conventional ways of reacting to it (buy a bottle of champagne, get the other fellow's license number and the name of his insurance company). There are of course individual differences in behavior, and there are moments when we do act spontaneously and unpredictably. But for the most part people spend their day-to-day lives acting according to accepted patterns. Individuals who depart from the patterns, even if only slightly, are often considered rather odd.

In fantasy, however, all the patterns, all the rules, all the conventions can be overturned. We may fantasize ourselves acting in ways that would be unacceptable or disastrous in daily life. We may insult or physically attack people with whom we are normally restrained and respectful. We may imagine ourselves having sex with people who are unavailable or simply peripheral to our lives: a movie star, a bank teller, our best friend's wife. Moreover, in our fantasies, we frequently perform actions that we would never dream of doing in real life. A mild-mannered person might imagine himself battering an enemy to pulp; a man may fantasize himself raping his female boss; a practicing heterosexual might imagine himself with a male sex partner. Generally, we do not share these fantasies with others, and so, with no basis for comparison, we are apt to think that our own fantasies are far more bizarre than anyone else's. But this could hardly be the case. The fantasy life of nearly everyone is strange, unpredictable, and chaotic, compared with the ordered, rational events that occur in the everyday world.

The trouble comes when we try to understand our fantasies in the same way we explain our everyday experiences. The attempt, as we quickly find, fails because fantasies simply do not fit rational modes of thought. Our natural reaction when we have trouble explaining any part of our experience rationally is to just put it out of our mind. Fantasy experiences cannot be dismissed so easily, nor should they be, for they are just as real as those we can explain in a rational way *and* just as natural. Moreover, fantasies have a definite value in and of themselves.

   The way we respond to our fantasies depends largely on cultural and educational backgrounds. In Western cultural tradition, until recently, fantasy has been viewed with considerable apprehension. The Judeo-Christian tradition has always held that a "good" person is good not only in action but also in thought. Thus, "impure" thoughts—especially sexual fantasies—were considered the work of the devil. The New Testament states in no uncertain terms "That whosoever looketh on a woman to lust after her hath committed adultery with her already in his heart." Such an attitude tends to blur the crucially important distinction between thought and action, between fantasy and reality. While the struggle of a St. Anthony to purge his mind of the sensual images that plagued him may be impressive as spiritual drama, it is perhaps somewhat less relevant for most of us today. A far more productive attitude would be one that allowed us to be comfortable with our fantasy life as well as to use it to promote our greater happiness and pleasure.

   While few of us still believe that every time we have a sexual fantasy we are under the influence of Satan, there does remain a good deal of confusion about the relationship of fantasy to everyday life. Specifically, most of us are unsure whether, or to what extent, our fantasies represent what we actually *want* to do. Do a married man's fantasies of having sex with other women mean that he really does not love his wife? Do a man's fantasies of rape mean that he really wants to commit sexual assault? Do a heterosexual's fantasies of sex with other men mean that he is really a latent homosexual? These are the sort of questions that cause the greatest anxiety for most of us where fantasy is concerned. We are aware that there is some sort of relation between fantasy and behavior, that in some sense fantasy expresses our unfulfilled desires and needs. But few of us can say just what that relationship is. How closely does fantasy approach the behavioral interface of day-to-day existence? To what extent are we responsible for our fantasies?

   In dealing with these questions, we should keep in mind that there is a profound difference between thinking about doing something and wanting to carry it through to behavior. Almost everyone has aggressive, antisocial, and bizarre sexual fantasies at one time or another, but relatively few people ever act out any of these fantasies. The fact is that the worst danger of antisocial fantasies is not that they will be acted out, but rather the guilt feelings they usually engender. Guilt is a powerful and dangerous emotion. While sexual fantasies themselves need not have any appreciable effect on a person's behavior, guilt experienced as a result of these fantasies frequently has a strong and negative effect. It can serve as a motivating force that keeps a person obsessively focusing on a particular fantasy, or it may become strong enough to influence our actual sexual behavior, making us uncomfortable with our sexual feelings or leading us to avoid situations in which the fantasies are suggested. Besides, such feelings of discomfort may distort a person's sexual behavior and can discourage open communication between partners.

Thus, in trying to come to terms with our sexual fantasies, we should be concerned not with finding a way to "purify" our thoughts, or to impose some sort of rigid control or limitation on our fantasies, but rather with effectively desensitizing ourselves to the guilt we may feel about having fantasies. As we shall see, we can learn to put our fantasies to good use. But for guilt, there is no positive use whatsoever.

When a particular thought or idea is associated in our minds with guilt, fear, or anxiety, the thought takes on a power and importance it ordinarily would not have, and we thus have less control over it. In some cases, a single fantasy may assume the central focus in a person's life, displacing other forms of sexual enjoyment. In such cases, the fantasy may produce intense arousal, but also intense guilt—an unfortunate combination of emotions. For example, a man who has intense and guilt-laden sexual fantasies about little girls would probably experience great discomfort each time he is alone with a young girl. Carried to this extreme, obsessive fantasies may lead to fetishism, the centering of sexual feelings on some inanimate object which then becomes the sole stimulus capable of triggering a sexual response. Fetishists are sometimes portrayed humorously as roguish old gentlemen gloating lasciviously over their collections of women's shoes or lace panties. But fetishism is a sad affair in real life, for it represents a severe limitation of the range of sexual stimuli a person is capable of responding to. A man's obsession with women's underwear is not bad because it is morally wrong; it is bad because it is the only thing he has, because without it he would probably become incapable of responding sexually to any other stimulus. While fetishism is the most extreme form, all guilt-laden, obsessive sexual fantasies should be avoided, not on moral grounds, but because they drastically reduce the pleasure we derive from our sexuality.

I believe that the best general course for you to follow, then, with regard to sexual fantasy is not to suppress your erotic imaginings or to reject certain types of fantasies, but to deliberately cultivate as widely varied a repertoire as you find enjoyable. To return for a moment to my cinematic metaphor, it makes little sense to watch the same film over and over again when you have at your disposal the enormous resources of a private Hollywood inside your head. The important thing to keep in mind is that whatever erotic entertainments we invent, the vast majority of us are in no danger whatever of wandering outside the bounds of normalcy. There is no such thing as unhealthy sexual fantasy, as long as it remains a fantasy and doesn't become obsessive.

Not only are sexual fantasies normal and healthy but they also serve a very useful purpose. We all need an occasional vacation from the rationality of everyday life, and fantasy provides just that. Dreams—perhaps the most common mode of our fantasy lives—are a case in point. Just about everyone dreams, although many people may not recall having dreamed. In the course of an average night's sleep, approximately one and a half hours are spent dreaming. Studies have shown that people deprived of their dreams become irritable, easily upset, and depressed. If the deprivation continues over a period of time, a condition similar to psychosis can develop. Thus, it has been suggested that dreams provide a nonrational "pressure-valve," without which our rational, controlled, waking lives would be impossible.

Perhaps because they intuitively recognized the great importance of dreaming to the natural health and balance of the mind, other cultures have paid serious attention to the content of dreams, valuing them as a source of knowledge and a portent of future events. In the Old Testament, Joseph found favor with the Pharaoh by interpreting his dreams. There is a Malaysian culture that still teaches its children how to dream "correctly"; the family members share their dreams each morning, and the parents instruct their children in how they might improve them. But we tend to write off dreams as unimportant unless, of course, we are undergoing psychoanalysis, in which case we report them to our analyst. In any event, we certainly do not consider our dreams to be an integral part of our lives.

Most of us do take dreaming seriously, though, when the content of our dreams is particularly disturbing or guilt-provoking. When this happens, we usually react by making the same mistake that we do with waking fantasies—that is, we blur the dividing line between fantasy and reality. This is particularly true, as we have already seen, when our dreams contain themes of a bizarre or antisocial sexual nature. Actually, bizarre sexual dreams are very common—dreams of incest, dreams of homosexuality, dreams about intercourse with a variety of sexually proscribed personages ranging from one's mother-in-law to the family dog. One type of dream, for example, that many men find extremely disturbing—that of having intercourse with a hermaphrodite, a woman who has a penis—is actually an extremely common motif found in the art and literature of many different cultures. We must learn not to expect dreams to make sense in waking terms, to deal only with permissible, commonplace subject matter. If we hope to be comfortable with our sexuality, we must learn to accept the bizarre nature of our dreams and fantasies as a normal part of our sexual functioning.

The person who wishes to do so can go a step further than merely accepting his sexual dreams for what they are. He can learn to regulate and control his dreams to some extent. Given the proper technique and a little practice, we can "program" our dreams, introduce themes and characters of our own choosing, and thus bring our dreams, along with our fantasies, within the province of our personal, imaginary Hollywood. The technique involved is quite simple. Decide whom and what you would like to dream about on a particular evening. As you fall asleep, keep that idea fixed in your mind. Chances are the chosen material will appear in your dreams in some form that night. The result may not be exactly what you ordered, but the fact that the technique can often be used with some success shows that it is possible to gain control of something that is potentially distressing and remove its threatening aspects. It also shows that if we can separate our propensity to impose moral judgments from the enjoyment connected with our dream activities, then our sexual dreams can become a free and harmless source of entertainment and pleasure of unlimited variety.

Sexual fantasies differ from dreams in that they are generally more rational, occurring as they do during waking life when we have more conscious control of our minds and are better able to choose what part of our thoughts to give our attention to. Like dreams, however, waking fantasies can serve as a bountiful source of pleasure and a convenient safety valve to draw off the accumulated pressures of our restricted, rational lives. If we keep in mind the distinction between fantasy and reality, between thought and act, then fantasy can be a way of allowing ourselves to fulfill those wishes and desires which may, for one reason or another, seem inappropriate or unacceptable to us or our society.

Two of the most common fantasies a man may have when he sees a sexually attractive woman are to imagine what she would look like naked and what it would be like to have intercourse with her. Mentally undressing a woman and fantasizing intercourse with her may substitute for the actual behavior, which may be socially inappropriate in the circumstances. Many men experience a degree of conflict between their professed attitudes of respect for women and the content of their fantasies, but if the distinction between enjoying a fantasy about doing something and actually wanting to do it is kept firmly in mind, then the fantasy can be enjoyed without any accompanying guilt or anxiety. Having such fantasies does not mean that you are a male chauvinist who wants to rape every woman he sees. A man can have an active fantasy life that contradicts every personal ethic he subscribes to without ever violating his beliefs in terms of actual behavior.

The opportunity to indulge in forbidden or impractical relationships is just one of the possible uses of sexual fantasy. It may also serve as a way of enhancing a relationship between two people who are in the process of becoming sexually involved. Sexual fantasies a man has about a woman he is dating may be a source of excitement and gratification for him and may strengthen his interest in her. This is equally true whether the relationship is new or longstanding, whether it is intimate or merely at the flirtation stage. In fact, many older married men could probably improve their relationships with their wives by deliberately incorporating them into their fantasies. For men who desire greater novelty and spontaneity in their marital sex, fantasizing about these things may be the first step toward making them happen. In an intimate relationship, a great deal of pleasure may be derived from the sharing of sexual fantasies. For example, telling your wife about a fantasy of yours in which she comes into your office and seduces you in front of your colleagues can serve to heighten the erotic feelings between the two of you—though it is obviously highly unlikely that either of you would want to act out this fantasy at your office.

A man's sexual fantasies about a woman can enhance their relationship in another, quite different way. Fantasy may serve as a rehearsal, a learning experience that can be particularly helpful for younger, inexperienced males. Depending on his capacity for making his fantasies vivid and detailed, a man may rehearse an entire lovemaking scene again and again, revising and editing to his heart's content. As a result, the real-life event may go more smoothly when it actually occurs.

Fantasy can also be used as an accompaniment during sexual intercourse. The experience of imagining that one's sexual partner is another person is a fairly common one, yet most people feel an acute sense of guilt at indulging in this type of fantasy. Such guilt is unnecessary, however, since changing a partner's identity in your imagination does not necessarily mean that you want to change it in real life. One of my students, a married man named Bob, liked to evoke a particular fantasy of multiple sex partners during intercourse with his wife. He would imagine that six women, one of whom was his wife, were making love to him. Two of them would be taking turns sucking his penis, another would be moving her finger in and out of his anus, a fourth would be massaging and sucking his nipples, a fifth presenting her vulva for him to explore with his tongue, while a sixth would be wildly rubbing her body against his. Other images would flit in and out of his mind, such as two of the women making love to one another while admiring his body, or three or four of them fighting to perform fellatio on him. Far from proving disturbing or guilt-provoking, these fantasies served to heighten his arousal during marital sex.

As in the case of dreams, bizarre and antisocial themes are quite natural in sexual fantasies. Fantasy and reality are two distinct realms, and there is no need to feel guilty or disturbed about the content of any fantasy. It is natural, for example, to fantasize about having sex with women of a different race. Group sex, oral and anal sex, and sadomasochistic experiences are some other common subjects of fantasies. Violent and aggressive sexual fantasies are quite normal and are seldom acted out subsequently. In fact, it is probable that a man likely to commit rape would be more apt to suppress such fantasies rather than to rehearse them in his imagination. Homosexual fantasies are common, too, and do not necessarily mean that a man is a repressed homosexual. Tom, another student of mine, reported that he occasionally enjoyed having a homosexual fantasy. While masturbating, he would imagine that there were two handsome and muscular men who were his sexual slaves. One would perform anal intercourse on him while the other blew him. Although he found the fantasy quite arousing, it was not something that he wanted to carry through to behavior. He accepted homosexuality as a valid life-style for people who choose that sexual orientation, but he was quite satisfied as a functioning heterosexual who included homosexuality as a part of his fantasy life.

Summing up: Sexual fantasies, rather than being something to fear and avoid, can be a great source of pleasure for any man. No fantasy is "sick" or "immoral" as long as it remains a fantasy; in fact, bizarre and antisocial fantasies are very common. The danger is not in the fantasy itself, but in the guilt that may accompany it, for it is guilt which can make us focus obsessively on one particular fantasy, thus limiting the variety of sexual stimuli which we find arousing. My clinical experience has shown that the healthiest and most rewarding practice is to cultivate a number of different fantasies, to enjoy them all, and to feel guilty about none of them. In this way, fantasy can become a positive help to us rather than a threat. Fantasy can serve to amuse, to excite, to educate, and to refresh us. It can make the experience of being male and being sexual a richer and more rewarding one.

5
Loving and Learning: Sex and the Unmarried Male

UNTIL FAIRLY RECENTLY, sex among the unmarried in our society was strictly regulated by the sexual double standard. Unmarried men and unmarried women were expected to conform to quite different codes of conduct. For an adolescent boy, gaining premarital sexual experience was a goal to be sought after as part of his growing-up process. Virginity was an embarrassment, a mark of shame. The young man who had "scored" with the greatest number of women was an object of envy and admiration to his peers. Adolescent girls, on the other hand, were taught that their sexuality was a valuable possession to be protected—saved in a hope chest, as it were—until it could be bestowed untarnished on a husband. The limits to acceptable female sexual behavior varied from family to family and from community to community, but one rule remained constant: Unmarried women were not supposed to "go all the way." They were expected to remain virgins until they married.

This double standard created an interesting dilemma. If young men were expected to become sexually experienced before marriage while young women were not, with whom then were the young men supposed to acquire their experience? The solution to this problem seemed to depend on the existence of two different classes of unmarried women—"good girls" and "bad girls." Good girls were of course the ones who followed society's dictates and waited for marriage to experience intercourse. Bad girls were the ones who gave in—who had intercourse prior to marriage and thereby "cheapened" themselves. In actuality, this distinction was not so strictly maintained. Not every girl who had sex before marriage automatically became bad. It was only when a girl acquired a reputation, when she began to be known for being "fast" or "easy" that her social standing was threatened. Interestingly, under the double standard, this was the reverse of the situation faced by males; a young man's reputation for promiscuity enhanced rather than diminished his status.

Certainly, this pattern of behavior allowed far greater sexual freedom for unmarried men than it did for unmarried women. Yet it also imposed certain severe restrictions on male sexual expression. Because "scoring" was considered such an indispensable sign of masculinity, sex became highly competitive, performance- and number-oriented. There was a tendency to see women as objects, trophies in the game of sexual pursuit. A considerable degree of manipulativeness was condoned in the behavior of a young man who was in the process of trying to "make" a young woman. He was almost expected to be false and seductive, to pretend to a greater intimacy or responsibility toward the woman than he actually felt—all in the interest of getting her to "come across" and go to bed with him.

This persistent pushing for sex on the part of young men often won them the reputation of "only having one thing on their minds"—meaning, of course, sex. Yet it was not so much sex itself that spurred them on in their efforts; rather it was the glory of having had sex, that great initiating experience which was so crucial in confirming the manhood of an adolescent male. Sex as status, sex as accomplishment—these were often of major importance in motivating a young, unmarried male to seek out sexual liaisons with young women. Real sexual feelings played a part in these encounters, too, of course. But very often, the quality of the experience itself was overlooked or taken for granted. The real emphasis was on competition among the young men themselves. As in poker, bluffing was a legitimate tactic in this sexual game, and a young man would often fabricate or exaggerate his own exploits in order to advance himself in the eyes of his peers.

Most young men were so caught up in this pursuit of sex that much of the pleasure of sex was lost on them. Premarital sex was surrounded by such negative societal sanctions that young people, both male and female, were usually too anxious and ill-at-ease to enjoy the actual experience in anything remotely approaching its full potentiality. In part, the trouble was that the double standard not only imposed two separate codes of behavior on unmarried men and women but it made them rather ill-suited as sex partners as well. Both tended to identify far too strongly with stereotyped role models—that is, men were expected to be aggressive and women passive. Thus, whole areas of experience and pleasure were effectively closed off to both sexes. Males tended to be eager for sex, willing to try out variations in sexual behavior, relatively uninhibited sexually. On the other hand, they seemed to have an incapacity for tenderness and warmth, as well as an inability to integrate their emotions with the physical expression of sexuality. Women tended to be less enthusiastic about sex, less adventurous, and probably more afraid of and out of touch with their own sexuality. Yet they did seem to be freer and more responsive in interpersonal relationships, and to have a greater sensitivity to and appreciation for physical affection when it was not specifically intercourse-oriented.

During the past decade or so, however, there have been changes in many of our attitudes toward sexuality in general, and much of this change has focused upon premarital sex, with indications that the restrictive double standard no longer seems relevant in contemporary society. There has been a tendency for women to step out of their passive role and to take an active interest in sex. Moreover, the old sanctions against premarital sex have begun to break down, and it is now far more acceptable for an unmarried woman to have sex. Premarital sexual experience no longer brands a young woman as "bad"; in fact, among many groups of young unmarried people, being a virgin can now be as much of a burden to a woman as it is to a man. There has been a moderate change in the incidence of premarital sex for men during the past decade, and a more substantial change for women, although hardly revolutionary. Previously, about 80 percent of males had intercourse before marriage, as compared to approximately 50 percent of females. At present, best indications are that the figures are 85 percent for males and 75 percent for females. The average age for the first intercourse experience is now seventeen for males and nineteen for females. While it is true that the old double standard may be on its way out, there is some question whether the guidelines that seem to be replacing it are much of an improvement, in terms of an emotionally integrated and rewarding approach to sexuality.

The new sexual attitudes too often seem to require that both men and women live up to the aggressive, competitive standards that used to apply exclusively to men, and there may now be a danger that women as well as men are giving more importance to performance than to pleasure. This was ironically demonstrated when Masters and Johnson published their material on female multiple orgasm. Suddenly a new performance demand had come into existence, a new standard against which to measure sexual ability. Many women who considered themselves sexually liberated began to feel anxious if they had never been multiorgasmic. Current studies indicate that this new anxiety may manifest itself in the form of sexual dysfunction, for there seems to be an increase in women who have been orgasmic and are now nonorgasmic, very possibly as a result of their attempts to become multiorgasmic. How unfortunate it would be if that old double standard were being replaced by a new code of behavior that was coercive—in terms of exerting pressure to meet a particular standard of performance—rather than liberating.

Maybe part of the problem is simply that young, unmarried people have been placed too much in the sexual spotlight. Whether premarital sex is forced underground by societal sanctions as it was in the past, or whether it is celebrated and ballyhooed in the media as it is today, the result is essentially the same: premarital sex is overemphasized at the expense of mature sexuality. According to contemporary stereotypes, sex is seen as something glamorous, tantalizing, and rather explosive, which takes place primarily between unmarried people in their teens and twenties. Sex as an intimate sharing of pleasure between adult couples who are deeply committed to one another has been largely ignored. Whether they are operating under the old, repressive double standard or under the newer, coercive single standard, young people tend to feel entirely too pressured to "prove" themselves sexually. Perhaps we ought to cease focusing on questions of "should they or shouldn't they?" and look at premarital sexuality from the perspective of a person's lifetime involvement with sex. Instead of seeing the premarital phase as a time of intense sexual activity—a sort of sexual proving ground—we could regard it as an initial explorative foray into the world of adult sexuality, a kind of sexual apprenticeship.

A more honest, nonmanipulative single standard of premarital sexuality needs to be developed—one that would attempt to combine the man's eagerness for sexual expression and the woman's interest in relationships and communication about feelings. Rather than the woman copying the man in being sexually manipulative and exploitative, she would allow herself to be sexually expressive and comfortable in the context of a nonmanipulative relationship.

In turn, the man would learn to accept his sexuality as a means of expressing and sharing intimate feelings and of giving and receiving pleasure, rather than as an inherently self-centered demand to be satisfied through exploitation. Perhaps the most necessary adjustment for a young man to make is to see women as sexual persons rather than objects. A sexual object can be treated as someone to be given a line, manipulated, used, and eventually discarded. But if seen as a sexual person, a woman becomes someone whose needs, both sexual and personal, must be considered and accepted. In short, what I am advocating is a freer and more humanistic relationship between the sexes. Both men and women must be willing to change and to learn, and the best time for this learning process to begin is at the outset of a person's sexual career—during the premarital years.

A young man who is accustomed to being manipulative in sex, who has treated his sex partners as objects—as prizes to be acquired—and who has had little practice in communicating honestly and sensitively with women, will probably find it difficult to change much after he gets married. Nor do women automatically blossom sexually when they marry. Rather, if their premarital learning stressed that they were not to engage in sex too freely or enthusiastically, this attitude is likely to stay with them. Thus, the old double standard is an unpromising basis for a marital relationship, and one that is difficult to overcome. Nor is it much of an improvement if both partners are influenced by the newer, false, single standard in which both men and women are expected to conform to the aggressive, competitive standards that once governed the sexual behavior of males. Thus, for the sake of achieving fulfillment in later marital relationships, as well as for the sake of present satisfaction, it is particularly important that unmarried men (and women) establish guidelines for making decisions about their behavior that will allow them to feel good about their sexuality.

One of the basic difficulties of premarital sex is still the question of whom to choose as a sexual partner. In the past, the double standard of sexual behavior made it quite clear just what was expected of young people. But now that it has become generally acceptable for both unmarried men and women to express themselves sexually, new problems have arisen. In a society where the choice of behavior is left largely up to the individual, the burden of making decisions that accord with your personal value system becomes far greater. We no longer have the dos and don'ts of society to fall back upon. In a sense, we are like children whose mother has given us free run of the cookie jar; the question has suddenly changed from "How many cookies can I get?" to "How many cookies do I want?" Are we obligated to prove the vigor of our appetites by gobbling as many as we can get our hands on? The problem is greater for males because it is we who have been schooled in the doctrine that a real man never turns down an opportunity to have sex. Thus, it is particularly important for us to establish some basic guidelines for managing our sexual relationships.

We might start by examining our normal social relationships. If we think about the people whose lives touch on our own, it becomes clear that we are involved with many people on several different levels, and that these relationships can be categorized according to the degree of intimacy they entail. Human relationships are, of course, highly complex, and any attempt to fit them into categories must be somewhat arbitrary. Nevertheless, it is worthwhile trying since, by doing so, we may gain a certain clarity and perspective on the situation.

The average person's relationships can be seen as fitting into five categories. We may visualize these categories as a series of concentric circles and the closer to the center, the more intimacy involved; the larger the circle, the less intimacy involved. As the relationship becomes closer, so the degree of trust, caring, and emotional involvement increases, but so also does the individual's vulnerability to being hurt.

In circle E—the outermost circle—we find all those people whose lives intersect with yours in some way, but about whom you know virtually nothing, sometimes not even their names. This group, whose number is potentially unlimited, might include a clerk in a store, an elevator operator, a bus driver, a receptionist in an office, people you pass in the street; your interaction with them is purely formal and involves no degree of intimacy at all. The next circle, D, contains all those people with whom you may have established a certain elementary degree of intimacy, but no real personal involvement—people you may see on a regular basis and chat with occasionally about relatively neutral topics. You may know their names and some facts about them, but if they were to suddenly disappear from your life, you would experience little emotional reaction. At any given time there could be a hundred or more people like this in your life, and during the course of your lifetime, perhaps thousands.

Relationships that involve a degree of real intimacy begin with circle C. These are people whom you would refer to as friends, people with whom you have shared some of your feelings and whose attitude toward you is a matter of some concern. You care about these people, and if *they* were to disappear from your life, a definite emotional gap would be created, although not a devastating one. The average person may have ten to fifteen such friends at any given time, and probably more than a hundred in the course of a lifetime. Circle B includes close friends, people who know a great deal about you and whom you trust enough to divulge your intimate feelings. The average person may have one, two, or three such special friends at any given time and perhaps ten to twenty-five during his life. When a close relationship of this sort comes to an end, there is usually a feeling of sadness and sometimes of hurt.

Circle A includes only very close, intimate relationships such as one has with a best friend, a lover, a spouse, or an adult who serves as a mentor or confidante. These relationships involve something more than intimacy—namely, a sense of deep commitment. We allow people in circle A to know our innermost thoughts, to gain an awareness of our strengths and weaknesses. When a circle A relationship ends, we are affected profoundly, experiencing a deep sense of loss, emptiness, desolation, and often hurt. In one's whole life there are usually no more than seven to ten circle A relationships, and for many people, there may be as few as one, two, or three.

We can use this circles-of-intimacy concept to examine the values that serve as a basis for making decisions about our sexual relationships. According to the old double standard, for example, which assumed that a man should be willing and able to have sex with any woman, anytime, anywhere, a woman from any of the circles would be a potential sexual partner. On the other hand, a woman would be expected to have sex only with a man occupying circle A—namely her husband or her fiancée. As we have seen, the double standard required a man to utilize deception and manipulation in his attempt to convince a potential partner that his feelings went much deeper than they really did, that his level of caring and emotional involvement approached that of circle A.

But such manipulativeness is a poor preparation for the intimacy and emotional sharing of a mature relationship. Thus, it is to our advantage to try to be completely open and honest about which circle of intimacy a particular woman who attracts us occupies. This does not necessarily mean that we should have sex only with women from circles A and B. What it does mean is that we should not enter into a sexual relationship under false pretenses. For example, it would be perfectly acceptable for a man and woman whose degree of intimacy placed them only within circle D to have sexual relations, provided they both knew just where they stood with respect to one another. If, on the other hand, the woman was dissatisfied with a circle D relationship and wished for a degree of intimacy characterized by circle B, it would be unacceptable for the man to pretend that such a relationship existed merely to have intercourse with her. This circles-of-intimacy concept is of course equally applicable to women as well as to men, and thus could prove useful in moving us closer to a single standard of premarital sexual expression, which would provide a better basis for adult sexual functioning for all of us.

While there is nothing really wrong with casual sex, so long as the participants have no illusions about it, sexual relations are generally more satisfying when a degree of intimacy exists between the partners, when the people involved are not only sex partners but friends as well. For one thing, it is easier in an intimate, trusting relationship to be more honest about your sexual preferences and responses, and this communication usually means increased sexual satisfaction. Therefore, assuming that you are interested in enhancing the quality of your sexual relationships, you would probably do well to limit your choice of partners to people from circle C or closer. Since circles C, B, and A are likely to contain no more than fifteen to twenty individuals *of both* sexes at any given time, such a decision goes a long way toward simplifying your sexual involvements. I might add that this guideline applies equally well to homosexual as well as heterosexual men. Friendship and intimacy are just as important in a sexual relationship between two men as they are between a man and a woman.

Using the circles-of-intimacy concept to plan and order your sex life may at first seem to be a strange idea. Most of us tend to think that sex should be a spontaneous occurrence and that deliberately planning our sexual activity must make it less enjoyable. Actually, planning can often make real spontaneity possible, for it can help you to avoid problems—VD or unwanted pregnancy, for example— as well as to increase feelings of comfort and self-confidence. The basic point to remember is that sex is an integral part of you as a person and that it can be used to enhance your life rather than to cause difficulties.

Nowhere is planning more needed—yet nowhere is it more often avoided—than in first intercourse experiences. Because it is usually so significant for a male whether it occurs at age fifteen or thirty-five, the first intercourse should ideally be planned, adequate contraceptive measures should be utilized, and it should occur in a leisurely, nondemanding situation. The experience would be further enhanced if the couple were comfortable with each other and had slept together several times and engaged in relaxed pleasuring activities before attempting intercourse. This crucial first experience should be seen not as a performance, but as a natural event arising out of increased intimacy and sexual arousal.

Unfortunately, very few men undergo their sexual initiation in such ideal circumstances. Typically, first intercourse experiences are characterized by intense anxiety based partly on the fear of failure and partly on the fear of being caught in the act. Only about one out of three couples use some form of contraception during first intercourse. The contraceptive device used most frequently is the condom, and it is generally put on in a hurried and clumsy manner. Since first intercourse is usually a time of high anxiety and low skill, it is surprising when it goes well at all. About 20 percent of males experience actual sexual failure during their first intercourse, generally due to inability to get or maintain an erection or to ejaculation before the penis enters the vagina. Also, the great majority of men ejaculate very rapidly during their first intercourse. It is important, therefore, not to overreact to an unsuccessful or unenjoyable first intercourse experience. Rather, you should be aware that sexual enjoyment takes practice, communication, lowering of anxiety, and cooperation. Above all, it is essential to remember that the human male is not a sexual machine that can be expected to function flawlessly whenever the button of sexual stimulation is pressed.

If a young man is able to think of premarital sex not as a "proving ground," but rather as a learning opportunity, a time of apprenticeship for the long period of mature sexuality to come, much of the pressure and anxiety of premarital sexuality will be automatically diminished. The less one thinks of sex as a performance and the more one thinks of it as a personally fulfilling and enhancing experience, the more enjoyable it will be. Once we are able to accustom ourselves to the fact that we are still at a learning stage with sex and that we are not alone in this, we can become more accepting of our own mistakes, confident in the knowledge that we are learning from these early experiences and that they will contribute to our later sexual adjustment. There is a joy to learning about any field, and sex is no exception.

Young, unmarried men should feel good that they are improving their sexual and interpersonal skills as a result of their experiences. There is a feeling of satisfaction in knowing that, from one relationship to the next, you are learning to overcome hang-ups, communicate more effectively, make love more skillfully and sensitively, and treat your sex partners as people. The real value of premarital sex is not in proving yourself a sexual superman, but rather in feeling that you are growing as a person and learning to make your sexuality a positive force in your life as well as integrating it more fully with your feelings and emotions.

The percentage of unmarried men who succeed in making such an adjustment is not great, but there are enough of them around to show that comfortable, pleasurable, and learning-oriented premarital sex is not an impossibility.

Jon, a student of mine, is one such example. A twenty-four-year-old graduate student who works as a trainee for a communications company, Jon enjoys his job, likes to travel, and is generally pleased with his sex life. Although he did not have intercourse until he was nineteen and was somewhat concerned at the time that he was lagging behind his friends, he soon gave up these fears when he became sexually active. Most of his relationships have tended to be fairly intimate ones. He has had four sex partners in about the same number of years, and he felt very little pressure to "score" with a greater number of women merely for the sake of achieving prestige among his male friends. In his first relationship, neither Jon nor his partner used any form of contraception, and there were two rather disturbing pregnancy scares. Since then, he has been careful about preventing unwanted pregnancy and uses a condom when his partner is not using the pill, IUD, or diaphragm. More recently, Jon has had sexual relationships of shorter duration—two one-night stands and two affairs lasting for only a few weeks. From these experiences he has learned that he generally enjoys himself more, both personally and sexually, when he feels a genuine sense of companionship with the woman. He has also discovered that the more he likes a woman on a personal basis, the more he will want to try to engage in a wider range of sexual acts with her, such as experimenting with

oral-genital sex. Moreover, he finds that his own pleasure is enhanced when a woman is responsive and really seems to enjoy sex.
Jon has decided not to marry until he is about thirty, and he is
looking forward to continuing to enjoy sex as a single man in the
interim period. He does not view marriage as a comedown from
premarital sex, but rather as an opportunity to use the sexual knowledge and skill he has acquired to develop and sustain a long-term,
intimate, committed relationship. I predict great success for him.

Perhaps not everyone can be as fortunate as Jon in managing their
premarital sexual relationships. Adolescence and young adulthood
are often confusing and conflict-filled times when negative sexual
experiences of one kind or another are almost certain to occur. But
if you remember that satisfying sexual relations require comfort and
a lack of anxiety, and that sexual experiences that do not go well
need not spell the end of your sexual life but can be used as learning
opportunities, you will have made important progress in achieving a
good sexual adjustment. The young, unmarried man, in accepting
responsibility for his sexuality, needs to learn not only to value
sexual experimentation and to be comfortable with sexual techniques but also to communicate his feelings and to enjoy the intimacy of relationships. All this could lead to the development of a
genuine single standard of sexuality.

6
Contraception: Pleasure, Not Paternity

UP TO NOW, we have been dealing with sex as a means of intimate communication, a sharing of pleasure. And certainly, for men and women today, this aspect of sex is by far the most important one. But there is, of course, another aspect we have not yet considered, and sooner or later we must come to terms with it because its influence on the pleasurable side of sex is extremely important. I am referring to sex as a means of reproduction.

From a biological point of view, you might say that reproduction is the purpose of sex. Sexual pleasure, then, is the prize that nature offers us for multiplying our kind. If this prize did not exist, if each couple had to go about reproducing themselves in a wholly rational, deliberate, and nonpleasurable way, it is unlikely that the human race would have grown to its present population.

Sex accomplishes the task of preserving the human race a little too well, however. Among primitive people, fatal diseases are commonplace, and the resulting high mortality rate serves to keep population in check. In advanced society, however, where widely available medical facilities insure that nearly all children will survive to reproductive age themselves, the biological function of sex presents a serious problem. A couple who pursues the prize of sexual pleasure without thought for the consequences are likely to find themselves with more offspring than they can afford to house, clothe, and feed. If all couples followed this policy, society as a whole would soon collapse under the sheer weight of numbers.

The answer to this problem is contraception. Contraceptive devices work by short-circuiting the reproductive process at some crucial point. In effect, they separate sex from procreation, making them two unconnected functions. Thus, contraception makes it possible for us to enjoy sexual pleasure without producing unwanted children. In a very real sense, then, effective contraceptive devices are one of the human race's greatest technological achievements, a significant victory in people's struggle to control their own lives.

Considering the benefits which contraception has conferred on humanity as a whole, it is difficult to understand the average man's attitude toward the use of birth-control devices. Many men, particularly those who are unmarried, tend to think of contraception as solely a female concern. Not only do we seem to assume that the prevention of conception is something we need not bother ourselves with but our whole attitude toward the subject is frequently characterized by aversion. This reaction is particularly evident when the birth-control method in question is one for which we ourselves must be responsible. "Why wear a raincoat in the shower?" typifies many a man's response to the suggestion that he use a condom. The specious logic of this attitude breaks down under rational analysis, though: wearing a raincoat in the shower would be a very sensible precaution if the consequences of showering in the nude were as catastrophic as an unwanted pregnancy.

Why are so many of us unwilling to assume responsibility for contraception? In part, the answer to this question relates to those exploitative masculine attitudes which formed the basis of the sexual double standard. If sex was viewed as something men must get from women under false pretenses, through the use of manipulative means, then it follows that the male would see little need to take responsibility for the consequences of his actions. If women were the victims in sex, then let them be the victims of its aftermath as well—so went the basic rationalization for the lack of male concern with contraception.

True, few of us are as blatantly insensitive as this. But the image of the exploitative, "macho" male has become, through popularization by the media, a sort of ideal toward which the rest of us have sometimes unthinkingly striven. Thus, by trying to conform to what we perceived as a socially approved male stereotype, we may have acted in ways that were a good deal more irrational and self-defeating than we have realized.

The "macho" ideal left no room for us to feel concerned or responsible for conception and contraception. Instead, we had to concern ourselves with playing the part of the uncommitted, footloose seducer with little or no feeling of caring or responsibility for his partner. This situation was likely to create a painful psychological bind, a conflict of loyalties, for while normal human concern and simple common sense might make us wonder whether we should be taking some precaution against an unwanted pregnancy, at the same time the socially approved masculine code would counsel us to "go ahead and damn the consequences."

Distorted notions of human reproductive biology may be another factor in some men's lack of concern with matters of birth control. Because pregnancy occurs within the woman's body and not the man's, the responsibility for preventing conception is automatically construed as lying entirely with the woman. In this view, the woman's tendency to become pregnant as a result of intercourse is seen as an inconvenient peculiarity of her physical makeup—an inherent weakness for which she has no right to expect special consideration. Pregnancy is an exclusively feminine worry. The logical flaw here of course is that, while pregnancy may indeed be a condition exclusive to women, conception is certainly not. Intercourse occurs, or should occur, by mutual agreement between a man and woman. Conception occurs when a male sperm and a female egg, each containing exactly half the number of chromosomes needed to create a human life, merge and begin to grow into a fetus. Thus it is clear that, wherever the embryo may actually grow, the responsibility for triggering its development lies equally with the man and woman—as does the responsibility for preventing its conception.

Even if a woman tells you that it is all right to have intercourse without using contraception because it is not her time to conceive, you should not feel that you are absolved of responsibility. There is a great deal of ignorance about ovulation among women as well as men, and since the majority of young women do not ovulate regularly, the most likely result of relying on an unsystematic use of the rhythm method is an unwanted pregnancy.

Another reason for the prevailing male attitude toward contraception stems from the erroneous connection some men make between virility and the ability to sire children. If a man believes that impregnating a woman is a way of demonstrating his masculinity, then he may secretly welcome the opportunity to do so since such an accomplishment would characterize him as a "real man." Actually, there is no correspondence at all between your sexual ability and your capacity to procreate, which depends chiefly on whether you have a normal sperm count, a factor that has no effect on either sex drive or sexual skill. A man may be a great lover and yet be sterile, or he can be quite fertile and still be unsuccessful in his sexual functioning and ability to satisfy his partner.

Some men may avoid taking responsibility for contraception because they feel that to introduce such a realistic subject as birth control may destroy the romantic mood they are counting on to sweep away their potential partners' objections to intercourse. In such a situation, the woman is often guilty of complicity, for she too may wish to preserve the fiction that both of them are so carried away by sexual excitement that they are unable to stop themselves for something so mundane as a contraceptive device. Such self-deception is particularly common in first intercourse situations where excitement, anxiety, and guilt are particularly pronounced. In fact, about two-thirds of the couples engaging in intercourse for the first time do not use any form of contraception.

The couple themselves may not perceive their lack of common-sense precaution as a function of their own guilt and confusion about sexuality, believing instead that they are acting according to romantic notions that sex should be spontaneous and unplanned. Certainly, there is no arguing with the proposition that a sense of spontaneity adds to the enjoyment of sex. But as we have already seen, spontaneity and planning are not necessarily mutually exclusive. And besides, an unwanted pregnancy is far too high a price to pay for the preservation of romantic illusions. But many are apparently paying this price because statistics indicate that approximately one out of three women engaging in premarital intercourse becomes pregnant. As a general guideline, if a couple is not able to make a committment to use effective contraception, they are not ready to engage in sexual intercourse.

Once you have become intellectually convinced that you should assume your share of the responsibility for contraception, how do you go about putting that conviction into practice? Admittedly, it may not be so easy for a man, particularly a single man, to actively concern himself with contraception. A couple's decision to have intercourse is most often expressed not in verbal terms, but in a language of glances, signs, and body language. "One thing led to another, and we found ourselves in bed," expresses the experience of many couples who become sexually involved. The problem is how to interrupt that nonverbal and highly enjoyable sequence of events with a consultation about birth control and yet avoid totally destroying the mood that has been created.

Unfortunately, there is no simple solution, but there are several things you should keep in mind that might make it easier for you to act. One fear you might have is that your partner will think less of you for bringing up a prosaic subject like contraception while in the heat of passion, that by doing so you might cause her to see you as an overcautious, unromantic soul. In fact, it is unlikely that a woman would react in this way. After all, it is she who is in danger of becoming pregnant, so any precautions taken to prevent pregnancy are definitely in her interest. She is far more likely to take your concern as a sign that you are interested in her welfare and that you care about her. Thus, rather than eliciting her scorn, your interest in contraception is far more likely to be comforting and reassuring.

It is certainly true, though, that bringing up the subject of contraception can break the romantic mood. There is no use pretending that a practical question about birth control can be worded in such a way that it will not jar the mood you want to create prior to intercourse. The point to remember, however, is that the more naturally, unself-consciously, and straightforwardly the subject is introduced, the less of an intrusion it will seem. Assuming that both partners are consenting individuals who are aware of what they are doing, a note of realism, introduced in good faith, should not present an insurmountable obstacle for either the man or the woman.

Another solution to this dilemma is simply for the man to provide the means of contraception himself. Of all the contraceptive methods available, only two are male-oriented—the condom and the vasectomy. This situation results chiefly from the fact that more opportunities to prevent conception exist after ejaculation into the vagina than before. But the preponderance of female-centered contraceptive methods may also reflect the attitude in our society that contraception is the female's responsibility. In the past, contraceptive research has focused on techniques involving the female rather than the male, as in the case of oral contraceptives, and there are few indications of prospects for significant change in the near future. There has been talk of a new technique for a reversible vasectomy in which a valve installed in the vas deferens could be used to turn the flow of sperm on and off; however, there are still many problems with this operation. There have also been rumors of an effective male contraceptive pill, but it will probably be quite some time before such a product is put on the market.

Nevertheless, the male has no cause to feel that technology has passed him by, for the contraceptive methods that are readily available to him happen to be two of the most effective and trouble-free of any that can be used. The condom has particular advantages in that it is the only method of contraception which also provides protection against venereal disease. For a single man, or a man engaged in extramarital relationships, protection against VD can be quite important, particularly if he has several different sex partners. Condoms are available in most drugstores, where they can be purchased unobtrusively, and it is also possible to purchase them through the mail. The quality of condoms has improved markedly in recent years so that they now interfere much less with penile sensations. They are available in both rubber and natural membrane, lubricated and nonlubricated, and the newest varieties even come in different colors. Contrary to popular belief, very few condoms are defective (provided you do not buy bargain brands), so there is no need to test them by blowing air into them or by filling them with water. In fact, this is likely to cause damage. Finally, the condom is one of the few contraceptive methods that is entirely free of side effects.

To be effective, however, the condom must be used properly. It should not be put on until just before intercourse is to begin and the penis is erect. Some men make a habit of entering the woman without the condom in place, then withdrawing and placing it on their penis when they feel they are near ejaculation—an extremely dangerous technique that I do not recommend. Even if the man is quite sure of his ability to control his ejaculation, there is still considerable risk involved. Well before ejaculation takes place, there is a clear discharge from the Cowper's glands which often contains enough live sperm to cause conception. This is why coitus interruptus is an unreliable contraceptive technique even if the male does manage to withdraw before ejaculation.

The condom should be put on so that there is about a half-inch of space left at the tip of the penis to accommodate the ejaculated semen without danger of bursting. (Some condoms are even made with a receptacle end to provide for this need.) Immediately after ejaculation, the penis should be withdrawn from the vagina, and while withdrawing you should hold the ring at the base of the condom to prevent spillage of the ejaculate into the vagina. Remember that condoms are made to be used only once; it's false economy to try to reuse them.

Vasectomy is a totally effective contraceptive technique, its only disadvantage being that so far it is essentially irreversible. Therefore, only a male who has had as many children as he wants (or has decided he wants no children) and has discussed the issue with his wife should consider having a vasectomy. (This topic is discussed in greater detail in the following chapter.)

The ultimate birth control method is abortion. It can hardly be said to be ideal since—religious and moral questions aside—it is expensive and can involve unpleasant emotional reactions and some risk to the woman's health. But it is often the only recourse. When an unwanted pregnancy occurs, and the man and woman decide that abortion is the best solution, the man should support his partner through the experience both financially and emotionally. The same principles apply here as with other contraceptive techniques. The man must assume his share of the responsibility for conception.

We have been focusing primarily on the use of contraceptives among the unmarried. The rationale for this emphasis is that it is among unmarried men that self-defeating attitudes and misconceptions regarding contraception tend to be most prevalent and pronounced. Also, we should be able to assume that married men do not share these uncaring, irresponsible attitudes to the same extent as unmarried men, if only for the simple reason that they cannot afford to. Because a man is legally responsible for the children his wife bears, he must take some interest in contraception. Unfortunately, however, many of the attitudes, feelings, and habits a man develops premaritally are carried over into the marital situation, and in no area is this truer than in the case of contraception.

The majority of married couples have a difficult time reaching an understanding about family planning and deciding on an effective means of contraception. This fact is vividly demonstrated by statistics showing that one in four brides is pregnant at the time of marriage. Moreover, approximately 40 percent of children born to married couples are conceived without planning, and fewer than 5 percent of married men accompany their wives to the gynecologist for the purpose of discussing contraception. Research on marital adjustment indicates that it is best for a couple to wait at least two years after marriage before having their first child. Yet the average couple has their first child after being married for only a year to a year and a half—probably because of their failure to deal realistically with the question of contraception.

The main point that we, as men, need to internalize is that contraception is a *couple responsibility* for the very simple reason that procreation and child-rearing are couple functions. To duck our share of the responsibility on the excuse that the woman's body happens to be the receptacle in which conception and pregnancy take place is both unrealistic and irrational. A couple should be able to discuss their feelings about whether they want children, how many they want, and at what intervals they want them. "Letting nature take its course" may seem to be a more emotionally satisfying policy, but, as research has shown, there is no surer way to turn a relationship sour than for a couple to have children before they are ready for them. After discussing their feelings about children, a couple should then share their thoughts and attitudes regarding the contraceptive methods available to them. One thing both must realize is that there is no such thing as the "perfect" contraceptive, and each couple needs to be aware of the possible dangers and side effects of the particular contraceptive technique used in their individual case.

The birth control pill—the most popular contraceptive utilized by women—is also the most effective method of birth control available if the woman follows directions for its use and is careful not to skip doses. The synthetic hormones in the pill prevent ovulation (the releasing of the egg by the ovary), and therefore pregnancy cannot occur. However, the woman taking the pill does continue to have her regular menstrual period. It is crucial for a woman who is using the pill to undergo periodic examinations by her gynecologist because for some women the pill can have disturbing or serious side effects, some of which are still being studied.

The intrauterine device (IUD)—which ranks second only to the pill in effectiveness—is a steel, polyethylene, or copper loop, coil, bow, or ring which is placed in the uterus by a physician. Once in position, it remains in the uterus until there is some reason for taking it out (for example, if the couple desires a pregnancy), at which time it must be removed by a physician. One of the advantages of the IUD is that it does not entail a daily routine, as does the pill, or application before each sexual encounter, as do the diaphragm and condom. However, the nylon strings should be checked occasionally to make sure that the IUD has not been spontaneously expelled.

Although no one is certain of how the IUD prevents pregnancy, the most widely accepted theory is that it prevents implantation of the egg in the uterus. It should be noted that some women experience unpleasant side effects from the IUD such as irregular bleeding, and that the copper IUD sometimes leaches into the woman's system, with as-yet-to-be-measured side effects that concern doctors.

A dome-shaped, thin rubber cup stretched over a flexible ring, the diaphragm is designed to cover the entrance to the cervix and is inserted in the vagina prior to intercourse. A spermicidal cream or jelly is placed in the rubber dome and around the rim of the diaphragm; the cream or jelly is toxic to sperm and keeps them from entering the cervix. When used properly, the diaphragm is a safe and highly effective contraceptive. It must be put in place not more than two hours before intercourse, and if you are going to have intercourse a second time, another application of jelly or cream must be used; also, the woman must keep the diaphragm in place for at least six hours after intercourse. The most common complaint about the diaphragm is that to some extent it affects spontaneity in sexual relations because it must be inserted shortly before intercourse takes place.

Since the three most popular and effective forms of female contraception all require a gynecological exam and a prescription, the next step, if one of these is chosen, should be to consult with a gynecologist. The man should try to accompany his partner to the doctor's office and share in a discussion of the issues involved. If this is impossible, then he could discuss her visit with her afterward and offer support for whatever contraceptive method has been decided upon, for he should never delude himself into thinking that she alone is responsible for it.

Suppose, for example, that a couple has decided to use the pill. The man should accustom himself to the idea that, if his partner skips a day, it is not *she* who has forgotten to take her pill, but rather *they* who have forgotten to take *their* pill. The same is true for the use of the IUD and diaphragm. Instead of the woman inserting the diaphragm by herself in private, the man could learn to insert it for her as part of their pleasuring and foreplay activities. If she uses an IUD, he could make a habit of checking the strings to make sure it is in place. There are at least twenty-two different types of pills and at least five different types of IUDs. While the major responsibility for advising the couple on what kind to use should fall on the gynecologist, the man should be prepared to take an intelligent part in the decision. This sense of working together as a couple on contraception might well enhance feelings of mutuality in the sexual aspect of their relationship as well.

It is important to realize also that the question of providing effective contraception is not settled forever after the initial visit to the gynecologist. A woman is fertile until after menopause, which usually occurs between forty-five and fifty-five, and a man is fertile into his sixties and often beyond. Therefore, a couple needs to periodically discuss and reevaluate the contraceptive methods they are using in order to insure that they continue to suit their needs and life-style. Family planning and contraception are complex issues, from both a physical and a psychological point of view. Thus, there is all the more reason that they be seen as couple issues, where the male is involved as a committed, caring, and responsible partner.

7
Contraception Continued: The Case for Male Sterilization

ALTHOUGH MANY METHODS of contraception are effective, as we have seen, none is entirely without disadvantages. We judge contraceptive devices according to several criteria: reliability, convenience, the extent to which they interfere with sexual pleasure, freedom from undesirable side effects, and, finally, the ease with which their influence can be reversed. A method that scores high marks in a majority of these categories is surely worthy of our favorable consideration. We should therefore carefully examine the advantages of the contraceptive method known as vasectomy, or male sterilization.

The idea of sterilization suffers, unfortunately, from some rather negative connotations. As Shakespeare pointed out, "From fairest creatures we desire increase." The corollary to this proposition is that we do not desire increase (i.e., offspring) from creatures which are not so fair. Consequently, sterilization has at times been used as a measure to prevent individuals judged to be socially undesirable, such as criminals or mental defectives, from reproducing themselves. Hence, in the popular imagination, sterilization has come to be thought of as something which is basically punitive in nature.

The distaste with which many of us view sterilization can also be traced to a confusion between vasectomy and castration, a deeply ingrained fear in most males. Even though a man might understand intellectually that the two operations are totally different, he may retain an emotional aversion for anything that bears even a superficial resemblance to the dreaded "loss of manhood." The fact that castration is often used as a means of sterilizing pets and farm animals may also tend to add unpleasant emotional connotations. In thinking about sterilization, a man might be reminded of the family tom cat who was sent to the vet to be "altered" and thereafter became overweight, docile, and uninterested in sex. On the basis of these associations, he may conclude that it is wisest to avoid any and all situations involving the close proximity of his testicles and a sharp instrument.

While such fears are quite natural and understandable, it must be stressed that vasectomy has nothing in common with castration, either in terms of the mechanics of the operation or in its aftereffects. Castration involves the removal of the testicles. Vasectomy, on the other hand, is a simple and safe procedure in which the vas deferens, two small tubes leading from the testicles, are cut and tied so that sperm produced in the testicles does not proceed to the penis. The testicles still continue to produce sperm, but it is absorbed back into the body rather than becoming part of the ejaculate. The total volume of semen does not diminish noticeably, even though it no longer contains sperm because the sperm themselves are so small. The sensations accompanying ejaculation do not change at all, and there is no loss of pleasure. Nor is there the slightest change in the male's desire or capacity for sex.

Sex drive is regulated by the supply of testosterone, a hormone which is also produced in the testicles, but which enters the body, not through the vas deferens, but through the bloodstream. Testosterone production and distribution are completely unaffected by the sterilization process. Hence, it would be extremely unusual for a male who has had no potency problem to develop one after a vasectomy, and in those rare cases the cause is almost always psychological rather than physical. In fact, sexual desire often increases after vasectomy for both the man and the woman simply because their sexuality is no longer inhibited by the fear of pregnancy. To repeat, the only physical effect of a vasectomy is to eliminate the male's ability to have children; there is no effect on potency, sexual ability, or desire.

There are some common misconceptions about vasectomy—that it is a lengthy and expensive operation, that it requires a general anesthetic, that it involves painful aftereffects, and that it requires time for convalescence. Actually, men undergoing vasectomies are often amazed that an operation whose effect on their lives is so profound can entail less pain and discomfort than a visit to the dentist. The vasectomy is, in fact, a minor surgical procedure which is performed in the doctor's office; the operation itself takes about fifteen minutes, and the total time spent in the office is usually less than an hour. The majority of vasectomy operations are performed by private urologists in their offices at a cost of $150 to $250, often covered by medical insurance. However, many cities have developed outpatient vasectomy clinics where the operation is performed for a lower fee.

After administering a local anesthetic, the doctor makes two small incisions in the scrotum, cuts and ties the vas deferens, and the operation is over. The potential for side effects and postoperative complications is minimal. In approximately one out of 300 cases, a hematoma (blood clot) may develop on the testicle. When this does occur, the hematoma is either allowed to drain or is removed surgically, a low-risk, rather simple procedure. Aside from this relatively rare and easily corrected problem, present research indicates that there is little evidence of any serious problems developing from vasectomies.

Moreover, the vasectomy operation involves little or no subsequent discomfort or interruption in the patient's activities. There may be some slight soreness lasting for no more than a day or two after the surgery. During this time, the patient is advised to refrain from strenuous activity, and he may want to wear an athletic supporter. In any case, there should be no reason for him to miss more than one day of work, if even that. Usually there is a swelling on each testicle about the size of a small nut, but this disappears in about a week and is no cause for concern.

The man does not become sterile immediately after the vasectomy operation. Because the sperm remain lodged in the upper part of the vas, in the seminal vesicles, and in the *ejaculatory ducts*, from ten to sixteen ejaculations are required to "clean out" all the sperm from the semen. During this time, other means of contraception must be used to prevent pregnancy, and they should not be dispensed with until after the patient is checked by his physician to make sure his semen no longer contains sperm. For this test, the vasectomy patient must have intercourse using a condom, or masturbate (or have his partner stimulate him) to orgasm and collect the ejaculate in a jar. He then brings the sample to the urologist for analysis. A similar examination should be conducted again six months later to make sure that the vas has not accidently grown back together. This is an extremely rare occurrence, but it has been known to happen. So it pays to be careful.

One question often raised is the possibility of a "reversible vasectomy." There is some research and experimentation on methods to accomplish this, but at present a vasectomy should be considered essentially an irreversible procedure. One technique that is being developed and tested is a spigot that could be implanted in the vas and used to start and stop the flow of sperm. However, along with the technical difficulties of perfecting the spigot, there is an added problem that when the sperm are not being used, there seems to be some decrease in sperm production and the viability of the sperm produced. Thus, even if the spigot were turned back on, the sperm might no longer be effective and the male would still be unable to impregnate a woman. However, if this technique is perfected in the future, it could make the vasectomy the best birth-control method ever devised.

The irreversibility of the vasectomy procedure is, in fact, its only major drawback. According to all the other criteria by which we judge the overall worth of contraceptive devices, vasectomy rates extremely high. It is almost 100 percent reliable, it is convenient, it does not diminish sexual pleasure, and it has no undesirable side effect. One possible way of dealing with its irreversibility is for the male to deposit sperm in a sperm bank prior to having a vasectomy. Then, if the couple later decided to have more children the husband's sperm could be used to inseminate the wife artificially. There is some question, however, as to how long sperm remain viable under such conditions, so that one cannot be altogether certain of success. Of course, there is always the possibility that the wife could become pregnant by using sperm from a donor other than her husband. However, the husband and wife would be well advised to examine their feelings carefully before choosing this course.

For many couples in their middle years, the husband's decision to have a vasectomy can be the beginning of a rejuvenation of their sexual relationship. Alan, a forty-two-year-old client of mine, married twenty-two years and the father of three children, is a case in point. Two of Alan's children had been unplanned, and the problem of finding an adequate contraceptive method had been a major inhibiting factor in his relationship with his wife. They had tried almost everything and were now using the rhythm method along with a spermicidal foam. However, sex for them could never be really spontaneous under these conditions. Alan had never thought of having a vasectomy until a friend of his had one. At first he was reluctant even to discuss it because of his fears that the operation would make him less masculine or less sexually potent. Even though he realized that these fears were irrational, he could not dismiss them from his mind. His attitude improved when he read some literature about vasectomy and learned the facts about the operation. After much thought and several discussions with his wife, he decided that it would be the best contraceptive method for them to use. He felt anxious on the day of the operation, but found to his surprise that it was "easier than having a tooth pulled." There were no complications, and three months later Alan and his wife found themselves able to have sex spontaneously, without worrying about pregnancy. In no time, they were having intercourse more often and their enjoyment of it increased to a level they had not experienced since their first child was born.

Like Alan, the majority of men who have vasectomies find that the operation has a positive effect on their sexual relationships and on their lives in general. I know that this is true in my own case. One of the most difficult elements in my decision to have a vasectomy was the fact that I had been very much involved in Emily's two pregnancies and had thoroughly enjoyed the whole process of having children. A vasectomy meant giving up the possibility of becoming a parent again. However, we finally decided that two biological children were enough for us, and I went ahead with the operation. I have had no regrets whatsoever since then, and I find that being voluntarily sterile has given our sexual relationship a freedom it had never quite had before.

As Emily and I did, a couple should frankly and maturely discuss the factors involved, and only when they are quite satisfied that vasectomy is the best answer to their contraceptive needs should the man take steps to have the operation performed.

Clearly, vasectomy is not for everyone. It would not be a wise choice for a young, unmarried man or for a man who is uncertain whether he and his wife want more children. Nor would it seem to be the best choice for the man who is either divorced or contemplating divorce and who may wish to have children with a new wife in the future. But for a man who has decided along with his wife that they have as many children as they want, and who wishes to be free of the possibility of causing an unwanted pregnancy, it may be the ideal alternative. Single, widowed, or divorced men who are certain that they wish to father no more children may also be excellent candidates for vasectomy. Apparently, the number of men who see themselves as belonging to these categories is increasing. In 1970, there were approximately 320,000 vasectomies performed in the United States, and by 1974, the number had risen to approximately 555,000. Vasectomy is also gaining in popularity in other parts of the world.

The fact that vasectomy is a male-oriented contraceptive method, that it allows the male to take the initiative in birth control and family planning is very much in its favor. As noted in the previous chapter, some men are apt to willfully ignore the fact that baby-making is a fifty-fifty enterprise and to consider contraception the exclusive responsibility of the woman. Male sterilization allows us to correct this distorted view by taking the major portion of the responsibility on ourselves. In this way, we can make a major contribution toward establishing that atmosphere of trust and sharing which is essential to a good sexual relationship. When undertaken in a spirit of mature understanding and cooperation, a vasectomy can serve as a means by which a man lets his wife know how much he cares about her and is committed to their relationship. Of course, if there are serious problems in the marriage to begin with, it is unlikely that a vasectomy will resolve them. But if the relationship is already a good one, the husband's decision to have a vasectomy can and often does improve things by providing greater trust and freedom.

The objection might be raised that the man should not necessarily be the one to undergo sterilization since such a procedure is also available for the woman. The two most common female sterilization techniques, however, known as tubal ligation and laparoscopy, are major surgical procedures compared with vasectomy. They entail hospitalization, far more discomfort, and greater risk. If for no other reason than that vasectomy is so much simpler and safer, it makes sense for the male to be the one to undergo the sterilization procedure.

Of course, sterilization for either a man or a woman should always be a joint decision, and there may be cases in which female sterilization would be the best alternative—if, for example, the man had a strong aversion to vasectomy, while the woman felt strongly committed to sterilization. In any case, a thorough discussion of the matter by the couple, as well as a consultation with a gynecologist, should precede any such action.

The same holds true for men. No man, whatever his situation, should allow himself to be pressured into having a vasectomy. If he feels ambivalent about undergoing the sterilization procedure, it would probably be best not to go ahead with it. It is important that his decision to have a vasectomy be based on his true feelings and that there be no margin of doubt. The most undesirable consequence of a vasectomy would be for the man to be sorry afterward and to be left with a feeling of having been victimized. The choice of a vasectomy should be made freely, with the man understanding the operation and its effects and feeling comfortable with his sense of himself as a man both before and after the operation. But above all, he should remember that sterility is an unfortunate condition only for men who want to father children. When parenthood is not desired, sterility becomes a positive good because it confers upon a man a rare degree of freedom to express himself sexually.

8
Dealing with VD

VD. VENEREAL DISEASE. Venereal: from *Venus*, the Roman goddess of love. Hence, venereal disease: the disease of love. A depressing idea, that you can get a disease from making love. And yet, VD is a very real thing. It is, in fact, the most prevalent infectious disease next to the common cold. To leave it out of a discussion of sexuality would be unrealistic. One of the major premises of this book is that a person must take responsibility for his behavior and accept the consequences of it whether pleasant or unpleasant. VD can be an unfortunate consequence of sexual behavior, and thus it is an eventuality that may have to be dealt with by anyone who engages in sex.

But it is important to keep one distinction firmly in mind. You don't get VD *because* you have sex. It isn't a judgment, a punishment, a bacterial sword of Damocles waiting to fall on the sexual transgressor. Rather, you contract VD *through* sexual contact, which is a very different thing. The idea that VD is one of the penalties of sex has long been used by moralists for the suppression of sexual activity. It is an old and tenacious fallacy, akin to the medieval notion that plagues came about as a direct result of the sinful behavior of the populace. The fact that such ideas often gain such widespread acceptance attests to the capacity of human beings to feel irrational guilt rather than to the idea's validity. The medieval plagues were caused not by sin but by poor sanitation. Similarly, the current epidemic of VD is not a punishment we have brought down upon ourselves through increased sexuality, but the result of ignorance and lack of responsibility. It is the consequence of our failure to face the problem squarely, to plan our sexual activities, and to take responsibility for our sexual behavior.

Avoiding sex because it can give you VD is not the answer. After all, you can contract influenza by breathing in viruses that have been exhaled by an infected person, and you can catch hepatitis by eating contaminated food—hardly valid reasons for either avoiding the company of other human beings or refusing to take in nourishment. The situation with VD is virtually identical. The answer is not to avoid sex, but to be aware of ways of preventing, detecting, and treating VD so that this medical problem does not interfere with your sexual functioning.

Connected with the idea that VD is a punishment for sexual activity is the notion that only morally "degenerate" and "dirty" people contract VD. It is common for people to think that VD "can't happen to me," that it is contracted only by a vaguely defined group of people who are considered to be morally and socially inferior to oneself. When a person who thinks in these terms contracts VD, his usual reaction is one of intense surprise and shame: "This can't be happening to me—not *me!*" He may feel that having VD brands him as precisely one of those undesirable individuals whom he previously scorned. He may also turn upon the sex partner whom he suspects of having given him VD and accuse her of being a "whore." Such an attitude makes little sense when one considers the extreme prevalence of VD. In 1974, there were seven hundred thousand reported cases of gonorrhea alone, and since most cases go unreported, it is estimated that the actual figure was more like two and a half million. In the face of such numbers, it becomes clear that VD must be taken seriously by *all* of us.

If there is any group more prone to VD than others, it is the young, for the highest incidence rate is found among individuals between the ages of fifteen and nineteen. But VD attacks people of all ages, races, religions, and socioeconomic groups. If you think for a moment about the extent of the networks formed in our society through sexual contact, it will become obvious that there are very few people who are not potential VD victims. Clearly, VD is a medical disease, not a moral judgment or a sign of the kind of person you are.

How does one contract VD? In order to answer this question, it is necessary to distinguish between the two most common venereal diseases, gonorrhea and syphilis. Gonorrhea (also known as "clap," "dose," and "strain") is passed from person to person through genital contact. Heterosexual intercourse is not the only way the disease is transmitted, however. It is also possible to contract gonorrhea through oral and anal sex. It follows that it can be transmitted through homosexual as well as heterosexual contacts, and, in fact, the recorded VD rate among homosexual males is considerably higher than among heterosexual males, but this may be partly the result of the greater reluctance of homosexual VD victims to report sexual contacts to medical authorities, so that other infected men may continue unknowingly to transmit the disease. Syphilis (also known as "pox," "bad blood," and "syph") is transmitted by close, intimate contact that is usually but not always sexual. It is quite possible, for example, for syphilis to be transmitted by kissing if one of the people has an infection or chancre in his or her mouth. The germs that cause both syphilis and gonorrhea die very quickly if they are not in a warm, moist environment. Thus, contrary to the popular notion, it is impossible to catch VD through contact with unsanitary toilet seats.

Statistics indicate that about one out of every four men in our society will contract venereal disease at some point in their lives. Since it is impossible to be certain that you will never become a victim to VD, it is a good idea to know how to recognize whether you have it or not.

Gonorrhea is the most common venereal disease (the cases outnumber syphilis by ten to one) and, as we have seen, it is passed from person to person through genital contact. Major symptoms in men are a burning sensation in the urethra during urination, and a heavy discharge of whitish or yellowish pus from the penis. These symptoms occur in most cases, but some males contract gonorrhea without developing any discernible symptoms. Untreated or improperly treated gonorrhea can result in kidney problems, bladder infections, blood poisoning, and even arthritis.

Gonorrhea is considerably more difficult to detect in women because they usually experience no symptoms whatever, although some do feel pain while urinating and have a vaginal discharge. Untreated gonorrhea in women can lead to even more severe problems than in men, including permanent sterility and uterine infections. The incubation period for gonorrhea in both men and women is from two to ten days. The symptoms, if any, begin to appear after this period.

The only sure way to determine whether or not you have gonorrhea is to go for a test at a doctor's office, a Planned Parenthood clinic, or a public health clinic. The test used, a smear and culture, is the only definite way of determining whether a person has the disease. A blood test, or VDRL, which is used to test for syphilis, will not reveal the presence of gonorrhea. It is a good idea, by the way, to specifically request a VDRL test in addition to a smear and culture, even if the symptoms you display point to gonorrhea rather than syphilis. It is quite possible to have both diseases at the same time. Fortunately, gonorrhea can be easily cured by treatment with penicillin or by another antibiotic drug when the patient is allergic to penicillin.

Syphilis is more difficult to detect because its first symptom, a painless sore or chancre, does not show up until ten to ninety days after contact with the infected person and often appears on a part of the body that can escape casual notice, such as the anus. In most cases, however, the chancre appears somewhere near the penis. If left untreated, syphilis progresses through four stages. Primary syphilis is signaled by the appearance of the chancre. Secondary syphilis may take up to six months to develop, and its symptoms include body rashes, loss of hair, sore throat, headaches, and fever. In some cases, however, these symptoms may be mild or non-existent.

As with gonorrhea, the disease is much more difficult to detect in women than in men. During the third stage, known as the latent stage, the spirochete (the organism that causes the disease) enters the bloodstream. There are no symptoms at this point at all, and the victim may thus be led to believe that the disease has gone away of its own accord. The last stage, however, usually brings a rude awakening from this false sense of well-being. It may occur as early as two years or as late as fifty years after the initial infection and can produce heart failure, blindness, paralysis, insanity, and, eventually, death. An ordinary blood test, of the sort given as a regular part of a physical examination, is not designed to detect syphilis, so if you have any reason to suspect you may have syphilis, you must specifically request a VDRL. Penicillin and other antibiotic drugs can completely cure syphilis in its early stages. The disease can be cured in its later stages as well, but whatever damage has already been done to the body is permanent and cannot be repaired.

There is no doubt about the fact that VD, because of its peculiar symptomatology, is frequently difficult to detect and therefore often goes untreated. However, the medical difficulties of treating the disease are insignificant compared with the psychological resistance which prevents the majority of its victims from dealing with it in a rational manner. Most of us feel that particular diseases affect our images as people in particular ways. Certain diseases are considered socially acceptable while others are not. Thus, a person who has suffered a heart attack may feel affronted or despondent that his body has failed him, but it would probably not occur to him to hide the nature of his malady from others. In fact, since heart disease is usually connected with psychological strain and overwork, some sufferers may even feel a subconscious pride at being able to display incontrovertible proof that they have dedicated themselves to the work ethic so unstintingly. But as has already been pointed out, most people feel intense shame when they find that they are suffering from VD. They feel that the disease identifies them with the world of prostitutes, of seamy, lower-class characters slowly rotting away from the consequences of their immoral lives. So intense is this shame that many victims will not allow themselves to believe that they actually have VD, even after the symptoms manifest themselves unmistakably. How could they have VD when they are simply "not that sort of person"?

Because of this view of VD, many people who contract it either avoid having it treated or wait so long before seeing a doctor that complications set in that lead to permanent damage. Other victims may seek treatment in time, but go to great lengths to see that the matter is "hushed up." Unfortunately, many doctors are willing to cater to this anxiety. The law requires all VD cases to be reported to the health authorities, and the victim is obligated to furnish the names and addresses of all his recent sex partners. This information, embarrassing as it may be to divulge, is necessary so that those people who may have been exposed to infection can be notified and treated. But many private physicians comply with their patients' request not to file such a report, and as a result, others with whom the victim has had sex are left to discover the disease on their own. Because the symptoms are not always noticeable, especially among women, it may be quite a while before this occurs. Meanwhile, the infection may spread from one person to another until dozens, perhaps hundreds, have been affected.

It is obvious that the microorganisms that cause the disease have no interest in the social status of their victims. As far as VD is concerned, we are all one big family, and it makes no more sense to be ashamed of catching VD than it does to be ashamed of catching measles. Moreover, whatever shame may be connected with VD should be more than outweighed by your sense of responsibility to your own well-being, to society in general, and especially to the people whom you choose as your sex partners. Responsibility ought to be the keynote of all our sexual involvements.

In view of the ease with which VD can be cured once it is detected, there is really no excuse for the fact that its occurrence has grown in our society to epidemic proportions. Lately, there have been public information and advertising campaigns aimed at providing the public with accurate information concerning VD. Free VD clinics have been set up which treat all patients confidentially, including those under legal age. And a Public Broadcasting television special called "VD Blues" was given national exposure for the purpose of alerting people to the realities of VD.

Despite all these efforts, however, the incidence of VD is still on the increase. Apparently, the shame connected with the disease continues to be intense, and until steps are taken to correct this situation, irrational and self-defeating behavior will remain the rule. In some ways the public's attitude toward VD resembles the syndrome of fear, denial, and embarrassment that until recently surrounded breast cancer and prevented many women from being tested and seeking treatment. The turning point in this case occurred when, in rapid succession, Betty Ford and Happy Rockefeller announced their operations for breast cancer. The example set by these two leading public figures—the wives of the President and the Vice President—encouraged many women to learn more about breast cancer and to begin having themselves tested periodically. As a result, there has been a dramatic increase in the detection of breast cancer in its early stages. It would be a great step toward bringing the disease under control if a comparable public figure were to perform a similar service with respect to VD. Considering the prevalence of the disease, there should not be any lack of opportunity, and the example of one or two courageous persons might be all that would be needed to bring about a wholesale change in the public's attitude toward VD.

In a sense, we men are fortunate because the male symptoms of VD are more distinct, and the chances of detecting it in its early stages are much greater than in women, who usually have no symptoms. And in most cases, reservations about seeking treatment are overcome by the obvious physical discomfort a man experiences when he has gonorrhea. Whatever a man's motivations in seeking treatment, though, the responsible and compassionate thing for him to do if he finds out that he has gonorrhea or any other form of VD is to inform anyone with whom he has had intimate contact. By doing so, he may help her to detect VD in its early stages and avoid the consequences of the later forms of the disease.

The effects of untreated gonorrhea are particularly severe in women; moreover, since nine out of ten women exhibit no noticeable symptoms, the danger of permanent damage occurring before the disease is identified is great.

The problem of how to tell a sex partner that she should be tested for VD is often complex, however, particularly if informing her of the facts involves revealing that you have had other sexual contacts she was unaware of. There is no "right" way to do this, but for the sake of your partner's health it is crucial that you give her the information. You can either take the responsibility yourself or have the medical authorities contact her. The latter alternative is, of course, the less courageous one, but at least it gets the job done, and that is the main thing. Whichever way you choose and whatever the possible negative consequences to the relationship, the only sensible course of action is to tell your partner since the health hazards of untreated VD are so great.

The discovery of VD can often present difficult problems in addition to the obvious medical ones. A student of mine named Ralph, a twenty-eight-year-old salesman, was engaged to be married, but often indulged in casual affairs while on sales trips away from home. Six months before the date set for the wedding, during one such trip, he had sex with a woman whom he had met in a bar. He came home on a Friday and spent a sexually active weekend with his fiancée. Several days later Ralph noticed a burning sensation in his penis during urination. Suspecting gonorrhea, he went to his physician for tests. The tests were positive, so the doctor treated Ralph with penicillin, but he did not urge him to supply the names of recent sex partners. Thus, Ralph had to decide for himself what to tell his fiancée. For a day or two, he was tortured by doubts and indecision. Actually, he had no way of telling whether he had caught VD from the girl he'd met on the business trip or from his fiancée herself. If his fiancée was responsible, then this meant she had had another sex partner, and despite his own infidelities, Ralph found this infuriating. But whether she had infected him or not, chances were she now had the disease herself and would have to be told sooner or later. For several more days Ralph attempted, through indirect questioning, to determine whether she had had sexual relations with anyone besides himself. Finally, getting nowhere with these questions, he decided to tell her straight out. He did so, and she accepted the news far more calmly than he had anticipated. Ralph went with her to her gynecologist for tests, which turned out to be positive. The episode was not pleasant for either of them, but on the whole, Ralph's fiancée felt more reassured about Ralph's concern for her welfare than she felt hurt by his having had sex with another woman. The wedding took place on schedule.

There are four primary methods of preventing VD. The first is to be discriminating about the people you have sexual relations with. But since no particular class of people is immune to VD, this method can never be totally successful. The second method is to use a condom when having intercourse, particularly with someone you do not know well. The third is to wash the genitals with soap as soon after sexual contact as possible. The fourth is to take a dose of penicillin or other antibiotic immediately after sexual contact. Since antibiotics are generally available only with a doctor's prescription, this last method may be difficult to put into operation. A secondary method of dealing with the possibility of VD is simply to take steps to insure early detection. In addition to being alert to the onset of the physical symptoms, a man who is sexually active with a number of different partners should have a smear and culture as well as a VDRL test administered at least once a year and preferably every six months. These tests are not typically given as part of a regular physical examination, so it is necessary to request them specifically.

Throughout this book it is assumed that the best and most realistic criterion for judging if a particular sexual practice is acceptable or not is whether it is harmful in some way to either your partner or yourself. It seems indisputable that you cannot do yourself much good by harming others. VD greatly enlarges the possibility of your harming others through sex or of being harmed by them. But basically, the ethics governing one's attitude toward VD need not be any different from the ethics of sexuality in general. Behavior that is based on caring, compassion, and responsibility will serve equally well in all cases.

9
Developing Sensual Awareness: A World Regained

HOW IMPORTANT is a hug? A kiss? A caress? It's impossible to place a specific value on physical affection, but if you are like most men, your impulse is probably to rate these activities fairly low on the scale of things which are essential to your survival.

You didn't always feel that way, you know. In fact, when you were a baby your expectations were quite different. Your need for affection was taken as much for granted as the food you ate or the air you breathed. And if you had suddenly been deprived of physical tenderness, the effect would probably have been almost as devastating as the absence of food or oxygen, though not, of course, as immediate. It is an established fact that babies usually do not develop normally and sometimes sicken if they are not regularly picked up and given physical warmth and affection. This is why nurses in orphanages are encouraged to cuddle parentless babies in addition to caring for their physical needs. To an infant, the physical expression of love is as important as nourishment.

It isn't difficult to put oneself in the place of an infant and to imagine why this need should exist. To a baby, physical affection, besides being a source of pleasure, means that it is being protected, cared for. To a certain extent, of course, we outgrow this need, or rather, we develop the capacity to be reassured through other means besides physical ones. To an older child, a smile or a kind word may have a positive effect equal to that of a physical display of affection. And yet we never entirely lose our need for physical warmth and tenderness. Whether we are eight or eighty, it is nice to be touched.

Unfortunately, as we grow older, we seem to touch and be touched less and less. This is especially true with males. Studies have shown that from a very early age, boys are treated with far less physical expressiveness than girls. Such sexual differentiation is part of society's campaign to make us strong, tough, self-reliant, even stoic, to prepare us for the rigors of adult male competition. Whether this training really does make us more fit to compete is a matter of debate, and one which need not concern us here. What does concern us are the side effects of this deprivation with regard to our adjustment to adult sexuality. Here the outlook does not seem to be very positive.

As we have seen in previous chapters, the tendency is for males to regard nearly all sexual situations as basically competitive and goal-oriented. In his relations with women, the man is encouraged to seek the goal of intercourse. The man who "scores" with a woman is regarded with admiration by his male friends, and the one who scores with many women is accorded special respect and envy. In the sex act itself, the goal is orgasm; this brief, intense sensation is considered by most males to be the only really worthwhile part of sex. The average man achieves orgasm rather quickly—usually within one to two minutes of intromission. Even when he learns to prolong the experience, he usually does so with the understanding that it is for the sake of his female partner, whose responses are usually not as quick as his own. As for the physical expressions of affection which precede intercourse, the very name that has been given to them by male writers—foreplay—conveys the idea that they are something of lesser importance, and mere preliminaries leading up to the "real thing."

It seems undeniable that this tendency of ours to sell short all sensual experience other than orgasm is related to our early training, to the fact that from an early age, males are often encouraged to do without physical expressions of affection. This early learning has apparently convinced us to dismiss kisses, hugs, spontaneous caresses as having little value if they are not followed by intercourse. We tend to forget that such behavior is highly pleasurable in itself. Furthermore, the fact that women seem to place a higher value on nongoal-oriented pleasuring reflects in part the greater freedom they are permitted in the physical expression of affection as children and adults. This disparity between the values that men and women place on physical affection is frequently a source of contention and misunderstanding between couples.

It is common for women to express dissatisfaction with the amount of intimate contact and physical affection they receive from their partners—not only in bed but at other times of the day. Men are often confused by this criticism because it is difficult for them to think of affectionate behavior as being particularly enjoyable or worthwhile. They tend to regard the expression of physical love as a specialized activity which is circumscribed spatially by the four walls of the bedroom and temporally by the time between lights-out and sleep. The fact of the matter is that we men have imposed on ourselves a state of sensual impoverishment. All is not lost, however. By opening ourselves to the possibilities of nongoal-oriented pleasure, we can regain that childhood world of spontaneous physical affection. Moreover, we will find that this world is even richer and more rewarding now that we are adults. Affectionate touching can convey not only the sense of protection, security, and comfort, which we enjoyed as children, but also mature emotions such as respect, gratitude, and sexual attraction. As well as providing a heightened sense of physical pleasure, the development of sensual awareness can have a positive effect on a couple's personal and sexual relationship. It is a skill well worth learning.

Many men would define sexual pleasure as the enjoyable sensations experienced through the genitals during intercourse. But a moment's thought will reveal that this definition is an extremely narrow one since it eliminates all the nongenital pleasures that we experience during sex. For example, what about the pleasure of seeing our partner's body, either nude or in various stages of undress? What of the pleasure of whispered words of love, or the excitement of hearing our partner's moans and heavy breathing? What of the smell of our partner's body mingling with our own? What of the sense of movement as we engage in coital thrusting? What of the tastes experienced during oral-genital sex? What of the infinite number of ways in which one human being can pleasurably stroke and caress another?

Nor is sexual pleasure by any means limited to the bedroom. For example, there is the exquisite thrill of touching knees under a table when the person attached to the knee happens to be someone we are attracted to. There is the erotic reaction we have to sniffing a particular perfume in the street or in an elevator. And there are the peculiar pelvic sensations we may experience in response to a certain word or phrase spoken in a certain tone of voice. If we are honest with ourselves, it becomes obvious that we are sexual creatures twenty-four hours a day, that sexual pleasure may occur anytime, anywhere, and that we are susceptible to it through all our five senses. Thus, we see the folly of trying to limit sex to a strictly delineated time and place and to a specific range of physical sensation. What makes a certain sensation sexual is the interpretation we place on it and the feelings that result. Thus, it is the mind which is the ultimate sex organ, determining what will turn us on and what will turn us off.

Unfortunately, this mind of ours, this central switchboard of sexual pleasure, too often acts as a sort of censor, closing down circuits, forbidding certain types of messages. Touching, caressing, and kissing are usually most exciting at the beginning of a relationship, probably because the couple has shared relatively few of these experiences. Each person is still learning how the other expresses his or her affection.

Discovering new things about one's partner can be a stimulating and exciting experience. For a couple who has not yet had intercourse, the fantasies about it are often rich and varied. But as a couple becomes increasingly involved sexually, simple gestures of affection often begin to lose their significance. Intercourse, enjoyed on a regular basis, tends to become the sole means of displaying physical affection. Kissing, caressing, and other pleasuring activities, once so exciting and important, now become mere "foreplay," a brief, hurried prelude to coitus.

While there is no disputing the fact that intercourse is the ultimate in sexual expression, there is certainly something wrong with the idea that other sensual and affectionate behavior is worth engaging in only when it is followed by intercourse. In fact, if intercourse is to continue to be exciting and satisfying, there must be experimentation, spontaneity, variety, and novelty. Naturally, trying new intercourse positions, of which there are dozens, is one of the chief ways of introducing novelty into sexual relations. But there are countless ways of expressing affection through sensual behavior which does not necessarily lead to intercourse. If we want to introduce new energy and enjoyment into our sex lives, what better way than to concentrate on reopening our closed circuits, expanding our consciousness to include modes of affectionate behavior that we have allowed to fall into disuse, and thus opening up a whole new world of sensual and sexual experiences?

One of the main reasons that we lose our capacity to experience pleasure freely and spontaneously is that we have allowed ourselves to become too damned grown up. As children, we responded intensely to the world because each experience was new and there was little to detract from our concentration. But as we mature, we become absorbed by our responsibilities, we assume that our knowledge of the world is complete and that there is little that we can learn. If we could recapture that openness of mind and senses we enjoyed as children, though, we would find that the world is still full of novel and surprising experiences. The number of ways to experience physical affection are almost limitless and, of course, part of the fun is discovering new activities that are pleasurable and exciting. But here are some suggestions that may help to add a new dimension to your relationship with your partner.

Learn to concentrate on and to increase your awareness of ordinary acts of physical touching such as hand contact. Pick up your partner's hand and spend some moments examining it as though you are seeing it for the first time. Tenderly explore each aspect of it, allowing yourself to become engrossed by the tiny details of construction—the nails, the cuticles, the knuckles, the loose folds of skin between the fingers, the veins on the back of the hand. Turn the hand over and trace the lines of the palm with your fingertip. Be aware of the delicate tactile messages that you are sending to your partner through this contact. It goes without saying, of course, that you should pick an appropriate moment for this activity. It may be part of a session the two of you have agreed to set aside for sensual exploration, or it may be entirely spontaneous. If the latter, your partner may be initially surprised by your attentions, particularly if you are not in the habit of acting this way. But provided that you are genuinely tender and affectionate, it is likely that your partner will be pleased and responsive. In fact, the pleasant surprise caused by a spontaneous act of affection often enhances its impact and may serve to trigger the release of sexual feelings whose intensity can be quite startling.

The eyes can also be organs of sensual communication. In everyday life, we observe strict rules about the amount and type of eye contact permissible with other individuals. Thus, allowing ourselves to gaze long and deeply into another person's eyes can be an experience of unique intimacy. Prolonged eye contact may be combined with other forms of affectionate expression such as touching, caressing, and hand holding. This can serve to create a moment filled with poignant and romantic sensuality.

A back rub or a massage is another effective way of expressing affection as well as being a pleasant, relaxing experience for your partner. It is an excellent method of projecting a sense of caring and of promoting relaxed, happy feelings between you. Massage can be even more enjoyable if both of you are nude. In fact, this is a comfortable way to experience nudity in a nonintercourse situation. The point of massage is to relax the muscles of the body through kneading, pressing, and stretching motions. You can't go far wrong if you use your hands sensitively and gently and if you follow your partner's suggestions about what does and does not feel good. Try to make your touching slow, rhythmic, and tender, with no demand for response other than the experience of pleasure. If you like, you can learn the fine points of massage—the special movements designed to relax specific parts of the musculature. Consult the various books available, or you could even take a course in the subject— preferably you and your partner together. One way of making massage even more enjoyable is to use a scented oil (or even something like baby oil) as a lubricant. It is most satisfying if both partners learn to practice massage on each other and if you can integrate it into your life so that either of you can ask for a massage without feeling self-conscious. Besides being relaxing, enjoyable, and invigorating, massage is an excellent way of becoming at ease and familiar with your partner's body and of learning about physical and sensual communication in ways that can be beneficial to sexual functioning.

Another highly pleasurable and exciting experience is to bathe or shower with your partner. If you are not in the habit of doing this, there may be some embarrassment and discomfort the first time you try it. Most of us think of bathing as a solitary activity, and while the idea of doing it with a partner may be appealing, there may be a reluctance to break the accustomed pattern. Try suggesting it to your partner casually. For example, the next time she takes a shower, you might say, "Do you mind if I join you?" If the initial response is negative, you will have to use your judgment about what to say next. If your partner has a splitting headache and wants to spend a quiet hour in a warm tub, your best bet would be to desist. But if the negative response seems to be based more on self-consciousness, you might try countering by saying, "Come on, it'll be fun," or "We don't have to do anything else except just enjoy a shower together." Showering or bathing is a sensual, relaxing experience even when done alone, so it is the perfect way of exploring new possibilities of physical pleasure. You can take turns slowly soaping each other. The addition of warm water and rich, soapy lather enhances the feeling of touching and caressing your partner's body in a novel way. You can extend the pleasure of this experience by drying each other off. Brushing each other's hair is another way of turning a commonplace, personal act into a shared sensual experience. Showering or bathing together can also be an excellent preparation for mutual pleasuring and intercourse because it is a wonderful way of becoming relaxed, intimate, and open to physical sensations. And it has the advantage of making the body clean, fresh, and sweet-smelling so that it is a particular pleasure both to touch and be touched.

Although most methods of physical expression are suited to conveying a message of caring, affection, and tenderness, this need not always be the case. Many healthy relationships have a degree of aggression built into them, and it is usually better to express such feelings in a playful, physical way rather than to let them fester inside us. There are many ways we can do this, such as having a pillow fight or a wrestling or tickling match. Sometimes, when giving your partner a massage, you may want to bear down hard or rub rapidly. Expressing tensions and aggressions in one of these harmless ways can be stimulating sexually as well as providing an emotional release.

Couples should also feel free to express themselves in other ways, even if they seem childish or foolish. You might try playing roles, indulging in fantasy and pantomime, just as children do. The major difference will be that your role playing will probably be considerably more adult in content. The prostitute and her client, the princess and the slave, the sultan and the harem girl are just a few of the more conventional possibilities. The fact that both you and your partner recognize that these are fantasies and not reality should allow you to express yourself freely and to give vent to feelings and attitudes that you ordinarily avoid and you may even disapprove of in real life.

These are just a few of the many ways available for developing your sensual awareness and adding new excitement and meaning to your relationship with your partner. As we have seen, the situations in which we are apt to experience sensual or sexual feelings are potentially unlimited. Thus, there is no limit to the ways we can introduce sensuality and sexuality into a relationship. Imagination, sensitivity, and a willingness to try new and unusual activities are the qualities we should strive for in order to expand our pleasure quotient. There is little doubt about the fact that bringing greater sensuality to your relationship with your partner will have a positive effect on the quality of your sex life. But the pleasure to be derived from introducing spontaneous, novel, and affectionate behavior into a relationship is a substantial reward in its own right.

10
Pleasuring, Intercourse, Afterglow

I'VE ALWAYS THOUGHT IT ODD that people should consider it a compliment to a man's sexual prowess to compare him with certain male animals—a bull, a stallion, a billy goat, or a rooster—or to describe him as a "stud." The truth is, of course, that most animals are simply not very good lovers. Take the rooster, for example.

Anyone who has spent time on a farm is probably well acquainted with the mating habits of fowl. The male bird spends his time strutting about, surrounded by his flock of hens, pecking at the ground and every so often giving out with a strident call of pure, mindless self-affirmation. When the urge strikes him, he will pursue one of the hens and mount her. After a few seconds of rapid thrusting, he ejaculates, and it is all over. The hen moves off to continue her search for bugs while the rooster ruffles his feathers and chortles with satisfaction. True, he repeats this performance several dozen times a day, a feat that no human male could duplicate. But what is the good of such sexual capacity if it means settling for a total lack of variety and intimacy in sex?

The point is that the mating behavior of the rooster is completely instinctive. Its purpose is simply to produce more fowl, and it serves this purpose quite well. It never occurs to either the hen or the rooster that there should be anything more to sex; they just haven't got the brains to realize that they are missing anything. And so they keep on having intercourse in the same old way, giving birth to more hens and roosters who reach maturity and follow their own mating instincts just like their mothers and fathers, *ad infinitum.*

Unlike the mating habits of hens and roosters, the sexual behavior of human beings is only partially biologically based. A large part of it is learned, and it is this capacity for learning that allows for the possibility of infinite variety in human sexual expression. Moreover, we humans do not engage in sex purely for the purpose of creating duplicates of ourselves. In fact, sex for procreation is a relatively rare occurrence for most of us. Most of the time, we have sex for pleasure, for the communication of affection, warmth, and intimacy. Thus, sex between humans is a far more complex and emotionally significant act than sex between animals. Although we sometimes use the phrase, "You bring out the animal in me" to compliment a lover with whom we have been particularly responsive, in view of the peculiarly human capacity for imagination, variety, and emotional involvement in sex, it would actually be a greater compliment to say, "You bring out the human in me."

But while it seems obvious that human sex differs drastically from animal sex, apparently many humans haven't heard the news yet. Many of us haven't gotten past the rooster stage of lovemaking. Men in particular are apt to be addicted to a type of sexual expression which is goal-oriented, penis-oriented, and orgasm-oriented. Many of us, like the rooster, think of sex as something we do *to* a female. This attitude is reflected in some of our slang expressions, such as "I laid her" or "I made her." Other men, a little more advanced, are aware that women have a right to derive pleasure from sex as well. They have been persuaded by the sex manuals that a woman's sexual responses are slower than a man's and that women need special stimulation to make them "ready" for intercourse.

Most men, however, think of this stimulation as being exclusively *for* the woman and having little meaning or pleasure for them. But actually, neither *to* nor *for* accurately describes what sexuality can or should be. A much better word is *with*. Both the male body and the female body are enormously complex structures, gloriously endowed with the capacity to experience pleasure. The most satisfying sexual expression is a cooperative enterprise in which two people not only give each other pleasure, but guide their partner in the gratification of their own sexual needs. This sharing, this affectionate give-and-take, is the essence of human sexuality. It is the quality that distinguishes our sexual behavior from the blind, instinctive demands of the rest of the animal kingdom.

Male and female sexual responses have many more similarities than differences. But there is a major difference that must be understood: female sexual response is more complex—not necessarily better or worse, just more complex—than the male. The woman may be nonorgasmic, singly orgasmic, or multiorgasmic, and this can occur during any phase of the sexual experience. But the male typically has a single orgasm which occurs during intercourse. There is new tentative evidence that some males might experience multiorgasmic responses, although they would ejaculate only once. However, this is by no means characteristic of men, and it would be unwise for you to pursue multiple orgasms to the extent of spoiling your sexual pleasure with performance anxiety.

The title of this chapter—"Pleasuring, Intercourse, Afterglow"—is meant to emphasize the fact that there is more to sex than just "getting it in, and getting it off," rooster-fashion. Intercourse—that part of sex between intromission and ejaculation—may be the high point, but it is not the be-all and end-all of sexuality. It is, rather, one of the many activities in which a couple may cooperate to give each other pleasure. It can be even more rewarding if we allow ourselves to freely explore and enjoy all the other possible methods of sexual expression.

In this chapter, we will consider pleasuring, intercourse, and afterglow as three separate aspects of sex. Each of them is characterized by distinct feelings as well as some which are common to all three. Each can be enjoyable in its own right, for its own sake, as well as being part of the total sexual encounter. The three experiences may be enjoyed in different combinations, depending on the feelings of the couple and on the limitations imposed by the external situation. For example, pleasuring may lead into intercourse, or it may be engaged in for its own sake without intercourse ever taking place. Intercourse, on the other hand, may begin at once, without the prelude of a pleasuring session. Afterglow activities may follow intercourse, or they may be dispensed with—all according to the wishes and needs of the couple. The three aspects will be considered separately, but with the awareness that, like the courses of a fine meal, they may be combined at the discretion of the partners to form a satisfying overall experience.

Pleasuring

In many sex manuals, the term used to describe the erotic activities which precede intercourse is "foreplay." I prefer to use the word "pleasuring," and there is, I think, a very good reason for this shift in terminology. "Foreplay" suggests something that derives its significance from what follows it. Just as it is difficult to conceive of a foreword without the book that it is meant to introduce, then it is difficult to think of something called "foreplay" as anything else but as a prelude to intercourse. Moreover, foreplay, as it is presented in most sex manuals, is generally a procedure whose purpose is to arouse the woman, to bring her to the same pitch of excitement as the man. The problem here is not with the activity itself, but with the spirit in which it is undertaken. Usually, the man who is told that he must engage in foreplay feels that he is not doing something for his own enjoyment, but rather fulfilling an obligation. The woman, meanwhile, may experience discomfort and self-consciousness because she feels she is forcing her partner to do something he would rather not waste his time on.

Pleasuring, on the other hand, is a mutual activity. It refers to all the behaviors that a couple may engage in to produce sensual and sexual enjoyment—everything, in fact, except intercourse itself. Pleasuring is not goal-oriented like foreplay; it is an activity that is engaged in for its own sake. In most pleasuring experiences, the activities will lead to more and more arousal and will eventually culminate in intercourse. But this need not be so. Pleasuring experiences that are not followed by intercourse can be particularly erotic and tantalizing. Emily and I have found that an occasional session of pleasuring—say, every month or two—in which we agree beforehand *not* to proceed to intercourse, no matter how turned on we become, provides an excellent way of re-exploring our erotic responses and of retaining variety and novelty in our sexual relationship.

Pleasuring can be particularly important for men since most of us pay little attention to the nuances of our feelings. We are well acquainted with the pleasure of orgasm, but we are often unaware of what else can make us feel good. We have a tendency to rate the value of our sexual responses in terms of intensity, and, since orgasm is the most intense physical sensation we have experienced, we are usually orgasm-oriented. But the intensity of a sensation depends to a great extent on how well attuned to it we are. When we learn to increase our sensitivity to the range of sensual feelings other than orgasm, the intensity of these sensations will increase in our perception. In order to develop this sensitivity, we need to change our approach to sex, to accept that there is more to our body than just our penis, and that there is more to sexuality than the three to ten seconds of orgasm. Once you make this change, I think you will find that developing sensitivity to a broader range of sensual stimuli is one of the best favors you can do for yourself. And, of course, the effect of this heightened sensitivity on your relationship with your partner will also be extremely beneficial.

Probably the most difficult concept for most men to comprehend in relation to pleasuring is that it need not lead to intercourse and orgasm. It is common for men (and women) to place an implicit demand on themselves and their sex partner that every affectionate or erotic encounter *must* culminate in intercourse. For many men, the fulfillment of this requirement becomes a matter of pride, a test of their masculinity. Thus, when a particular sexual encounter does not end in intercourse, they may feel that there is something wrong with them. Or they may consider extended, nonorgasmic sex play as somehow immature, reminiscent of the sessions of necking and petting which they experienced as adolescents. But if you are honest with yourself, you will probably remember that you enjoyed those sessions very much. There is no reason why you shouldn't enjoy them again, perhaps even more so since your greater maturity as well as the comfort of a stable relationship allow you to introduce much greater sensitivity and experimentation into nongoal-oriented pleasuring. Many of us tend to feel that the consummation of each sexual encounter with intercourse and orgasm is a special privilege we have earned by becoming adults. What we forget is that true maturity means freedom, the right to choose, to be self-directing. The mature person may occasionally choose not to press for intercourse in a particular sexual experience, or when he or she might choose to experience orgasm through manual or oral-genital stimulation.

The varieties of pleasuring techniques are endless, but here are some suggestions drawn from my own experience and the experience of some of my clients. If you and your partner decide to devote some time specifically to learning techniques of pleasuring, be sure to give yourselves at least an hour free of interruptions or obligations. Take the phone off the hook. Make whatever preparations you like to set the mood. Turn the lights in your bedroom down if you wish (but not off—you'll want to see what you're doing). You might want to put a favorite record on the stereo or light some incense. Emily and I have a scented candle in our bedroom which seems to create just the right sensual atmosphere for us, but the choice of such paraphernalia depends entirely on individual tastes.

One effective way to structure your pleasuring is to designate one partner as the pleasurer and the other as the pleasuree. These roles are arbitrary and might be determined by flipping a coin. The role of the pleasuree is to receive and accept pleasure passively and you will probably find this a great deal harder than it sounds. As the pleasuree, you might want to try closing your eyes during the experience. This will make it easier for you to concentrate on your own sensations as well as cutting down on whatever self-consciousness you may feel. The pleasurer's role is, of course, to actively give pleasure, and also to explore and learn about his or her partner's body and to be aware of his or her own sensations and responses to the stimulation. The pleasuree needs to receive a wide variety of sensual experiences so that he or she can discover which are most arousing. So the pleasurer should feel free to use both hard and light massage, just barely touching with the fingertips, kissing, licking, biting, or any other technique which the pleasuree might find enjoyable.

At some point during the session you should switch so that each partner gets a chance to experience both roles. Many couples find that their learning is facilitated when they begin with a clear idea of their roles. But as they become more comfortable with the pleasuring concepts and techniques, the process becomes more mutual and interactive.

You might begin with the pleasuree lying face down. The pleasurer can then stroke and caress the partner from head to toe, experimenting with different kinds of touching, kissing, massaging, all the while being aware of the look and feel of the various parts of the body. Later, the pleasuree can turn over and the pleasurer can continue touching and exploring the front of the body. It may be a good idea to begin your pleasuring sessions with nongenital touching and then to proceed in later sessions to stimulating the genitals and breasts. (Many men are also highly sensitive in the breast and nipple area; you may not have been aware of this because you have been misinformed that only the woman's breast is an "erogenous zone.") Although looking at your partner's body is an important part of pleasuring, an interesting variation of the pleasuring method is for both partners to keep their eyes shut. This has the effect of heightening your other senses and of making you aware of feelings which you may have missed otherwise.

Both men and women who have not engaged extensively in pleasuring activities may be somewhat ignorant of one another's sexual anatomy. For example, many men who are aware that the clitoris is a particularly sensitive area may not realize that direct clitoral stimulation can be unpleasant and even painful. It is generally more effective to apply stimulation around the clitoral shaft and inner lips. However, let your partner guide you as she is the expert on her own sexual responses.

In subsequent pleasuring sessions, the pleasuree can participate more actively by putting his or her hands over those of the partner and guiding them to those areas which are particularly sensitive and by showing the partner the particular kind of touch that is most arousing. This type of nonverbal guidance can be very important. Sometimes the difference between a pleasant and an unpleasant sensation may be a fraction of an inch to the right or left or a bit more or less pressure. A very effective way to give such guidance is through touch. During these later sessions, both partners can keep their eyes open and communicate their responsiveness and affection through visual contact. If something the partner does produces discomfort, the pleasuree should not call a halt, but rather suggest some alternative activity. By the same token, if the pleasurer notices stress or uneasiness in the partner, he or she should not stop, but rather go back to a previous activity which they are more comfortable with. In this way, negative feedback can be incorporated into the couple's interaction without interrupting the current of erotic responsiveness that has been created between them.

There are other positions, of course, that are effective for pleasuring—in fact, quite a few more than there are for intercourse. In a particularly satisfying one, the pleasurer sits upright with back against the wall or headboard and legs spread apart, and the pleasuree sits with back leaning against the pleasurer's chest. This position not only allows the pleasurer full access to the partner's body, but it also makes it easy for the pleasuree to guide the pleasurer's hands to those parts of the body which are particularly sensitive and to demonstrate the kind of touch that is most effective.

Pleasuring activities can often be enhanced through the use of emollients such as Allercream, baby oil, hand lotion, or even powder. In fact, you can use anything that your imagination suggests so long as it is stimulating and fun for both of you and not physically harmful. External devices—anything from a vibrator to a feather—might be interesting to experiment with. One thing for you to remember about pleasuring is that getting an erection need not be interpreted as a sign that pleasuring should be ended and intercourse begun. When an erection occurs during pleasuring, be aware of it, enjoy it, but do not feel that you are obligated to do anything about it. Nor, on the other hand, should you feel alarmed if you do not get an erection. Think of pleasuring as an exercise in whole-body stimulation and response. In these terms, the penis is just a part of the big sex organ known as the human body.

Intercourse

There is no sharp dividing line between pleasuring and intercourse. Pleasuring does not stop when intercourse starts. Many kinds of pleasuring such as kissing, caressing, breast stimulation, and, in some positions, clitoral stimulation, may continue during intercourse. In fact, intercourse itself is really an ultimate form of pleasuring. It is an activity in which a couple gives each other pleasure through the intromission and movement of the penis in the vagina.

Thinking about intercourse in this way can be an eye-opening experience. Studies have shown that the average intercourse experience lasts only about two minutes, and the male orgasm takes up only three to ten seconds of those two minutes. For many males, then, intercourse consists of a mad rush for orgasm. Not that such an intercourse style is necessarily bad. An occasional frenzied "quickie" can, in fact, be highly exciting and satisfying. However, when "quickies" constitute the entirety of a couple's sexual repertoire, the result is usually monotony and frustration. If, on the other hand, a man learns to take his time, to savor the intercourse experience in a leisurely manner, he will find, first, that there are a thousand nuances of pleasure to be enjoyed along the way and, second, that his orgasm is still waiting faithfully for him at the end of the line—and usually better than ever after the slow, tantalizing build-up.

The average man may think of his pattern of sexual arousal as simply a steady increase to orgasm, and that is the way it may be experienced. Actually, though, there are four phases in the sexual arousal cycle: excitement, plateau, orgasm, and resolution. In the first, or excitement phase, the penis becomes erect and the testes are elevated. If stimulation continues, the male enters the second, or plateau, phase, where his excitement increases, his erection becomes firmer, his breathing becomes heavier, his skin may break out in a "sex flush," and he may begin sweating. Usually intercourse itself begins either at the end of the excitement phase or sometime during the plateau phase. The intensity of stimulation (both physical and psychological) is the variable that determines the man's experience of his arousal. If he is consistently stimulated, without pause, he might well progress through the excitement and plateau phases and reach the point of ejaculation in a short time, perhaps in a minute or two. If, however, variations in the amount and intensity of stimulation he receives are introduced, then corresponding variations in the pattern of arousal are possible.

But how to introduce these variations? What can you do to prolong the experience of intercourse? There are some common folk remedies for rapid ejaculation such as biting down hard on the corner of the pillow or fixing your mind on something unpleasant and nonsexual like your income tax. These methods might actually be effective in temporarily reducing the intensity of stimulation, but at what cost? Certainly the feeling of a pillow between your teeth or the thought of your tax debts adds nothing positive to the intercourse experience. And using these methods might even cause you to build up a sense of resentment against your partner by making you feel that you are depriving yourself of pleasure for her sake.

Luckily, however, there are better ways of achieving ejaculatory control. The first step in prolonging intercourse is to discard the demand for quick orgasm. This may seem to be more easily said than done, but there is an established psychological principle which you can use to achieve the desired end. The human mind can be fully occupied with only one thought or sensation at any one time. If your attention is fixed on something else besides the demand for orgasm, then that demand subsides. Actually, this principle is the same one you employ in the other methods, but the important difference is the object you choose to use to distract yourself from the demand for orgasm. It makes far more sense to choose a pleasant distraction than an unpleasant one, and the most pleasant distraction, as well as the most effective, is the stimulation you are experiencing at that particular moment. The more fully you concentrate on the sensations of intercourse and are absorbed in the nuances of pleasure you are experiencing, the less intense will be your demand for orgasm and the longer the experience will last.

The difference in approach is roughly that between a sprinter straining to reach the finish line and a person strolling at a leisurely pace through a lovely, enthralling countryside and using all his senses to take in as much of the experience as he can.

The next most important thing for a man to do in order to prolong his enjoyment of intercourse is to learn to recognize his point of ejaculatory inevitability, the point at which he loses control and will ejaculate, no matter what. If you can learn to anticipate this point, then you can reduce the amount of stimulation of the penis just before the point is reached and thereby make the intercourse experience last virtually as long as you wish. (The specific techniques which a couple can use to achieve this goal are described fully in Chapter 18, "Learning Ejaculatory Control.")

Variety is also important in intercourse. Of the many possible positions for intercourse, most couples use the male superior exclusively or almost exclusively. There is nothing wrong with this position: it is comfortable, intromission is fairly easy, the penis seldom slips out, and, since the couple face one another, it allows them to kiss and caress each other freely. Other positions, however, offer advantages just as great, and there is no reason to consider the male superior any more natural or basic than any other.

The point of trying a variety of positions is not to prove yourself a sexual contortionist or to show that you are not afraid of exotic sexual practices. Rather, it is to introduce a sense of novelty and discovery, which is as important in sex as it is in all other aspects of a relationship. Discovering and sharing a new restaurant, a new hobby, a new book or movie, a new friend, or a new way of making love are all experiences that enrich and deepen a couple's feeling for each other. Just as rigidity and monotony can have a deadly effect on a couple's enjoyment of other activities, it can also have a dampening influence on their sex life, eventually making it seem like something kept up out of habit or duty alone.

Since this book is not meant to be a sex manual, I will not attempt to describe the many other possible positions for intercourse, the most common of which are female superior, side-by-side, and rear entry. There are many excellent books available that provide this information. It is important to emphasize, however, that for optimal sexual pleasure, a couple ought to feel free to experiment with positions they have not tried before and to choose from the great variety available, those which they find particularly comfortable and stimulating.

You may find that there are two or three positions which become your favorites and which you use time and time again. There may be others which require a particular mood and which you utilize only on occasion. There may be still others which you use even more rarely, when you are feeling especially adventurous. But you will never build up this repertoire unless you make a special effort to experiment and to find out which positions suit you and which do not.

You can also introduce variety in the type of coital thrusting. Many men rely primarily on a rapid in-and-out thrusting movement in which they control the rhythm. You might want to experiment with a more circular or up-and-down movement, a slow, tantalizing movement, a movement that slowly increases in tempo and then holds steady. Also, at times the woman might set the tempo for the coital thrusting. You could also try a minimal, slow movement (the "quiet vagina" exercise) for a period of time to enjoy the feelings of vaginal containment.

In addition to positions, another aspect where variety is important is the matter of who makes the first move. In our male-dominated society, it is usually the man who initiates a sexual encounter. But there is no reason why this pattern should be accepted as the norm. There are times in the relationship of any couple when a reversal of the traditional roles can be a turn-on for both partners. In fact, the most satisfying relationship may be one in which both partners feel free to initiate and both feel free to say no. The key here is for the man to develop a relaxed, positive attitude toward *accepting* pleasure. In this way he can encourage his partner to express herself in initiating sex and taking the aggressive role.

Just as there are times when you experience such urgent sexual desire that you feel almost like devouring your partner as though she were a sumptuous meal, there are doubtless times when she feels exactly the same way about you. You should not be shocked or intimidated by this, but learn to accept and enjoy it. Most men feel uncomfortable being passive in sex. Actually, there is nothing wrong with being either aggressive or passive in sex, as long as you don't assume you *always* have to be one or the other.

Afterglow

Afterglow is the most neglected phase of the sexual experience. In fact, the period immediately following orgasm has frequently been characterized in the past as a negative state. There were considered to be only two exceptions to the Latin maxim, *"Omne animal post coitum triste"* ("All animals are sad after intercourse")—the lion and our friend the rooster. These lucky beasts are supposedly able to bang away with scarcely an unhappy afterthought while the rest of creation, including man, is doomed to sink into the doldrums after each ejaculation.

This is, of course, utter nonsense. There is absolutely no physiological reason for the concluding phase of sex to be an unhappy one. It can, in fact, be a very pleasurable time when both partners bask in their feelings of relaxation and satisfaction, savoring the nuances of their bodily sensations as they return to an unstimulated state. From a physiological viewpoint, the afterglow period is the experiential component of the fourth stage of sexual response, the resolution phase, when the man's sexual arousal decreases and his erect penis becomes flaccid again. Although the physical reactions— that is, the erect penis becoming flaccid again—occur rather quickly, the entire resolution phase actually takes up a considerable amount of time. In a young man, the vasocongestion of the tissues in the genital area may take three to four hours to disappear completely; in an older man, the period is about a half hour.

Most men assume that intercourse is over with orgasm and that the only possible activities for a couple to engage in afterward are either to get up and go about their business or to fall asleep. The first pattern may be the result of early experiences with clandestine lovemaking, when it was important to quickly erase all evidence of intercourse for fear of discovery. The second pattern is probably a conditioned response based on the mistaken notion that intercourse is a highly taxing activity and that a man needs to sleep afterward in order to recuperate. Indeed, when intercourse takes place late at night, it may be perfectly acceptable to go to sleep afterward. There is, however, no physiological need for sleep after orgasm, and the man who invariably goes to sleep following intercourse is cheating both himself and his partner of the warm and intimate sharing of sensations which characterize the afterglow period.

For women who are nonorgasmic during intercourse, the afterglow phase may provide an opportunity for their partners to manually or orally stimulate them to orgasm. In such a situation, however, a man must realize that his partner may find it difficult to request additional stimulation and that he needs to be especially sensitive and responsive to her needs.

One couple whom I had been treating for sexual dysfunction—a military officer and his wife—provides an excellent example of this problem. The couple had been following a program of pleasuring and had been making rather good progress. The wife had been nonorgasmic during intercourse, however, and her husband had flatly turned down her requests for manual stimulation. We talked about her need during one session, and he agreed, rather reluctantly, that the next time he would try to help bring her to orgasm. But when they next had intercourse, he fell asleep afterward, as usual. Then remembering his promise, however, he roused himself and said in a grumpy voice, "Oh, yeah, I almost forgot. Is there anything you want me to do for you now?" The wife became livid. "That's it," she replied. "I'm leaving you!" She did in fact leave him, but came back shortly afterward, and the two of them returned to therapy. I concentrated on teaching the husband not to fall asleep after intercourse and to be more sensitive to his wife's needs, and eventually, as she began to respond to these efforts, she did become orgasmic.

Another impediment to a man's enjoyment of the afterglow phase may stem from his feeling that any sort of touching or caressing implies a demand for further sexual activity. There is a physiological phenomenon among males called the "refractory period," when it is physically impossible for a man to respond to sexual stimulation and to get an erection. This period is typically at least fifteen minutes and can extend to an hour (and longer for an older man). A man may feel that any sort of touching is best avoided during afterglow since it cannot lead to anything; perhaps he fears that if he fails to respond with an erection, he will be seen as lacking in virility. But if he understands that no further performance is expected of him, he will be able to relax and engage in the nondemand touching, kissing, and holding activities that make the afterglow experience such an enjoyable and rewarding one.

Although comfortable tenderness and relaxation are the most common responses during afterglow, other feelings and activities are also possible. As with pleasuring and intercourse, variety, experimentation, and spontaneity are of prime importance. After orgasm, a couple may find themselves in a playful, happy mood and might express their exuberance by having a glass of wine, taking a shower together, or raiding the refrigerator. As with other phases of sex, optimal satisfaction will result when both partners endeavor to get in touch with their true feelings of the moment and to act on them in a free, spontaneous, and mutually sensitive way.

If this chapter has had a consistent theme, it is that if a man is open to variation in his sexual experiences, then he will be in a position to discover his sexual likes and dislikes and choose those activities that are most enjoyable to him. The basic principle of sexual satisfaction is really quite simple. Anything that expands and intensifies a couple's enjoyment of themselves and of each other is good and ought to be encouraged. Anything that limits or nullifies that enjoyment is bad for them (though not necessarily for others) and should be eliminated. The rest is up to you. Sexuality is yours to make of it what you will. Why not make the most of it?

11

New Tastes, New Pleasures: Getting into Oral-Genital Sex

CONSIDER THE MOUTH. What a marvelously sensitive and expressive part of the body it is! Say the word "elephant" aloud very slowly. Notice the series of fine and smoothly integrated adjustments your mouth makes. We say thousands of words, each consisting of different sounds in different combinations, hardly ever making a mistake. If we work at it, we can learn a second language, even a third or a fourth, teaching our mouths to adjust to a whole new collection of sounds. Our mouths also have a wonderful ability to receive and analyze sensations. Best of all, our mouths have an enormous capacity for experiencing pleasure. Think of the enjoyment of biting into a juicy porterhouse steak or of downing a chilled beer on a sweltering day.

Like our mouths, our genitals are richly supplied with nerve endings and exquisitely receptive to pleasurable sensations. Isn't it natural and fitting then that, in seeking to experience and to impart sexual pleasure, we should employ oral-genital stimulation? For our mouths and our sex organs, which have so much in common and so much to offer one another, can unite to produce a very special and intense sort of enjoyment.

We are accustomed to using our mouths, our lips, our tongue, and teeth to make love, to kiss, suck, lick, nibble, bite. Oral-genital stimulation is not more than a normal extension of this. It is a coming together of the two most sensitive pleasure-giving and pleasure-receiving areas of the body. This is equally true of fellatio, the oral stimulation of the penis, and cunnilingus, the oral stimulation of the vulva area. Both are natural and healthy activities which are not only well within the normal range of sexual expression but also represent a comfortable, integrated attitude toward sexuality.

Unfortunately, however, a whole complex of prejudices and misconceptions has grown up around the subject of oral-genital sex, causing many people to shy away from this method of sexual expression or, if they indulge in it, to feel anxious and guilty about their activity. Let us consider some of these negative attitudes toward oral-genital sex and try to understand and to dispel the inhibitions that prevent this form of sexuality from being more freely and comfortably practiced.

One of the major misconceptions about oral-genital sex is that it is unclean—that is, unsanitary. Americans in particular have an over-concern, practically an obsession with oral cleanliness, which is plainly reflected in the endless succession of ads for toothpaste, mouthwashes, and breath mints seen in magazines and on television. The genitals, on the other hand, are generally considered a "dirty" part of the body, not only because of the lingering puritanical attitudes toward sex but also because of the close connection between the sex organs and the organs of excretion. The male urethra serves as a channel not only for semen but for urine as well; and the female expels urine through the urethral meatus, located between the clitoris and the vagina. Thus, in contemplating the idea of orally stimulating the genitals of his or her partner, many people may be dismayed by the prospect of taking into the mouth organs that have been contaminated by bodily wastes.

But such concerns are quite unfounded. If a person washes properly, then no remnant of urine will remain on the genitals. With ordinary hygiene, the sex organs can be as germ-free and clean-smelling as any other part of the body. In fact, the mouth usually contains a great many more germs than the penis or vulva. Sexual secretions—the male semen and the lubricating fluids of the female—are antiseptic and perfectly harmless protein substances, and, if anything, are healthful if swallowed.

Probably, the factor most responsible for negative attitudes toward oral-genital sex is an ignorance of the structure and function of the genitals—your own and those of your partner. It is for this reason that mutual and self-examination of the genital area can be an enlightening and often liberating experience for a couple, and may serve to change their attitude toward oral-genital sex.

One of my clients, a young married law student who had been very active sexually and was proud of his masculinity and prowess, experienced such a psychological breakthrough. He often requested that his wife fellate him, but he refused to engage in cunnilingus. Originally, they had come to me for therapy to reduce their anxiety about childbirth, but as things progressed, the wife's dissatisfaction about her husband's attitude toward oral-genital sex emerged as a significant problem. He claimed to be disgusted by the fact that the urethra was located in the vulval area. "Piss just doesn't turn me on," was the way he expressed it. At my suggestion, he agreed to make a thorough visual inspection of his wife's genitals. The experience was a turning point for him. He realized that while the urethra was indeed located in the vulval area, he could avoid it if he chose to by concentrating on the clitoral shaft, inner lips, and the vagina. Subsequently, his anxiety was reduced considerably, and he was able to enjoy orally stimulating his wife and found it particularly arousing if she fellated him at the same time.

This example shows not only the value of direct knowledge of sexual anatomy in overcoming hang-ups but also the importance of choice in oral-genital sex or in any phase of sexuality. While therapy techniques like the one described above can be helpful in changing our attitudes and behavior, we should not allow ourselves to be forced by outside pressure into any sexual activity that we feel uncomfortable about. Our sex lives should be motivated by genuine desire and the wish to experiment and increase our sources of pleasure, not by a sense of duty. You may decide that oral-genital sex is just not for you, but why not at least be adventurous enough to give it a fair chance?

Vaginal secretions have a definite flavor of their own—a salty, tangy, complex taste which is really not quite like anything else. Many men enjoy this taste enormously and find it highly arousing. Others may not find it quite so appealing. While it is useless to try to persuade someone to like something he does not enjoy, it is nevertheless true that tastes may often be acquired, particularly when the surrounding circumstances are positive and nonthreatening.

The key to learning to enjoy the experience of cunnilingus is to approach it in a gradual way. For example, a man might begin by caressing the woman's vulva with his lips closed. Later, when he feels comfortable with this form of stimulation, he might progress to using his tongue and open mouth. There are several products on the market—flavored vaginal sprays—which are meant to appeal to women whose partners have ambivalent feelings about oral-genital sex. Some of these products are of dubious value from a health point of view, probably increase the potential for vaginal infections, and should therefore be used with caution. Besides, it seems more honest to cultivate an appreciation for the real thing rather than to try to make it palatable with synthetic peppermint or strawberry flavoring.

A common misconception is that men who enjoy fellatio are really latent homosexuals. While it is true that homosexual couples of both sexes use oral-genital techniques—often very skillfully and satisfyingly—it is not the technique employed that makes the act a homosexual one, but the fact that the people involved are of the same sex. When two males erotically kiss each other, the activity is homosexual, but certainly kissing in and of itself is not a sign of latent homosexuality, and neither is the enjoyment of fellatio.

Oral-genital sex has been unjustly maligned in other ways. One frequent contention is that oral-genital sex is a sign of immaturity—the basis of this charge being the idea that heterosexual intercourse in the male dominant position is the only truly "adult" form of sexuality. This, of course, is nonsense. As we have seen in previous chapters, the hallmark of fulfilling, healthy sex is the ability to experiment freely and to communicate and cooperate in mutual pleasuring techniques. A couple who limits their sexual activity to a single method or position is not proving their maturity; they are merely stuck in a rut. Their lack of imagination probably increases the possibility of their becoming bored with sex altogether.

Oral-genital sex represents a major area a couple may explore to add variety to their sex life. In fact, surveys have indicated that those couples who practice oral-genital sex, rather than being characterized by immaturity, tend to be better educated and more sexually well adjusted. Approximately 75 percent of couples do experiment with oral-genital stimulation, and approximately 40 percent use it with some frequency.

Some men, who mistakenly think of oral-genital techniques as a substitute for intercourse, believe that the use of the mouth in sex is an indication of a lack of virility. This is particularly the case where cunnilingus is concerned. The assumption—based on a very narrow and rigid conception of sexuality—is that a man who orally stimulates a woman does so because he is incapable of satisfying her with his penis. Actually, a man who employs cunnilingus as part of his sexual repertoire is likely to be more relaxed and confident about his sexual ability. Consequently, he will probably be more competent, both in intercourse and in oral-genital techniques, than a man who limits his lovemaking to conventional methods.

There is also a fear, held by a surprising number of men, that a woman might become "addicted" to oral-genital sex and begin to prefer it to intercourse. While it is true that many women find oral sex extremely pleasurable since it provides more direct stimulation of the clitoris, there is no evidence that they become indifferent to penile stimulation. On the contrary, the chances are that couples who use oral-genital techniques are more likely to enjoy other methods of sexual activity, including most definitely, intercourse. For intercourse and oral-genital sex are complementary, not either-or, activities. Most couples use fellatio and cunnilingus as pleasuring activities which generally lead to, and indeed whet the appetite for, intercourse.

Learning to see oral-genital sex as a natural, healthy, and permissible activity is an essential prerequisite to deriving the optimal degree of pleasure from it. Only in this way will we be able to approach it in the sort of mutually cooperative and guiding way that characterizes the most satisfying sexual functioning.

Too often, men who desire oral-genital sex think of it as a forbidden pleasure that they must procure either by coercion or else outside the realm of their normal sexual relationships. The prevalence of this feeling is demonstrated by the fact that the majority of married men who go to prostitutes request fellatio rather than intercourse; apparently, they find it impossible to ask their wives to fellate them. These men seem to set up a strict dichotomy between the kind of sex allowed within marriage and the sex they seek outside of marriage, where anything goes. There is no conceivable reason, however, why such a dichotomy should exist. In fact, the idea that there are sexual activities that are not permissible for married couples undoubtedly has a great deal to do with perpetuating sexual dissatisfaction in marriage.

Other men may try oral-genital sex with their wives but give it up when it does not go well the first time. The man may tell himself that since the woman does not seem particularly turned on by it, he is doing her a favor by not asking her to go through with it again. Such an attitude denies the woman's potential responsiveness to oral-genital sex as well as ignoring the complexity of fellatio and cunnilingus as sexual behaviors, requiring communication, comfort, guidance, and feedback which clearly cannot be achieved at the first opportunity. If couples reacted to their first intercourse experiences as they often do to their first attempts at oral-genital sex, many of them would probably cease having intercourse altogether.

A man needs to feel that oral-genital sex is something he has a perfect right to request from his partner, just as she has a perfect right to request it from him. Not only should they feel comfortable asking for oral stimulation, but they also ought to be able to guide one another in achieving the most satisfying kind of stimulation. A sympathetic give-and-take between partners will enable them to find the best way of pleasuring one another. Too many men think of fellatio as a "symbolic" act rather than as a mutually pleasurable activity. They feel that just getting their partners to "go down on them" is really all they can reasonably expect. But there is much more to oral-genital sex than this.

The point is well illustrated by a couple who were clients of mine in sex therapy. The man had been pressing his wife for a long time to fellate him, but she could not get up the courage and kept refusing. Finally, he convinced her to try it one evening when she was drunk. After overcoming her resistance this one time, she was able to repeat the act on a regular basis. Her husband, however, feeling that he had gotten what he wanted and had no right to request anything further from her, offered no advice or guidance. She, meanwhile, had worked out her own method of fellating him, according to what seemed arousing and comfortable to her. Rather than taking the head of the penis into her mouth, she concentrated on sucking and stimulating the shaft. When I asked the man privately whether he was satisfied with the stimulation she had been giving him he became very embarrassed. "Please don't tell my wife this," he said, "but actually I hate the way she fellates me—it hurts!" He later agreed to communicate his dissatisfaction to his wife, and eventually they did manage to work out a style of oral-genital stimulation that was satisfying to both of them.

There are many other potential problems in oral-genital sex that are apt to arise chiefly because of a failure to communicate. For example, many women are reluctant to fellate their partners because of a fear of gagging on the penis. Rather than urging his partner to continue despite her discomfort or withdrawing his request out of a misplaced sense of compassion, the most appropriate response a man can make under these circumstances is to encourage his partner to experiment until she is able to fellate him with comfort. For example, she could try placing the penis to one side of her mouth rather than in the center, or she might try holding the shaft in her fingers as she took it in her mouth. These techniques tend to give the woman a greater sense of control and prevent the penis from going too deep so that the gag reflex is not triggered. A relaxed, nondemand atmosphere is best for reducing anxiety in both partners. Often the ability of the couple to laugh at the situation can be invaluable for relieving the seriousness of the occasion. After all, sex—of whatever variety—is supposed to be fun!

Another problem that may arise in fellatio is the woman's lack of desire to swallow the man's semen once he ejaculates and the man's subsequent feeling that by rejecting his semen she is rejecting him. Here, again, we encounter a too rigid approach to oral-genital sex and a failure of the partners to honestly and sympathetically communicate their feelings. First of all, the man should realize that the woman's swallowing his semen has very little to do with the pleasure he receives from fellatio. Our main concern in sex should be pleasure, not symbolism. Besides, the woman's willingness or unwillingness to swallow the semen relates to what is comfortable and pleasurable for her, not to any personal acceptance or rejection of her partner. There is no reason to expect fellatio to follow some set format, ending with ejaculation. Rather, the question of whether it should be used simply as a pleasuring technique or whether it should be continued until the man reaches orgasm is one that should be decided according to what is pleasurable and acceptable to the partners themselves.

Of course, understanding and communication between the partners are just as important for successful cunnilingus. Frequently, men who have not taken the trouble to examine their partner's anatomy or who have not received adequate guidance from their partner may use oral stimulation in ways that are ineffective. Two distinct problems may arise here. On the one hand, the man might be concentrating all his attention on the vagina or the outer lips, where the concentration of nerve endings is rather sparse, and thus producing a minimum of pleasurable sensations. Or he might be stimulating the clitoris in a way that is too rough and thereby causing more pain than pleasure.

The clitoris is an extremely sensitive organ, particularly at the tip, or glans. Most women prefer stimulation of the clitoral shaft rather than a direct stroking of the glans. Different women respond to different types of oral stimulation. Some like slow, quiet stroking while others prefer a rapid, tickling movement. Still others like the man to run his tongue over the clitoris and then suck on the clitoral shaft. You should discuss with your partner the kind of stimulation she prefers and then follow her guidance. In any case, the ideal situation for sexual functioning is one in which this information can be imparted frankly and openly, in which it is recognized that each partner has the right—in fact, the responsibility—to instruct the other in what sort of stimulation is most effective for him or her.

For the couple wishing to get into oral-genital sex, the best approach to follow is a gradual one. Begin with manual stimulation of the genitals, with one partner taking the role of pleasurer and the other that of pleasuree. Begin slowly to use oral stimulation, concentrating at first on the insides of the thighs and the area surrounding the genitals. Over the course of several sessions, you may work up gradually to direct oral stimulation of the genitals, experimenting with different types of movements such as licking, sucking, kissing, and a darting movement of the tongue. Feel free meanwhile to tell your partner what sort of stimulation is effective and what is not. Be open to the same sort of response from her. Once you have begun to feel comfortable with oral-genital sex, there is no end to the variations that can be improvised between you. Many couples find mutual, simultaneous oral stimulation—the famous "69 position"—to be extremely satisfying. Others find they are not comfortable receiving and applying stimulation at the same time and prefer to confine themselves to one or the other.

One of the most important things to remember about oral-genital sex is that the reason for engaging in it should be to enhance your pleasure, not to prove anything to yourself or anyone else. We should be wary of the new sexual conformism in which people feel pressured to show that they are free of sexual inhibitions by demonstrating their readiness to engage in every possible form of sexual behavior.

Often a particular sexual technique becomes the "in" thing, and there is a tendency for people who like to think of themselves as being sexually liberated to feel that they must try it and like it or else jeopardize their self-image. The latest of these sex fashions seems to be analingus, the oral stimulation of the anus. There is nothing abnormal or "bad" about this particular sexual technique as long as proper hygiene is utilized, and many couples find it quite arousing. What would be unfortunate, though, would be to do it simply because you feel it is expected of you or out of a fear of being thought inhibited or unsophisticated.

Whether the sexual experience is analingus, group sex, bondage and discipline, swinging, or watching hard-core pornographic films in your bedroom, the same basic guideline applies. In my view, as long as a particular sexual activity is not forced, does not involve children, is not carried out in public, is not compulsive or clearly destructive, it falls within the range of normal sexual behavior. However, when you feel pressured to engage in certain acts to prove that you are liberated, you are no longer using your sexuality in your own best interests. The goal of sexuality should be pleasure, not performing according to a certain standard—whatever that standard may be.

I want to emphasize once again that the key to effective, satisfying oral-genital sex is gentleness, comfort, and communication. If you approach it in this way, you will soon find that it ceases to be a "heavy scene," potentially threatening and frustrating to both partners, and becomes a normal and healthy part of sexuality which greatly enlarges the range of techniques you can use to express your love for one another.

12

"Within the Normal Range"— Understanding Male Homosexuality

BEFORE THE LAST DECADE, most books on sex treated homosexuality, if they dealt with it at all, primarily as a problem to be solved. It was assumed that the homosexual was abnormal, that something had gone wrong in his development, causing him to prefer a type of sexual expression which was unnatural and could never bring him any real happiness or fulfillment. Homosexuality was generally thought of as a sickness, and, like any sickness, it was considered to have an etiology (i.e., specific causes) and a cure. The only trouble was that no one seemed to be able to identify very convincingly either the cause or the cure.

But there has been great change in a very short time. Along with the liberalization of our attitudes toward sexuality in general, there has been an active homosexual movement (much like the various other militant minority groups) to demand the respect and equality that have been denied them. Many prominent people have openly declared their homosexual orientation, and great numbers of other individuals have proudly "come out of the closet." Phrases like "gay pride" and "gay is good" have become commonplace. Meanwhile, recent findings by psychologists and other researchers have cast doubt on most of the assumptions the straight world has so smugly held about homosexuality. This research indicates that homosexuality is in no sense a disease, but rather a normal variant of human sexual expression, no less "natural" or "healthy" than any other form of sexuality.

The only sense in which homosexuality is "abnormal" is in the context of the values that are held by people of a particular society. Societies everywhere tend to approve of certain patterns of behavior and to disapprove of others. What is normal and desirable in one society may be abnormal and undesirable in another. Although homosexuality has existed in all times and in all cultures, the attitudes of different societies toward it have varied widely. In some instances it has been accepted as healthy behavior (as, for instance, in ancient Greece); in other instances it has been condemned as sinful and perverse. But homosexuality has remained constant—nothing more nor less than a preference for sexual partners of the same sex as oneself. Whether this preference is considered an abomination or an ideal has depended upon the values and attitudes of the people doing the judging.

In the United States, the laws and attitudes toward homosexuality are in a stage of reevaluation and change. The increasing strength and visibility of the gay movement and the more liberal general attitudes toward sexuality lend impetus to this newer and more accepting view of homosexuality. However, there are still a bewildering number of misconceptions, superstitions, and glaringly myth-based notions about homosexuality, even among the most sophisticated strata of the population. The aim of this chapter will be to attempt to dispel these mistaken ideas, particularly with respect to male homosexuality, by exploring the subject in as factual and nonbiased a manner as possible.

One widely held but erroneous notion is that people must be either exclusively heterosexual or exclusively homosexual. Alfred C. Kinsey, a pioneer in the area of sex research, made the point, based on numerous case histories, that homosexuality and heterosexuality can be envisioned as falling along a range or continuum, rather than being an either-or proposition. He found that the sex histories of many men revealed both heterosexual and homosexual feelings and experiences, whatever their basic orientation might be. For example, a man might have homosexual experiences during adolescence and later become a practicing heterosexual as an adult. And another man who has most of his sexual relationships with other males might occasionally become very aroused by a woman and have intercourse with her.

Well over 50 percent of men have had at least one fantasy, thought, or feeling about another male which caused them to become sexually aroused, and it is estimated that one out of every three men has had at least one homosexual experience leading to orgasm sometime in his life. About one in ten has been predominantly homosexual during a portion of his life—usually in adolescence or in his early adult years—and later has become predominantly heterosexual. About 4 percent of all males are chiefly homosexual during the whole course of their lives. These facts are particularly important for heterosexual men who mistakenly believe that their sexual orientation must be pure and untainted and that if they have homosexual thoughts or an isolated homosexual experience, this makes them "latent homosexuals." The much overused term "latent homosexuality" is neither very accurate nor particularly useful since it tends to negate the elements of choice in sexual orientation.

Another common misconception is that homosexuality is a form of mental illness, a notion that is firmly entrenched in the public consciousness. Many people regard it as a matter of common sense that anyone who prefers partners of the same sex to partners of the opposite sex must be sick and in need of psychiatric help. But in fact, this assumption is a good deal less self-evident than it might seem. True, many books and articles have been written by psychiatrists maintaining this point of view. But these studies are usually based on theorizing rather than factual evidence, and the case studies cited are drawn from the ranks of the psychiatrist's own patients—clearly a biased sample.

There is quite a bit of solid scientific evidence to indicate that homosexuals, as a group, do not show any more psychological pathology than heterosexuals, although the family pressures and the societal and economic discrimination they have to deal with add considerably more stress to their lives. In acknowledgment of such evidence and in response to pressure from the gay movement, both the American Psychological Association and the American Psychiatric Association have recently taken as their official position that homosexuality is not deviant behavior, but rather lies within the normal range of human sexual expression. This view of homosexuality has been accepted by many sex researchers and sex educators, including Masters and Johnson and the Kinsey Institute. They agree that for some men a gay orientation is the healthiest and most normal possible life-style.

Basically, homosexuality is a *preference* on the part of a man for engaging in sex with other men. Such a preference might be transitory, it might be interspersed with heterosexual interactions, or it might be a relatively enduring pattern. But whatever the circumstances, homosexuality should be seen as a matter of choice, rather than as an illness or a social problem. The only time homosexuality can legitimately be seen as problem behavior is when it causes problems for a particular individual. But as long as homosexuality (or any other form of sexual activity, for that matter) is freely agreed upon by both partners, is performed in private, is not coercive, does not cause physical injury, does not involve children, and is not used to inflict guilt or punishment on oneself or one's partner, it can be said to fall within the range of normal and acceptable sexual behavior. This is not to say that homosexuality is in any way *better* than heterosexuality or that everyone should try it. Homosexuality is simply a valid choice of sexual orientation. It would be equally erroneous to hold it up as a sexual norm or to denigrate it as an inferior or unacceptable form of sexual expression.

Many heterosexuals believe that homosexual men can be identified by certain physical characteristics or peculiarities of dress and behavior. Some people may congratulate themselves that their ability to identify homosexuals shows a degree of perceptiveness or sophistication, but in reality it is more likely to be a sign of prejudice similar to that of the anti-Semite who is convinced that he can "always spot a Jew." Actually, most homosexuals cannot be identified by outward signs. Most gays have no wish to stand out and consequently keep a rather low profile, looking, acting, and dressing virtually the same as heterosexual men. Nor is it true that homosexuals are to be found exclusively in certain characteristic occupations such as interior decorating or hairdressing. There are homosexuals in every field of endeavor, including stevedores, business executives, machinists, doctors, truck drivers, and college professors. Some homosexuals, of course, do dress and act in a flamboyantly effeminate manner, but these exhibitionists are definitely in the minority and are often looked down upon and avoided by other gays who have no desire to flaunt their sexuality.

Despite the recent liberalization of our attitudes, society does continue to be hostile to gays. Homosexuality is still accepted as grounds for discharging a man from the armed forces, and, in spite of a movement among the clergy to incorporate homosexuals into the religious community, the Roman Catholic Church, along with other religious groups, continues to regard homosexuality as a perversion. Moreover, the attitude of most people toward homosexuality is still a negative one, ranging from disapproval to outright disgust. What are the reasons for this widespread and persistent antagonism?

It may have something to do with the notion that homosexuality is on the upswing and that unless it is kept down by force it will threaten the integrity of the family unit and the structure of society as a whole. But there is no real basis for this fear. Research indicates that there has been no real change in the percentage of men who adopt a homosexual orientation. Rather, homosexuality has become more visible as more and more individuals openly declare themselves. Homosexuality does not pose a threat to the family unit. The majority of males have been and probably will continue to be heterosexual; they will continue to marry and to produce enough children to ensure the perpetuation of society.

Another reason many people fear homosexuality is that they are convinced that most homosexuals are child molesters. The homosexual who goes about seducing impressionable young boys is a figure of fear for many an anxious parent. Actually, it is an established fact that the vast majority of child molesters are heterosexuals preying on young girls. Although there undoubtedly are homosexual child molesters, they constitute a very small minority of homosexuals.

A related but more subtle fear is that the increased acceptance of homosexuality will cause the male role to become less clearly defined, and this in turn will make it more likely for young boys to become homosexual. Many people are particularly opposed to homosexuals as teachers because of the fear that they might steer a young boy toward homosexuality at the point in his life when he is most impressionable and his sexual orientation is in the process of formation. However, the data argue that these concerns, too, are largely groundless. Increased toleration and awareness of alternatives do not necessarily lead to increased homosexuality.

Perhaps the most significant reason heterosexual men are hostile to homosexuals has to do with an apprehension that their own heterosexual orientation is somehow ambiguous or fraudulent. Many heterosexual men seem to be afraid of being "contaminated" by contact with homosexuals. The heterosexual may feel threatened because he fears that there is a homosexual part of him that the gay male might recognize and make a play for. This misapprehension is probably responsible for most cases of overreaction on the part of heterosexual men to sexual overtures by gays. Often the heterosexual feels that he has to protect his manhood from imagined contamination by reacting rudely or threateningly, or even by beating up the homosexual. A man who is secure with his heterosexual orientation, however, feels no need to react in this way. He recognizes the invitation of the homosexual for what it is—a mistake, a misdirected attempt to attract a sexual partner—and he replies to it simply by saying straightforwardly and assertively that he is not interested in a homosexual encounter. Following such a reaction, the overwhelming majority of homosexuals would have no wish to pursue the matter further.

It may also be true that heterosexuals are particularly threatened by gay men because of the subtle indoctrination nearly all men in our society receive against excessive physical contact between males. We learn early on that male contact should be strictly limited (i.e., to competitive sports, a slap on the back, a handshake, etc.). Even in father-son relationships, touching, playful roughhousing, and kissing usually come to a halt as the boy grows older. Supposedly this restraint is in the interests of maintaining the social ideal of being "male." In contrast to this process of achieving "male identity," women are given freer reign to express themselves physically and emotionally. The demonstration of affection between women is generally accepted and does not seem to arouse fears that it will promote lesbianism or undermine "female identity."

Although many theories have been put forward to explain why certain individuals become homosexuals, the question remains largely unanswered. Some writers ask, "What went wrong to cause homosexuality?" Such an approach implies a biased and unscientific view since it assumes that homosexuality necessarily involves a psychological or physical malfunction of some kind. The most popular psychiatric theory suggests that homosexuals are the products of homes in which there is a dominant and seductive mother and a weak or absent father. Although the backgrounds of some homosexuals conform to this pattern, it is by no means true of all or even of a majority. Thus the validity of the theory is open to serious question. Another leading theory is that homosexuality has some physiological basis such as a hormonal imbalance or a genetic flaw. These factors might play a decisive role for a small number of homosexual males. However, research has found that for the great majority of homosexual men, hormonal or genetic factors have no appreciable influence.

A more constructive approach to the question of what causes

homosexuality is to bear in mind that the choice of a sexual orientation, whether homosexual or heterosexual, is a complex phenomenon which is influenced by many interconnected factors—child-rearing practices, the nature of peer interactions, sex education, (or the lack thereof), ways of dealing with affection, general comfort with one's own body and sexuality are some possible influences on sexual orientation.

It is possible that a series of "pleasure events" in the presence of a member of the same sex might culminate in a later preference for male sex partners—a process analogous to what we hypothesize happens in the development of heterosexuality. The experiences of early orgasmic responses might be particularly important. Also the kind of sexual fantasies males use during masturbation might have a strong reinforcing effect on the development of sexual orientation. According to the way we understand the nature of sexual development at the present time, it appears that people *learn* to be sexual, and that the nature of the learning determines whether one ultimately prefers opposite- or same-sex partners.

But regardless of what causes homosexuality, it seems that the most sensible and least prejudicial way of regarding sexual orientation is as a matter of choice or preference, of committing oneself to a life-style that is in accordance with one's basic needs and desires. Whether a person chooses homosexuality, heterosexuality, or bisexuality, this choice ought to be respected by other individuals, regardless of whether they share or approve of that particular orientation. It may be some time before such complete toleration is reached in our society, but when it comes it is sure to bring much greater happiness and fulfillment than was ever achieved under the older prejudiced and repressive attitudes.

A great many misconceptions center around the methods used by homosexuals to obtain sexual pleasure. It is often assumed that the sexual practices of homosexuals include strange rituals, "kinky" and perverse acts. Generally speaking, these notions exemplify the tendency of most people to impute strange behavior to any group of whom they have little direct knowledge. Although some gays do practice "exotic" sexual behavior, the percentage is probably no greater than that found among heterosexuals. Most of the sexual techniques used by gay couples are identical to those used by heterosexuals—a fact that underscores the absurdity of identifying any particular sexual technique as a specifically homosexual act. A homosexual interaction is defined by the fact that two same-sex people are involved, not by the nature of the techniques employed.

Thus, as we have seen, oral-genital contact between a man and a woman is not an indication of latent homosexual tendencies. Oral-genital contact is heterosexual if opposite-sex partners are involved and homosexual if same-sex partners are involved.

Fellatio is one form of sexual behavior commonly enjoyed by homosexuals. Fellatio might be mutual ("69 position"), or it might be performed by one partner at a time. It might be used solely as a sexual-arousal technique, or it might be carried through to orgasm. Anal intercourse is another sexual technique engaged in by some gays and also tried by one out of four heterosexual couples. Contrary to popular thinking, it is not the rule among homosexuals practicing anal intercourse for one partner to assume the female role and the other the male. It is more common for them to alternate in assuming the receptive and penetrative positions. Other forms of sexual expression used by gays include mutual masturbation, frottage (a simulation of intercourse involving mutual rubbing of the penis against the partner's abdomen), and interfemoral intercourse (thrusting the penis between the partner's legs).

It is important to note that all of these activities can be and often are engaged in by heterosexual as well as gay couples. In fact, the only activity exclusive to heterosexuals is penis-vagina intercourse. It should also be noted that homosexuals generally use these techniques with as much variation and imagination (or lack of it) as do heterosexuals, and that the kissing, caressing, and other pleasuring activities which form a part of heterosexual lovemaking are commonly incorporated into gay encounters as well.

Of course, some sex between gays—such as anonymous sexual encounters in men's toilets or at all-male public baths—*is* devoid of affection and emotion. But then so are most encounters between heterosexual men and prostitutes. Just as men who have sex with prostitutes usually also have more long-term relationships with women, so the majority of gays who engage in anonymous one-night stands are involved in ongoing relationships as well. If anything, the men who limit their homosexual encounters to brief, impersonal meetings are probably most often those who are attempting to maintain a heterosexual facade and satisfying their preference for male sexual contact on the side. Thus, anonymity and lack of warmth among gays, insofar as it exists, may be blamed partially on the repressive intolerance of heterosexual society.

Homosexuals need and tend to seek out closeness and intimacy in relationships just as much as heterosexuals, and while a particular homosexual man might have dominant sexual preferences, he is not likely to be inflexible and to engage in stereotyped and rigid patterns of sexual behavior. Like his heterosexual counterpart, he feels the need for variety and for greater sensual and emotional satisfaction in his sexual encounters.

Life-styles among gays are diversified—a fact that runs counter to the idea that the majority of homosexuals are overconcerned with making sexual contacts to the exclusion of other life-experiences. Many men succeed in integrating their homosexuality into their lives, engage in productive occupations, have a multitude of social and cultural interests, and establish very satisfying interpersonal relationships. Because of the stigma still attached to homosexuality in this culture, many homosexuals choose to express their sexual orientation clandestinely, admitting that they are gay only to other homosexuals and to intimate friends, and meanwhile representing themselves as straight to the rest of the world. Thus, they effectively lead two separate lives, sustain two independent identities. The psychological stress of such a life-style can prove damaging to many men, especially those with a wife and children. They are not yet able or willing to join the growing movement of homosexuals who are open, vocal, and direct in affirming their sexual orientation, who proclaim that homosexuality is not a second-rate human condition and need not involve shame, guilt, or an apologetic attitude toward the rest of society.

Like any minority group, gays place a high value on social institutions that allow them to enjoy the company of others who share their own preferences, problems, and life-style. Hence, the continuing popularity of gay bars, where they can "cruise"—that is, seek out sexual contacts that may last only for a night or may develop into long-term emotional attachments. Essentially, the gay bar serves the same purpose for homosexuals as the singles cocktail lounge serves for heterosexuals. Not all gay men enjoy these bars; some, in fact, avoid them, preferring other kinds of social activities such as small dinner parties or sports. For some gay men, cruising might involve walking or driving around areas that have a heavy concentration of other gays seeking sexual liaisons. Cruising—whether it occurs in a bar, movie, party, steam bath, or at an intersection—involves a subtle and complex system of nonverbal cues not unlike the kind of seductive behavior common among heterosexually oriented people. In some areas, male prostitution or "hustling" may also be prevalent.

Generally speaking, sexual relationships between homosexual men tend to be less permanent than both heterosexual relationships and relationships between lesbians. To a certain extent, however, this impermanence can be attributed to the corrosive effect of society's negative attitude toward male homosexual attachments. Long-term relationships between heterosexual couples are, of course, encouraged in all kinds of ways by society, particularly when they are formalized by marriage and involve children.

Female homosexuality, while not approved by society, seems to arouse less hostility. Women are traditionally allowed to be more physically expressive with one another, unmarried women are almost expected to live together as roommates. Hence, a lesbian couple can maintain a relationship without attracting as much attention as a male homosexual couple. Nevertheless, many male homosexuals do establish relationships that last five, ten, or twenty years, and even longer. Some gay couples have, in fact, sought to legalize their relationships as formal marriages, insisting that to deny them the same rights and advantages which are accorded to heterosexual couples constitutes blatant discrimination.

Gays have attempted to organize in other ways as well. The Gay Activist Alliance, along with other militant groups, is working for an end to discrimination against homosexuals in hiring practices and other social situations. Gay religious groups are attempting to bring about the acceptance of homosexuals within the religious establishment. "Problem-centered" groups and services such as "Gay Alcoholics Anonymous," gay switchboards, and gay VD clinics have been established to deal with specific difficulties faced by gays. Such organizations underscore the fact that gays are human beings whose choice of sexual orientation and life-style is a legitimate one that should in no way exempt them from enjoying the same freedom and privileges accorded to other people.

As we observed at the beginning of this chapter, sexual orientation seems to fall along a continuum, with a significant percentage of men experiencing arousal in both homosexual and heterosexual situations. It might seem that, ideally, those men who have tendencies in both directions ought to be able to express themselves as homosexuals and as heterosexuals, according to the circumstances. However, for most people, such an adjustment is rarely possible. The majority of individuals find it quite difficult to function as active bisexuals. Straddling both worlds places serious social and psychological stresses on the individual that most people are unable to sustain. Thus, most men who feel strongly drawn toward homosexuality must make a conscious decision at some point whether to opt for this orientation or whether to attempt to reinforce their potential for functioning as heterosexuals.

Such a choice must ultimately rest with the individual himself, and it should be based on what he feels would lead to the greatest fulfillment, happiness, and pleasure on his part. His decision should *not* be based on what others want for him, whether those others happen to be parents, a wife, an employer, or society at large. While it is true that those who are closest to a person may feel that they want what is best for him, their very emotional involvement makes them unable to provide unbiased and nonjudgmental advice. It is the individual himself who must live with the decision, so it is he who must assume the responsibility of making it.

Nor is it advisable for a man to put off making a decision about his sexual orientation. Difficult as life may be for a homosexual in certain instances, there are few things more painful for a man than to go through the motions of heterosexual existence while fighting against the suspicion that his true sexual needs would be better fulfilled as a homosexual. One of the most difficult is the situation of the man who, fearing to confront his homosexual orientation, chooses to deny his sexual needs altogether and makes no sexual contacts with people of either sex. Such a person condemns himself to living a shadow existence in both worlds while enjoying the advantages of neither.

We are all sexual beings whether we admit it or not, and all of us have a right to choose some form of sexual and emotional expression. To deny this fact is to shut off one of the major sources of happiness in your life—but that, too, is an individual choice.

For a man making the choice of sexual orientation, professional guidance can often be invaluable. A professional counselor, if he is truly qualified to help in these situations, will not attempt to force a particular decision on the client, but rather help him to discover what his real needs are and then to assist him in planning a course of action designed to realize them. This counselor may be a psychologist, a minister, a psychiatric social worker, a psychiatrist, or an individual working for a gay counseling service. His effectiveness will depend much less on his professional qualifications than on his commitment to helping the client achieve a personally satisfying decision about his sexual orientation. In my own practice I have counseled quite a number of men seeking help in choosing a sexual orientation, and in each case my guiding principle has been that the needs and desires of the client come first. A solution to a sexual-orientation problem (or any other sexual problem) that is imposed from without is no solution at all.

One client, for example, was a nineteen-year-old college student who had been actively homosexual since he was thirteen. The summer before, Tom's parents happened to find out about his homosexual activities and insisted that he seek out professional therapy. He presented himself as a very reluctant client, making it clear that he was coming to me under duress and that he expected me to share his parents' disapproving attitude. My first task then was to make clear that I viewed homosexuality as a legitimate sexual life-style and that it was not my intention to force him to change. After some discussion we decided that we would spend two or three sessions reviewing his sexual development and preferences and then determine a plan of action. Eventually Tom decided that a homosexual orientation would be better for him since his sexual experiences, masturbatory fantasies, and sexual preferences all pointed toward an overwhelming attraction for other men. We then focused on how to describe this to his parents in a way they could accept without blaming themselves for the fact that Tom had chosen homosexuality. We decided that it would be unrealistic to expect them to be enthusiastic about Tom's choice, at least at first, and that simple acceptance was the most we could hope for. This decision turned out to be the right one as Tom's parents eventually became reconciled to his homosexuality, an adjustment that contributed greatly toward relieving the tension that had developed between them.

Another client, George, was a twenty-one-year-old man who felt very ambivalent about his sexual orientation. Since the age of fourteen, he had felt admiration and attraction for athletic and virile men. Convinced that he had a small penis, he had always been aroused by the thought of men with large organs. Although George masturbated frequently to a variety of homosexual, heterosexual, bisexual, and group-sexual fantasies, his sexual experiences with other people were rather limited. He had had two successful homosexual experiences in which he was fellated to orgasm by other males, and one unsuccessful heterosexual intercourse experience in which he ejaculated before he could get his penis into the woman's vagina. George decided to see me to discuss his confused sexual feelings. I began by telling him that I did not want to sell him on being heterosexual, but rather that the decision to be straight or gay would ultimately be his. After four or five sessions in which we focused on exploring his sexual experiences, feelings, and fantasies,

George decided that it would be better for him to try to make a heterosexual adjustment. We then engaged in a systematic program to increase his heterosexual arousal and skills and to decrease his homosexual desires and feelings. This relearning process proved successful, and George went on to function happily as a heterosexual.

For the sake of homosexuals and heterosexuals alike, it would be best if society as a whole could adopt the basic principle that serves as a guide for responsible therapists: sexual orientation is a matter which the individual himself must be free to decide in his own best interests. Those choosing to make a homosexual adjustment should be given as much respect as those who make the heterosexual choice. Homosexuality should be looked upon as a truly *alternative* life-style, not a second-rate one. We must remember that a homosexual is above all else a human being, and we should emphasize the positive aspects of his humanness rather than stigmatize him with the label of deviant. Contrary to what you may have heard, there *is* such a thing as a happy homosexual. I have met quite a few of them. Whether we will be meeting more of them in the future depends at least in part on the attitude that straights decide to adopt.

13
You and Marriage: Choosing the Intimate Bond

"SADIE HAWKINS DAY" is a holiday celebrated by the citizens of Dogpatch, the backwoods community in Al Capp's comic strip, "Li'l Abner." During Sadie Hawkins Day, it is open season on males, and any woman who manages to run down, corner, trap, or otherwise physically restrain any unattached man has the right to claim him as her spouse. The holiday is, of course, enormously popular with the unmarried women of Dogpatch, who look forward to catching a husband whom they would ordinarily be unable to obtain. But to the men, Sadie Hawkins Day is a time of pure terror, when each member of Dogpatch's bachelor population exercises to the utmost his talents of evasion in order to avoid what is generally referred to as "a fate worse 'n death."

What makes the Sadie Hawkins Day pursuit so funny, aside from the pure slapstick of the situation, is its devastatingly accurate caricature of the average man's attitudes toward marriage in our society. Like the men of Dogpatch, we often see ourselves as entering into marriage under protest. It is assumed that the rewards of marriage—closeness, intimacy, emotional security—are of interest chiefly to women. Men, on the other hand, value "freedom" and "good times." Women are supposedly involved in a continual effort to ensnare men into marriage, to deprive them of their freedom and turn them into tame, obedient husbands. How close we are to the Sadie Hawkins Day mentality can be seen from the way we respond to news of a fellow male's nuptials. It is amazing how often the language we use in these situations resembles that used to describe defeat in battle. "Another good man gone," we might say, or "Another man bites the dust." Or we might jokingly offer our condolences.

The contrast between the male and female attitudes toward marriage can be seen most clearly in the celebrations which generally precede the wedding ceremony. The bridal shower, a gathering confined to the bride's female relatives and friends at which the gifts are usually domestic in nature, clearly looks forward to the married state. The male counterpart, however, the bachelor party, which may feature drunkenness and salaciousness in varying degrees, is obviously a last look backward at the joys of the single life.

But isn't there a discrepancy here? Statistics show that 95 percent of the men in this country get married at some time in their lives. Contrary to popular myth, marriage is neither going out of style nor is it a dying institution. If we are really engaged in a battle against the efforts of marriage-minded women to enslave us, then we must be extremely ineffectual warriors, since our losses are so incredibly high. Either that or there is a good deal of hypocrisy in our attitude, and we do not really succumb to marriage as unwillingly as we pretend.

I think the second explanation is the more likely one. After all, it isn't only women who need the companionship, intimacy, and emotional security that marriage is designed to provide. These are human needs, not just female ones. Marriage holds out the promise of a sexual and emotional bond with another person that will be deeper and more satisfying than is possible in any other relationship. Women respond to this promise wholeheartedly because they have learned from childhood to think of marriage as a desirable goal. Men, on the other hand, feel they must hold something back because marriage does not coincide with the macho image they may have learned to accept as an ideal. Thus, the average man may inwardly desire the emotional rewards that marriage offers, but, for the sake of appearances, he must represent himself as simply another Sadie Hawkins Day casualty.

The trouble with this divided attitude is that a man who pretends to enter the married state under duress is apt to feel that merely consenting to marriage is all that should be required of him. In fact, it is typical of men in our society to feel that they need not put much emotional energy or commitment into marriage. For a woman, marriage is supposed to be everything, the very basis of her life. For a man, marriage is merely one of several obligations, and probably not the most important one. Many men feel that marriage is simply a matter of fulfilling certain set duties, and that carrying out these duties adequately automatically puts them above criticism. This attitude is typified by a cartoon in which a husband and wife are seated in their living room amidst all the accoutrements of comfortable, middle-class married life. The man glances over his newspaper with a look of consternation and says to the woman: "Of course I love you—that's my job."

A marriage conducted in this spirit is bound to be unsatisfying. A man may undertake the responsibilities of marriage in the same way he undertakes the responsibilities of his business, but there the resemblance between the two institutions ends. A large established company might be able to survive if the majority of people working for it do their jobs in an uninspired, routine way. A marriage is not likely to. There are no stockholders in a marriage, no federal subsidies, no way of borrowing emotional capital. All that makes up a marriage, all that keeps it going must come from the couple themselves. Entropy, the tendency of a system to break down if left to itself, takes effect very swiftly in the marriage situation. Or to put it another way, a love that isn't growing is probably dying.

Because marriage demands such unequivocal participation, it is foolish and self-defeating to enter into it with anything less than a total readiness to work toward making it succeed. True, there is great pressure to marry in our society. Beyond a certain age, unmarried people are looked upon as being a bit strange. Even our tax laws give certain advantages to the married person. Nevertheless, you should resist social pressure and view marriage simply as one of a number of options open to you (such as staying single, cohabitation, group living, and so on), and you should choose to marry only if you decide that marriage fits your own needs, wishes, goals, and values in life.

The first step in determining whether you are marrying for the right reasons is to ask yourself whether you are choosing marriage for its own sake or to escape from some other situation. For instance, a man may decide to get married because he wants to avoid the pressures of dating or the loneliness of being single. He may see marriage as the only way to get out of an unpleasant or boring family setting, or he may allow parental or peer pressure to influence him to give up his unmarried state. One of the worst reasons of all to marry is as an attempt to cover up a real or suspected homosexual orientation. In such situations, marriage is not seen as a positive choice, but as a kind of escape hatch.

Generally speaking, an individual should become extremely suspicious of his motives whenever any course of action appears as "the only way out." For one thing, when people seek marriage as an escape or because they feel that it is "time to settle down," they often do not give the time and attention they should to locating an appropriate marriage partner. Often they are so anxious to be married that rather than being at all selective they end up with whomever happens to be convenient or available at that time. If a partner has been selected in this way, a couple often finds sooner or later that they really do not care about or respect each other as much as they had thought or that their interests and values are so different that they are unable to pull together in life. These strains can add to the difficulty that any two people will have in adjusting to each other's idiosyncrasies and in handling the hassles and confusions of everyday life together.

An unplanned pregnancy is also a very poor reason for a couple to marry. Marrying the woman you have gotten pregnant may seem like the gallant thing to do, and such an action may have been laudable at a time when the price of giving birth to an illegitimate child was banishment from respectable society. But times have changed, and today it is a far greater kindness to consider marriage as a choice in and of itself, rather than as a way of avoiding possible shame and humiliation. On the other hand, it would be a mistake to go to the other extreme and automatically eliminate marriage as a solution to an unplanned pregnancy. The fact is that one out of four brides is pregnant at the time of marriage and that some of these couples make excellent marital adjustments—especially those who were already planning to marry and simply moved up the date because of the pregnancy.

Just as marrying the woman you've gotten pregnant is the gallant but unrealistic gesture from the male point of view, marrying a man to reform him is its equally foolish female counterpart. The woman who marries a man with a drinking or gambling problem or one who can't hold a job, thinking that her good influence will cause him to reform, is being extremely unrealistic. It is the man's responsibility to change his life. Dealing with problems such as these is the job of therapy, not marriage. No matter how well intentioned a wife may be, it is unlikely that she will be able to exercise the necessary amount of self-control to deal effectively with such problems. Nor is it her role to do so.

So much for poor reasons for marriage. Are there any good ones? Yes, there are some very real benefits to be looked for in marriage, benefits it would be difficult to realize in any other situation. Sharing as they do the high points as well as the everyday events of life, a married couple has a unique opportunity to develop a relationship of extreme intimacy. Within marriage, an individual's very human need to feel loved, important, and secure and to love and care for another person can be satisfied. Of course there is a dark side to marriage as well. The great amount of time married couples spend together can lead to boredom and psychological suffocation. The insights into one another's character that intimacy confers on a couple can be used to wound as well as to help. But when these negative effects occur, the cause can usually be traced to an insufficiently thought-out marriage decision, a lack of commitment to the marriage itself, or a lack of communication and continued sharing in the relationship.

Just as there are positive and negative reasons for getting married, there are also effective and ineffective ways of choosing a mate. The most important prerequisite to look for is probably the ability to communicate. Communication means a capacity and a willingness to share important aspects of your lives and personalities with one another, not just those that make you look good. A marriage partner should be someone with whom you can talk about your fears, angers, and other negative feelings as well as about positive feelings of love and attraction. Letting your partner know about your vulnerable areas as well as your strengths is an effective way of building intimacy into a marriage relationship. However, revealing his weaknesses to his wife—especially feelings of uncertainty and inadequacy, or of sadness and depression—is often one of the hardest things for a man to do. Males learn from an early age that they must always be, or appear to be, in control of the situation, and that women admire "the strong, silent type." Certainly, strength is an admirable quality in any human being, male or female. But no sensible person would expect a partner to be strong on all occasions. Your partner must be willing and able to accept you as you are rather than as what she wants you to be and to accept the difficulties and weaknesses you have without putting you down for them.

But at the same time, the relationship should be a reciprocal one. Your partner should not take the role of full-time therapist or confessor, but should also be honest and open with you about her thoughts and feelings, both positive and negative. Effective communication helps to locate the inevitable dissatisfactions and disagreements that occur in any marriage and also serves as a means of finding solutions to them. Partners should be able to communicate happiness and satisfaction also, since by doing so they can help one another to see the value and effectiveness of their positive actions.

Although it is true that after a few years of married life, most couples grow sensitive to one another's moods and emotional states, they still can't be expected to be mind-readers, and verbal communication remains extremely important. When joys and sorrows are not communicated and are in effect suppressed, the couple is able neither to fully share their pleasure nor to identify and work on problem areas. So above all, good potential marriage partners should be people who are able to share feelings and talk to one another.

Another important guideline to selecting a partner is to try to choose someone whose interests and values seem to be compatible with your own. If a couple share some interests, they will be more likely to spend more of their time enjoying life together. And while it is possible for a couple who have other things going for them to work out a compromise when a difference of opinion arises, major conflicts over values which are basically unresolvable create a degree of strain in any relationship. Of course your interests and values need not all coincide, and in fact it is an excellent idea to have some interests you do not share with your spouse. This gives you an area in which you can grow as an individual in your own unique direction. The strongest marriages seem to be those in which there are both shared and separate areas of interest, where the partners have a lot in common, yet each has some area of his/her own in which he/she can develop and bring something new to the marriage.

Before a couple marries, they should discuss realistically the major issues that will affect their relationship. Some of the questions that should be focused on are: Will there be children and, if so, when? How will the couple manage and spend its money, and what priorities will they have? Where will the couple live? What roles will each spouse take with regard to careers, housekeeping, and child-bearing? What sort of contact will the couple have with their in-laws? These are issues that need to be dealt with seriously before marriage, at least to the extent of laying down some workable guidelines for reaching a decision on any of them.

There is a great tendency for a couple anticipating marriage to minimize difficulties facing them. This is especially true of younger people, who often seem to feel that only by being wildly impractical and by insisting that problems will somehow take care of themselves can they preserve the romance in their marriage. Actually, a marriage that is to succeed and last needs more than romance—it needs planning of a highly realistic sort.

Functioning as a married person is, like other forms of behavior, something we learn to do. It often helps to facilitate the learning process if we have been exposed as a child or adolescent to good role models. Therefore, it is usually beneficial to a marriage if one or both of the partners was raised by parents who were themselves happily married. For such a person, a good marriage relationship will seem the norm, and he or she will follow the patterns of behavior that were in evidence in the home. A person who has not had such good fortune, on the other hand, must adopt the opposite strategy and try to learn from the weaknesses of his parents rather than from their strengths. Above all, he must work harder and more consciously to achieve a successful marriage himself.

Both Emily and I fit into the latter category. Our parents' marriages, while not disastrous, were something less than ideal. As a result of this early influence, I think a certain degree of complacency settled into our marriage during its early years. Both of us realized that we had reached a plateau, and that while we were reasonably satisfied, we weren't going anywhere and were in danger of stagnating. At this point we made the conscious decision to work at developing our relationship further. This proved easier for Emily than for me. Like most men, I had a lower expectation of marriage than my wife. Trying to communicate more effectively, being more affectionate, and thinking as a couple rather than as a single man who just happened to be married took a good deal more conscious effort for me than it did for her. I have found, however, in the long run, that this effort has been very worthwhile, both for me as a man and for us as a couple. Several times since then we've gone through similar periods of reassessment, and I believe that these can be of immense value in any marriage.

Too many couples think about doing something to improve their marriage only when their relationship seems to be foundering—a rather negative approach. If a marriage is thought of as an arrangement that is valued because of the emotional satisfaction and pleasure it gives, then it will seem worthwhile to try to make it even better, to increase the dividends it produces. It is a lot easier and much more fun to make a good marriage better than to try to lift a bad one off the rocks. Unfortunately, many couples do not try to change their marriages or go for counseling until serious problems have arisen and considerable anger and resentment may have accumulated.

So far we have said nothing specifically about the role of sex in marriage. Obviously, it has a very important place, but only by first viewing marriage in a larger context will we be able to see clearly what that place is. One encounters different attitudes about the importance of sex in marriage. One viewpoint is that sex forms a sort of bedrock of the marital relationship—that if sex is good, everything else will be good. By the same token, it is assumed that if trouble appears in a relationship, the cause can always be traced to a poor sexual adjustment. Another viewpoint is that sex is of secondary importance, and that the primary element is the couple's feelings and regard for one another. If their relationship is good in this respect, a poor sex life won't matter very much.

Both of these attitudes are actually rather simplistic. Sex serves a number of purposes in a marriage. For one thing, it is a means of helping to create and reinforcing the feelings of intimacy between a couple. It is also a kind of refuge, a source of pleasure that is always available even when all else fails. It also provides a form of affirmation of you as a person and as a couple. However, it is not by any means the sole and primary substrata of a marital relationship. It is quite possible for a couple to have a good sexual relationship and yet have serious problems in other areas which they are unable to handle and which may lead to the breakup of their marriage.

But on the other hand, sex is certainly not a secondary consideration in marriage either. It is best seen as one aspect of a couple's pattern of interaction and feeling for one another. It is not something separate, but rather an integral part of the relationship. Thus, it is possible for a couple to be intellectually and emotionally compatible and yet to have an unsatisfactory sex life, but it is not possible for them to remain in such a situation indefinitely, at least not without diminishing their relationship or putting it in jeopardy. If a couple is truly committed to making their marriage work and to getting as much joy and fulfillment out of it as they can, they will not be satisfied with poor sexual relations, but will work at improving them.

A feeling of closeness and intimacy is very important to a couple's sexual life. Feeling loved and loving is one of the chief factors that make a couple want to have sex. Many couples do not understand this. Men especially tend to feel that sex is a part of life that is completely unrelated to anything else. In fact, the closeness and affection a couple feel outside the bedroom is of the greatest importance to their sex life. For example, when a husband shows that he cares for his wife by expressing his hopes and fears to her, by sharing household tasks, by calling during the day just to say hello, or by planning a special evening out for them, he creates a feeling of closeness that will probably make both of them want to enjoy sexual experiences together more often. Just as we saw in earlier chapters that intercourse is only one method of sharing sexual pleasure and expressing affection, so in the larger context of marriage, sex itself is but one way in which a couple expresses their enjoyment of one another.

This point is especially important for men who feel that each act of physical affection must culminate in intercourse. Such an attitude, common to a surprising number of men, is really an outgrowth of the tendency to compartmentalize sexual expression, to see it as a specific act that must be played out according to an unvarying script. When the expectation of intercourse is attached to every hug, kiss, and caress, one or both partners may begin to avoid interacting physically because they feel that if they are not prepared to go all the way, it would be best not to start something. Paradoxically, this attitude of "intercourse or nothing" is often responsible for reducing the frequency with which a couple has sexual relations. When marriage partners do not feel free to express their affection in ways that do not lead to intercourse, the general level of affection and sensuality in their relationship is automatically reduced, and, eventually, they will probably have intercourse less frequently.

Communication is another area in which the importance of a couple's daily interaction is clearly related to their sexual relationship. Partners who are in the habit of communicating freely on a wide variety of subjects and who are able to relate negative feelings as well as positive ones, will be better prepared for the mutual communication and guidance that are necessary for good sexual functioning. Each partner has the right and the responsibility to let the other know whether a particular type of stimulation is pleasurable or not. No matter how good a lover your partner may be, there is no way she can possibly know what turns you on unless you can provide some sort of feedback. Men in particular tend to feel that they should know how to be good lovers and how to satisfy their wives without help or instruction. But of course the very point of writing this book is my contention that men *do* need to learn about their sexuality in order to realize it to its fullest potentials. And both men and women do usually have to put a lot of energy into communicating their sexual likes and dislikes before they are able to establish a maximally enjoyable sexual relationship.

If you doubt that this is true, then try this test on yourself. See if you can name all the parts of your partner's body that she enjoys having stimulated (breasts, lips, ears, shoulders, thighs, labia, clitoris, etc.). What sort of stimulation does she like in each of these areas (heavy, light, tickling, rubbing, kissing, licking, stroking)? If you feel unsure about any of the answers, then there are still things you have to learn, and the best way to learn them is by experimenting with different pleasuring activities and at the same time providing each other with feedback, either verbal or nonverbal. Partners often feel embarrassed to initiate such exploration because they are afraid of doing something awkward and being rebuffed. However, this sort of exploratory activity can not only increase your knowledge of each other's sexual responses and thus make you better sex partners, but it can also be an intimate and adventurous experience. And it is something that should be done continually as your marriage progresses. People's sexual preferences change as they discover new areas of sensitivity and learn to experience their bodies in new ways. A couple should try to communicate these changes to one another so as not to become sexually out of touch.

It cannot be emphasized too strongly that sexual communication in marriage must be a two-way street. Just as your commitment to the success of your marriage obligates you to be receptive to signals from your mate about what is enjoyable or not for her, so it is your responsibility to communicate your own preferences to her. To put it very simply: Sex is a pleasurable activity, and pleasure means getting what you want. Renunciation and self-sacrifice have little part in a sexual relationship. Making clear, specific requests for certain kinds of stimulation is a skill that must be learned to facilitate sexual communication. The first step, of course, is knowing what you want, and some exploration on your own as well as with your partner can help you discover this. The second step is making these preferences known to your partner. This not only increases your chances of getting what you want but also it diminishes your partner's uncertainty and anxiety as to how to please you. Showing your appreciation verbally and nonverbally can allay your partner's feelings of awkwardness, make her feel good about herself for pleasing you, and make her more willing to pleasure you in the same way again.

It is important to distinguish, however, between a request and a demand. A request takes your wife's feelings into account because it gives her the option of saying no. A demand does not. As important as it is for sexual partners to feel free to ask for the sort of stimulation they prefer, it is equally important they they not feel pressured into doing anything against their will. Obviously not all your partner's likes and dislikes will be consistent with yours, and it will be necessary for each of you to make some concessions to the other. Imposing your wishes on your spouse will probably produce anxiety and anger, and the sexual experience may then degenerate into a struggle of wills. In such situations, the anger that is unleashed can easily extend beyond the bedroom. Even if one partner capitulates to the other's demands, the loser's resentment is likely to sour the winner's enjoyment of the experience. Remember, the object of sex should be pleasure, not a struggle for power and control.

The importance of communication in sex can be seen most clearly in those cases where sexual relations between a couple stop entirely. The fault is rarely a simple lack of interest in sex, although one or both partners may pretend that it is. Nor is it usual that the couple find each other so personally unappealing that they have no wish to go to bed together. In most cases, in fact, they continue to remain on amiable terms in other areas of life. It is just that in the sexual realm communication comes to an end.

In some cases, the suspension of sexual relations may continue indefinitely, creating an iciness that gradually pervades every aspect of the marriage. In other cases, communication may resume at some point, and when it does it is often with a bang, attesting to the intensity of the feelings that have been suppressed. One middle-aged couple who had come to me for sex therapy represented such a case. The husband was an important businessman who was totally involved in his work. He and his wife had not had intercourse for thirteen years and had not touched affectionately for about eight; nor had either partner had any extramarital affairs during this period. The wife wanted to get a divorce, but her husband objected, claiming that it would damage his professional image. Finally, both agreed to try sex therapy as an alternative.

During the first session, we talked about sexual communication and the value of affectionate touching as a learning experience, and I described to them the exercise in nongenital pleasuring that I wanted them to start out with that night. Neither of them seemed to be very happy about the idea, but they promised they would try.

When they appeared for the next session, I was surprised to see the husband with a bandage over his right eye which did not completely cover a hideous, purple bruise. When I asked what had happened, they glanced sheepishly at one another, then, not without a degree of humor, began to tell me the story. Following my suggestions, they had begun their first pleasuring session by having a drink together, along with a few minutes of intimate talk. I had mentioned that they might hold hands at this point, but when the man reached for his wife's hand she jerked it away, saying that they had not held hands for years and she thought it was stupid to start now. They hurriedly finished their drinks and went on to the next step, which was to take a shower together. The wife entered the shower first and began soaping herself. Then the husband entered, and, while reaching for the washcloth, inadvertently brushed against her bare shoulder. This seemed to trigger something in her, for, without hesitation, she turned and rammed her knee into his groin, pushed him out of the shower, then grabbed his hair and smashed his head against the side of the tub.

Oddly, after the wife had gotten over her fury and began to apologize for what she had done, and after the husband recovered somewhat from his initial surprise and pain, their first reaction was a rather shocked realization of how physically and sexually alienated they had been. They both understood for the first time the strength of the emotions they had been bottling up inside them, and both felt strongly motivated to continue therapy and work out their sexual problems. As it happened, their ability to communicate improved so dramatically that they were able to make rapid progress in sex therapy and went on to make a highly successful sexual adjustment.

Not every marriage is suffering from a communication problem as severe as this one, but most marriages could profit from an attempt to make communication both in and out of the bedroom more sensitive and explicit. Communication, spontaneity, and a willingness to experiment are the key elements that can keep the sexual relations of a married couple from becoming boring and routine. Promoting these elements is the responsibility of both partners. Each has an obligation to communicate his or her own emotions, thoughts, feelings, and preferences, as well as to be receptive to those of the partner. Each has an obligation also to contribute to the variety and spontaneity of the relationship.

Where sex is concerned, this means refusing to fall into the rut of always using one sexual position. It means experimenting with different moods or styles of intercourse—serious, playful, quiet, excited, "quickie," or long and romantic. It means experimenting with making love at different times of day as the opportunity presents itself, rather than adhering to the arbitrary dictum that the time for intercourse is just before sleep. It might mean having sex in other rooms of the house besides the bedroom—for example, on the living room sofa, on the rug, or in front of the fireplace. It means taking the trouble and forethought to add creative touches to lovemaking sessions, such as music, incense, candles, or an after-sex bottle of chilled champagne. The point is that such variations and innovations are not extraneous trappings, but rather part of the act of love itself; they are an integral part of the effort to produce pleasure and express affection. They very much belong in the sex life of married couples.

A man should marry because he wants to, not because he feels he should. He should enter marriage willingly and with his eyes open, not as the victim of some Sadie Hawkins Day type of attack. He needs to have realistic expectations of marriage, not a romantic idealism or a cynical view that nothing ever gets better. Every couple goes through negative experiences, and a good marriage requires continued commitment, energy, and communication. Once married, the man should exert every effort to make his marriage succeed—not out of some consideration for marriage in the abstract, but because a good marriage can be a source of much pleasure, security, and closeness for him and for his wife. A successful marriage is well worth the thought, work, and energy needed to make it that way.

14
A Cost-Benefit Approach to Extramarital Sex

COMPARED WITH the unlimited sexual vistas that the single man is free to explore, marriage is a tight little world indeed. In our society, marriage usually means sexual exclusivity. For many men, raised on the belief that sexual conquest is the means by which a man proves his masculinity and obtains his fulfillment, the idea of being constrained to having sexual relations with one woman for the rest of his life may seem intolerable. Even when he has no real opportunity or desire for extramarital sex, a married man may still find himself obsessed by thoughts of an affair, simply because it is forbidden. He may feel that, sooner or later, the chance to engage in extramarital sex must arise. And since a "real man" never turns down a sexual opportunity, it may appear that an extramarital affair is something that will happen to him sooner or later, regardless of whether he actively pursues it or tries to avoid it.

The trouble with such a fatalistic attitude, however, is that it deprives you of the power to make rational decisions about your actions. In the case of extramarital sex, these actions may have far-reaching consequences, and so the ability to think about your values and feelings regarding marital sexuality and extramarital affairs and to make decisions that are good for you becomes extremely important. It would be worthwhile for you to look at extramarital sex in a more discriminating way, to distinguish among the different levels of extramarital involvement, and to be able to weigh the advantages and disadvantages of extramarital sex both for you as a person, for your wife, and for your marriage.

In doing so, we must try not to be influenced by the ready-made opinions and cultural stereotypes, whether they are liberal or conservative in origin. Each is liable to exert its own sort of tyranny over our thinking. One traditional attitude, for example, is that any extramarital affair, if discovered, is sufficient cause for ending the marriage. The offended party either leaves the house or forces the other to leave, and all communication between them ceases, except that which is carried out through their lawyers. There is another commonly accepted, traditional idea: that in any marriage the husband may be expected to have a number of brief, clandestine affairs, but that the wife will remain strictly faithful, preferring not to "really know" about her husband's activities.

Some liberal-minded couples take an entirely different attitude. An idea that has gained currency recently is that it is not extramarital sex but sexual exclusivity that is the enemy of marriage. Monogamy restricts the individual's ability to express himself and to relate freely to others; therefore, the ideal marriage is one in which neither partner questions how the other spends his time, or with whom. According to this view, "co-marital affairs," threesomes, mate-swapping, group sex, even bisexuality can be comfortably incorporated within the marital context, provided both partners agree to give up their selfish and old-fashioned feelings of jealousy and possessiveness. Hence, extramarital sex is seen not as a negative thing, but as an opportunity for both partners to liberate themselves from restrictions and achieve new freedom and openness.

If we look carefully at the traditional and the "swinging" attitudes, it becomes clear that they are both equally doctrinaire, equally unsuitable as guides for real-life behavior. To see how emotional and value-laden both really are, we only have to look at the contrasting terminology they employ. Those who are opposed to affairs use terms like "adultery," "cheating on your wife," "stepping out," "being unfaithful." Those who favor extramarital sex, on the other hand, prefer to use such terms as "personal and sexual sharing," "not being hung-up by jealousy and possessiveness," and "open marriage." In this chapter, we will attempt to avoid both value-laden terms and judgmental attitudes. We will try to take an objective, realistic, and constructive approach to the issue of extramarital sex. There is no blanket judgment—good or bad—that can apply to all extramarital affairs. Rather, each extramarital affair must be considered in the context of its meaning for the individual and his marriage situation. The individual's and the couple's religious and personal values must also be taken into account.

For the purpose of analysis, it is helpful to separate extramarital affairs into three basic categories: the casual encounter, the low-emotional-involvement affair, and the high-emotional-involvement affair. The casual encounter is the most common type for men. Generally it may begin during an out-of-town business trip or as a pickup at a bar or party. Although the desire for an exciting, illicit experience or the need for sexual variety may play a considerable part in motivating a man in such a situation, the main reason that most casual encounters happen is simply because it is *possible* for them to happen. The opportunity presents itself, and there seem to be few liabilities in accepting it. Very often, these experiences are with prostitutes. In the case of paid-for, totally impersonal sex, an added factor may be significant. The man may want to try some type of sexual activity with the prostitute that his wife is unwilling to engage in or which he feels uncomfortable about asking her to perform. This activity is generally fellatio; in fact, it is quite common for the married clients of prostitutes to request oral-genital stimulation rather than intercourse.

There are advantages as well as disadvantages to the casual encounter. One advantage is that since there is little or no emotional component to this type of affair, it is the least threatening to the marital relationship. A man may feel guilt as a result of an anonymous one-night stand, but such an experience is not likely to compete on a profound emotional level with the relationship he has with his wife. And in the event that the wife happens to discover the encounter, she may feel less threatened by it than by a more serious involvement. It is also possible for a casual sexual encounter to actually enrich the sexual relations between the man and his wife. The man might learn new techniques or acquire a new enthusiasm for sex which he can bring back into his marriage. It can also provide sexual pleasure for a man who, for one reason or another, receives little pleasure from marital sex, as well as adding an element of excitement and adventure to his life.

The disadvantages of the casual encounter include some that may exist for unmarried men as well—namely, the danger of venereal disease and/or pregnancy. People who meet casually and decide to have sex often do not bother to discuss contraceptive methods. The man may assume that the woman is on the pill, or he might just not care, and the result may be an unwanted pregnancy. There is also a chance that the woman has VD, and if the encounter is truly anonymous she may not be particularly concerned about infecting her partner. If the man does contract VD, he is almost certain to give it to his wife, and then he faces the extremely embarrassing task of having to reveal his affair so that he can alert her to the need for medical treatment.

Another disadvantage of the casual encounter is that although there is a chance that it may provide an input of sexual novelty into the marriage, it may also detract from the marital relationship. A man who finds his sexual excitement and variety outside the marriage may not have much motivation to try to improve the sexual interaction he has with his spouse. There is the danger that casual encounters or visits to prostitutes or massage parlors will become a habit, probably reinforcing a tendency that is highly detrimental to marital adjustment—namely, thinking of sex in marriage as being routine and unexciting and sex outside of marriage as being varied and adventurous. To consider one's marriage in this way not only sells short its potential for pleasure but also contributes to its deterioration.

The low-emotional-involvement affair is probably the next most common form of extramarital sex for men. Such affairs are generally based on an understanding between a man and a woman that they will meet periodically for sex, a little conversation, drinks or dinner together, but little else. There is no expectation that the relationship will develop, grow more serious or more intimate. Usually intimacy or possessiveness beyond a certain point is discouraged by one or both of the partners. Typical examples of this kind of affair are the salesman who spends the evening with a particular woman every time his business brings him to her area of the country; the man who visits a divorced woman every week or so for a sexual liaison; the executive who is carrying on an affair with his secretary. These affairs are often of short duration, but if they satisfy the needs of both parties and if they can be carried on comfortably without fear of detection, they may continue for many years.

The low-emotional-involvement affair has certain definite advantages. It allows for a certain degree of continuity and human contact as well as providing a supplemental sexual outlet. At the same time, it does not require an overwhelming emotional commitment or the expenditure of a great deal of time or energy. While the relationship is emotionally limited, it may provide a setting in which the man can talk about ideas, frustrations, and emotions which he feels he cannot share with his wife. Thus, the affair furnishes not only a sexual release but also a psychological one as well. If the man's marriage is irredeemable, yet he does not wish to get a divorce, this type of affair may help him to maintain appearances by assuaging his loneliness and his sexual needs. There is also the advantage that such a relationship, though it might settle down into a comfortable and familiar routine, can, at the same time, create a sense of adventure in the man's life. The experience of arranging a secret rendezvous, of leading a clandestine and illicit "double life" may provide a certain charm and excitement in and of itself.

The low-emotional-involvement affair has some of the same disadvantages as the casual encounter—namely, the possibilities of detection, of pregnancy, and of VD—but it also has some of its own. Probably the greatest danger is that it may lead to deeper and more personal involvement than was expected. Emotions are unpredictable, and there is no guarantee that they will remain at the level intended for them. Such unexpected emotional involvement may be mutual, or it may be one-sided. But in either case, it is sure to lead to other unlooked-for complications.

Most people's lives are not geared to handling sudden emotional overloads, and the consequences of being caught between a demanding, jealous mistress and an increasingly suspicious wife may be disastrous. Also, since this type of affair quite often ends up consuming more time and psychological energy than originally anticipated, it can detract from other areas of a man's life. One of the first effects of the time-squeeze is on his relationship with his children; he simply does not have the time to devote to the father role. He may also find that he has less time for his business, his hobbies, and other activities. Ironically, what was originally undertaken for pleasure and recreation can end up increasing the demands and restrictions on his time and energy. Unless the man can manage to break off the affair (usually an immensely harder and more complex task than starting it was), the situation may easily get out of control and could end in catastrophe.

Another real disadvantage of this type of affair is the loss of intimacy with one's wife. Not only is the low-emotional-involvement affair likely to have a negative effect on the man's sexual relationship with his wife but it is also likely to affect their emotional relationship as well. Often the man in this situation puts less energy into his marriage and shares his feelings less with his wife. Because of guilt and the fear of discovery, he might be particularly guarded or uncommunicative, and, as a result, his wife may become suspicious or simply feel that he no longer cares very much about her. She may withdraw her intimacy and affection, causing him to turn more and more to his outside partner for personal support as well as sexual gratification.

Brian and Ellen provided good examples of the toll that a husband's extramarital affairs can take simply in terms of the time and energy they consume. It was Ellen who came to see me in therapy originally. She was unhappy, dispirited, complaining that the responsibilities of caring for a home and two children left her feeling frustrated and inadequate. She felt that she needed some change in her life and was considering getting a job or returning to school. It soon became clear that one of her main problems was that her husband seemed too busy to give her much help or emotional support, and, at my suggestion, Ellen requested that he participate in the sessions as well. After talking to the two of them together and to Brian alone, I learned the story behind their present troubles.

Brian was a leasing agent who had relatively flexible hours and contact with a wide variety of people. During the first two years of their marriage their sex life had been fairly good, but after Ellen became pregnant their sexual relations stopped almost completely. Brian decided to seek a sexual outlet outside of his marriage and engaged in a number of casual affairs. He found extramarital sex more exciting than the "settled-down" sex he had with his wife and felt that he was recapturing the feelings and sensations he had experienced with women before he was married. He decided to keep these affairs a secret from Ellen. Brian continued in this pattern until, after the birth of their second child five years later, he felt that things were beginning to become too much for him. Between his job, wife, children, and the intricate circle of extramarital commitments he had formed, he had begun to feel that he was living life too fast with too little time left for himself. He was spreading himself too thin, and Ellen was suffering for it as much as he was. As these problems came out during our sessions, it became apparent that the best way of dealing with them would be to dissolve the marriage. There was simply too much anger and disappointment built up on both sides for them to devote the necessary energy to rebuilding their marriage.

The third category of affairs is usually the most complex as well as the most threatening to the *status quo*: the intimate, emotionally involving affair. In this situation, more of the man's personal and sexual needs are being met by the affair than by his marriage. There are definite advantages as well as disadvantages to be considered. .

Having an intimate affair can be a powerful ego booster, particularly for someone who is feeling down about a job problem, family troubles, or just middle-age blues. If love, excitement, and passion have been missing from one's life for some time, it can be very exhilarating to feel them again. Finding that he is still capable of loving and being loved may cause a man to feel that he has a new lease on life. It has been said that love is the best tonic, and this can be as true of an extramarital relationship as of any other. Having an intimate affair may have a profound regenerative effect on a man's whole life. It may galvanize him into taking things in hand in a way that he felt little motivation to do previously. For example, if a man's marriage has deteriorated beyond repair and he has been too apathetic to do anything about it, having an intimate affair may show him what he has been missing and thus spur him to take steps toward getting a divorce.

The disadvantages of an intimate affair, however, can also be great. Many of the dangers and problems associated with the other two types of affairs may result from this as well. In addition, the intimate affair has the most potential for ending disastrously. It places the greatest psychological stress on the man, since in effect, he is leading two separate lives. Usually one of the two women involved will end up feeling hurt and rejected, and there is the possibility that the man will eventually be deprived of both relationships. The emotional conflict can become intense, and it can affect family, job, and sense of well-being. Most men are incapable of sustaining this kind of double life, no matter what one reads in the recent spate of books and articles advising people on how to deal with multiple love relationships. The majority of men who become involved in an intimate affair eventually find that they have to choose between the affair and the marriage. And that choice will probably be accompanied by a considerable amount of turmoil and psychological pain.

There is naturally a good deal of simplification in this discussion of the advantages and disadvantages of different types of affairs. In real life each extramarital encounter is unique and will not fit neatly into any of the categories. Also, no matter how carefully we enumerate the pros and cons of a given course of action, we can never balance one side against the other in any truly objective way. In the end, we tend to choose intuitively and often on the spur of the moment. However, this is all the more reason for taking stock of our situation and our feelings beforehand so as to have some basis for future decisions. Ideally, a husband and wife, early in their marriage, should frankly and openly discuss the subject of extramarital sex in order to share and clarify their thoughts and feelings on the matter.

When Emily and I were married, part of the traditional, male-chauvinist baggage I brought with me into the relationship was the assumption that I would have clandestine affairs. I hadn't thought much about Emily in relation to extramarital sex, but I think I assumed that she would not follow my example. After a year of marriage, the subject came up in conversation and Emily told me that she would not accept my having affairs with other women. We discussed whether I would feel comfortable about her having emotionally involving affairs with other men, and I had to admit that I wouldn't. We then discussed whether we wanted to maintain a sexual double standard in our marriage. It seemed clear that, in our case at least, a single standard would be more satisfactory, and that intimacy would be better for me than a variety of partners. Thus, we made our feelings and expectations explicit. The advantage of this is that our agreement actually allows us more freedom in interacting with friends of the opposite sex than we would have if neither of us felt sure of the other's commitment. It also makes us more vulnerable to hurt if either of us does have an affair. If this did occur, it would cause hurt and anger and would naturally require a good deal of talking out, but because of our strong commitment to each other, it would not necessarily be devastating for our relationship. Our agreement has so far met the needs of our marriage quite well, but it does not necessarily mean that it would be good for you or your marriage. My work as a therapist has convinced me that each individual and each marriage is unique, and each person has to be aware of his own values, feelings, and experiences.

Besides being aware of the advantages and disadvantages of the different kinds of extramarital sex, you should also keep in mind some of the general guidelines that can be applied in such situations. Guideline number one is that the better the marriage, the less there is to be gained from having an affair. If a basically good relationship is beset with sexual or emotional problems, it makes far more sense to try to work these out together within the marriage rather than forming a new attachment and, in effect, resolving them unilaterally. If the problems seem overwhelming, then a therapist may be consulted. Many people reject the idea of seeking professional help because they see it as a sign of weakness, an acknowledgment that things have gotten beyond their capacity to deal with them. But if anything, the decision to consult a professional is an indication of a couple's commitment to their relationship, a sign of the value they place on it. Moreover, a therapist who has training and experience in dealing with marital and sexual problems can often provide the objective viewpoint and knowledge that are needed to resolve conflicts.

Another guideline is to beware of self-deception in extramarital affairs. It is very easy to convince yourself that what you are doing is motivated by the best intentions when actually it is not. For example, where extramarital sex is concerned, honesty is not necessarily the best policy. Confessing an affair to your spouse may appear on the surface to be a virtuous act. You may feel that you are promoting an honest and open marital relationship by sharing your experiences with your wife, but what you may actually be doing is trying to alleviate your own guilt. Living with the discomfort caused by keeping a part of your life secret from your spouse may be the price you must pay for having an affair. In most cases it is unfair to expect a spouse to accept the knowledge of an affair and to go on functioning as if nothing were out of the ordinary. For most of us, having an affair and enjoying a state of innocence at the same time is simply too much to expect. One strategy sometimes employed by men in this situation—persuading their wives to have an affair of their own to "even things up"—represents a form of coercion that reflects the husband's need to assuage his guilt more than the needs of the wife. It also might be a roundabout and therefore dishonest way of declaring a desire to split up the marriage.

Finally, there are certain patterns which nearly always indicate that the motivation behind the affair is a dishonest and destructive one. For example, there is the man who has a series of affairs, usually with younger women, in an attempt to prove his potency. This man may tell himself that his wife simply does not turn him on anymore, forcing him to seek sexual gratification elsewhere, but obviously there is a basic problem here which he is refusing to face. Sexual dysfunction is a very poor reason to seek extramarital sex. The more honest and productive approach would be to try to solve the problem within the context of the marriage, seeking professional sex therapy if required. Another example of a destructive behavior is the man who repeatedly seeks extramarital encounters with married neighbors, with his wife's friends, with co-workers, and with others whose relationship would make detection of the affair both extremely likely and extremely awkward. Such a man is probably using extramarital sex as a means of inflicting punishment on either himself or his wife and possibly on both.

In certain cases, however, where self-deception is not involved, extramarital sex can actually be a positive part of your life. Like a premarital affair, an extramarital affair can be a learning experience; it may show a person what is possible in a relationship, sexually or emotionally or both. Whether the knowledge gained in extramarital sex is used to enrich the marriage or to hasten its dissolution is a matter the individual must work out for himself.

Jack, a student in my course in human sexual behavior, wrote a personal sex history as part of a class assignment. His story illustrates the way in which extramarital sex may sometimes have a positive effect on a marriage. Jack was a twenty-nine-year-old accountant who had grown up in a rather restrictive Fundamentalist home. He had married at twenty-one, and although he had done a moderate amount of dating, he had never had sex with any woman besides his wife. Although he was reasonably happy with his job, house, and particularly his four-year-old son, he felt that his life was lacking in excitement. Sex with his wife was functional but routine. Although it took him two years to admit it to himself, what he wanted was an affair. It took another six months before the opportunity arose at an out-of-town business meeting.

Although the sex that first night was not great, Jack felt tremendously free and liberated. During the next year, he sought opportunities to travel away from home and to have sexual liaisons. One woman gave him his first introduction to oral sex, and when he got home he initiated his wife into this technique. After a year, Jack encouraged his wife to have an affair to "free her up sexually." They made an agreement not to talk about the details of their affairs, but did agree to share the new sexual techniques they learned. This pattern continued for several years, and their sex life prospered.

At present Jack has few affairs because his sexual relationship with his wife has improved so much. But if a really tempting opportunity presents itself, he doesn't turn it down. Their personal relationship has deepened, partly because talking about their decision to have an affair and their efforts to incorporate techniques learned in extramarital relationships brought them closer together and helped to reduce some of the doubts and fears that usually accompany such involvements.

Some couples claim that "swinging," the mutual exchange of sex partners, is one way of having extramarital sex without endangering the marital relationship. Swingers, who constitute about 2 or 3 percent of the married population, assert that by having extramarital affairs under controlled conditions, they are able to inject variety and excitement into their marriages while still maintaining mutual respect and trust. There is nothing necessarily negative or deviant about swinging—it depends on the couple, their goals, their values, and the nature of the relationship. It is worth noting, however, that few couples swing for more than about six months, and that it is usually the husband who is responsible both for making the decision to swing in the first place *and* for calling it off.

"Open marriage," an arrangement in which each partner is free to have extramarital relationships without having to hide these activities, has been advocated in some recent books. However, there has been very little research done on the viability of such marriages, which means that we have little real evidence that they actually work. It seems apparent, however, that there is a great potentiality in such relationships for both coercion and self-deception. The assumption behind the open marriage is that a mature and liberated person would not feel anger and jealousy about his or her spouse having a sexual relationship with another person. Since all of us want to believe that we are mature and liberated, we may deny having negative reactions toward our partner's extramarital affairs even if we feel them. The danger comes when these suppressed feelings suddenly burst forth, capsizing the marriage in a storm of resentment and violent emotion.

Statistically, a husband is more likely to engage in extramarital sex than a wife. Kinsey found that about 50 percent of all married men have at least one extramarital encounter, and more recent surveys indicate that the figure may now be nearer 55 percent. Compared with this, only about 33 percent of wives have extramarital sex. Some of the factors behind this discrepancy are probably that men generally have more opportunity for sex outside of marriage, that having affairs is seen as part of the male role, and that men are more inexperienced than women at turning down sexual opportunities. Nevertheless, women *do* have extramarital sex, and a man should learn to apply logic and understanding not only to his own real or potential involvements but also to those of his wife.

Generally, men react more strongly to their wives' extramarital affairs than women do to their husbands'. This is largely due to the sexual double standard, which assumes that men need variety and excitement in their lives while women do not. Therefore it is considered more acceptable for a man to have extramarital sex, but a woman who has an affair is regarded as being unfaithful and dishonest. This difference in attitude may also have something to do with the kind of affairs women tend to have—the most typical being a more intimate, longer-lasting relationship.

The casual encounter, the most common form of male extramarital sex, is rarer among women. Undoubtedly, this contrast reflects the profound and complex differences in cultural conditioning affecting the attitudes and responses of men and women, as well as the fact that men, in general, have more opportunities for casual sex than women do. Moreover, there is support, if not outright peer pressure, for men to engage in casual affairs, while this attitude is not found in most female peer groups. The average woman, unlike the average man, has an affair to fulfill important emotional needs which she finds lacking in the marriage. In other words, the wife's affair tends to be more significant in terms of its implications for the intimacy and stability of the marriage. This may be one reason men often find their wives' affairs so threatening.

Certainly there is no pat strategy for dealing with the discovery of a wife's extramarital affair. However, there are some practical guidelines which might prove to be of value. It is part of the traditional masculine role that when a man discovers his wife is having an affair, his response must be one of vindictive rage and possibly violence. For a man to react in any other way is to compromise his sense of honor and masculinity. This sort of reaction, socially approved as it may be, should be avoided. The fact that your wife is having an affair need not be interpreted as a put-down of your masculinity. Nor is it a sure sign that the marriage is destined to end in divorce. However, it does usually mean that the marriage is in trouble and that some important personal and/or sexual needs are not being met by the relationship.

Perhaps the best way to approach your wife's affair is to understand its significance in the context of the marital relationship. The affair may be, at least partially, a message drawing attention to some aspect of your marriage. Her decision to have an affair, for example, may reflect her boredom and dissatisfaction with her role as wife and mother. It may be an expression of her feeling that you do not devote enough time and attention to her, that she is neglected and unappreciated. Many men are threatened by the idea that their wives have greater sexual satisfaction with another man than with them. This fear can be heightened if there is a sex problem in the marriage. In the majority of cases, however, it is the need for emotional and psychological satisfaction that motivates women to have extramarital affairs, not simply the desire for better sex. Thus, the question the man should ask himself is not "How have I failed as a sex partner?" but rather, "What emotional needs have I failed to satisfy as a husband and lover?"

On the other hand, one should not make the mistake of interpreting a wife's affair too egocentrically, as though whatever she did could only have significance in terms of yourself. Sometimes it has more to do with her need for variety or a particularly tempting opportunity. Sometimes relationships deteriorate too much to be repaired. The message conveyed by the wife's affair may be not that she wants more love and attention from you, but simply that the marriage is unsatisfactory and she wants out. Then, of course, there is always the possibility that the chief reason for her affair is that she has become attracted to another man whose company she prefers to yours—not a pleasant turn of events, to be sure, but one that must be faced and dealt with should it arise.

If we begin with the assumption that marriage is a potentially viable institution which can provide great rewards for the couple willing to work at enhancing the quality of their relationship, then I think that we must regard extramarital sex with a certain degree of wariness. In most cases, the effect of an extramarital affair on a marriage is negative. For the man or woman who is dissatisfied with marriage, either sexually or emotionally or both, it is generally more profitable to work at solving these problems within the marriage than to seek escape in a second relationship or to leave the marriage hanging in midair. In and of themselves, extramarital affairs are neither bad nor good, but must be judged according to how they affect the marriage and each individual involved. In certain cases, extramarital affairs may have a positive influence on a marriage, and in other cases they may serve a useful purpose in a basically flawed marital relationship. However, a person thinking about engaging in extramarital sex should keep in mind that there is always some element of risk in any such affair.

15
Pregnancy and Childbirth: It's Your Baby, Too

JUST AS SADIE HAWKINS DAY expresses the idea that men are hapless victims of marriage-crazy women, a related cultural myth represents fathers as bumbling bystanders in the birth process, whose only real contribution is the sperm that starts things off.

The myth has been expressed in countless novels, movies, and TV shows, generally in a series of standardized scenes or vignettes. First we have the wife's coy announcement that she is pregnant and the husband's astonished response. Presumably at this point the decision to have a baby, the wife's missed period, and her visit to the doctor for a test have all gone on without his knowledge; he has been kept in a state of strict gynecological ignorance, which continues to be his most outstanding characteristic as the pregnancy progresses. We see him fluttering with exaggerated concern each time his wife climbs a flight of stairs or lifts anything heavier than a quart of milk. When the child finally comes to term, we find him pacing the waiting room like a caged beast and pestering the nurse with idiotic questions. Presented with his newborn offspring, he is all thumbs and can scarcely be persuaded that it will not break if he holds it. If it is a boy, he demonstrates his readiness to undertake its education by bringing a football or a baseball bat to the hospital. If it is a girl, he does nothing, for it is assumed that as a father he has nothing to teach her. His only task will be to provide for her and to keep her away from predatory males."

Throughout the entire procreative process, then, the father is portrayed as not only peripheral but superflous as well, allowed a place in the midst of things only because he is the one responsible for bringing home the paycheck that makes it all possible. The basic theme of this scenario is clear: women and women alone are responsible for the bearing and rearing of children; the male's presence is merely tolerated.

No man should allow his role as a father to be reduced to such paltry dimensions. Fatherhood is one of life's unparalleled experiences, and it can be replete with emotional rewards of a totally unique caliber. Because the experience is potentially such a rich and fulfilling one, it should be undergone deliberately, consciously, purposefully. Only by participating fully as a parent can a man assure himself of having taken the greatest advantage of the opportunity for emotional gratification which fatherhood offers. A man should *choose* fatherhood, savoring all that it has to offer, rather than just passively acquiescing in the experience.

But choosing fatherhood implies that a man must have the option of choosing nonfatherhood as well. In the past, before the widespread use of effective contraception, before the population explosion, before the opening of the job market to women, it was taken for granted that soon after a couple married they would begin to have children. Today, however, there is no longer any reason to make such an assumption. For a couple marrying now, having children is increasingly an option, not an obligation. It is no longer valid or realistic to insist that the purpose of sex is procreation. Sex happens to be the way we conceive children, but it also serves other equally important functions: as a means of experiencing pleasure and intimacy with a partner, an expression of love and affection. Sex, for sheer pleasure, is a normal, healthy, positive human activity. A couple should not feel guilty about enjoying sex for its own sake; nor should they feel that they have to have babies in order to justify their marriage or their sexual relations.

There are plenty of good reasons to decide not to have children. Having a child is a considerable expense. Hospital bills, visits to the doctor, baby furniture and other paraphernalia entail a sizable initial expenditure. As the child grows up, the expense gets even larger. Clothing, toys, entertainment, schooling, summer camps, college add up to an ever-increasing amount. Even if a couple has enough to live comfortably, they should realize that the addition of a child will reduce the amount of money they are able to spend on themselves and thus lower their standard of living.

A couple might also be unwilling to have a baby because it would mean that the wife would have to give up her career in order to stay home and take care of the child. Of course, an alternative could be for the wife to continue her career while the husband stayed home, and in some cases such an arrangement might prove ideal. If neither the husband nor the wife is willing to give up working time, though, a possible arrangement might be to hire professional help to care for the child and the home or to use a baby-sitter. But even with such assistance, the strain of raising a child while balancing two careers can be considerable, especially for couples in their twenties. The pressure often causes something to give way, usually either the marriage or the woman's career.

Couples who particularly relish the freedom and companionship they enjoy as a twosome might be unwilling to upset the balance of their lives by introducing a third member. Babies cut down enormously on the time and energy available for recreation, and a couple who consider their social life and "fun" times indispensable should think twice before having a child.

Finally, some couples may decide not to have children simply because they don't like them very much. Not being fond of children isn't something to be ashamed of. It doesn't imply that a person is unnatural or lacking in warmth. But if one doesn't like children or feel comfortable with them, it makes little sense to become a parent. A couple should also keep in mind that having a child represents a long-term commitment—for a period of at least eighteen years during which the parents are largely responsible for the child's welfare. A couple should take a long, sober look at this commitment and consider realistically all the obligations and limitations it involves before going ahead with the decision to have a child. They should also realize that there are several positive aspects of not having children, including greater freedom to travel, to try out alternative life-styles, to live where you please rather than choosing neighborhoods because of schools and child-related activities. Today there seems to be an increasing tendency for couples to weigh the advantages and disadvantages of childbearing realistically and to choose childlessness if that is what they decide is best for them.

But, if a man chooses fatherhood after thoroughly considering the question with his wife, his involvement in the childbearing process has only just begun. The next decision the couple must make is when to have a child, for ideally the arrival of children should be the result of planning rather than accident or chance. Potential parents should realize that the addition of a child to their family is no small event, but rather one that will place a great many demands on both the man and woman and will change their lives and their marriage considerably. Since the child will bring such great changes and demands, it is preferable that it be wanted, planned, and expected. If parents actively decide to have a child and are aware that its coming will involve considerable work and stress as well as joy and satisfaction, they will usually feel more positive about the child once it has arrived. This is especially true of the birth of a first child. They will also be more willing to work constructively at solving the problems that are an inevitable part of child care. Unfortunately, family planning is not as widely practiced as it should be. About four out of every ten children born today to married couples are not planned, and about one out of every four brides is pregnant at the time of marriage; for teen-age brides, the proportion is one out of every two.

About 15 percent of all couples who do decide to have a child will find that they have difficulty conceiving. If the couple has this problem, they should not feel embarrassed or think that they are abnormal. Rather, they should consult a gynecologist and/or a urologist to check out possible causes in both the man and the woman. There is a good deal of research being done in the area of infertility, and couples should try to understand the problem and work cooperatively with their physician. It is also very important that the man be clear about the difference between infertility and potency. Infertility simply means that the couple (the problem may be traced to the man, the woman, or both) is unable to conceive a child and has nothing to do with the man's sexual prowess, his identity as a male, or his ability to function as a lover. Fertility problems are stressful enough for a couple without adding to it inappropriate feelings of sexual failure. A man or woman who is physically unable to have a child is still as able as anyone to be a fully functioning sex partner.

When should a couple have children? Naturally, there can't be any hard and fast rule here, but studies indicate that the most satisfactory adjustment tends to occur with those couples who wait at least two years before having their first child. There is good evidence that it takes this long for the married couple to grow and develop into a close, strong unit. Waiting gives the couple time to work out a functional relationship based on intimate knowledge of one another's feelings, habits, and preferences. Thus, when the baby comes, they are better able to work through the demands that it makes on their life-style than they would have been if it had come earlier. A husband and wife who conceive a child either before or slightly after the date of their marriage have the task of learning about and adjusting to a third and extremely demanding person just when they have hardly begun to adjust to each other.

Of course, when we speak of family planning we do so with some qualification. Nothing in life can or even should be made to go 100 percent according to plan, and this applies to the conception of a child as much as to anything else. Accidents do happen, even to people who use contraception regularly and conscientiously. When a wife becomes pregnant accidentally, a decision must be made about what should be done. Should they carry through with the unplanned pregnancy, or should an abortion be performed? Husband and wife should face this choice together. An argument could be made that since the woman carries the child within her own body she should be the one to decide whether to allow it to be born. While it is true that it is the woman who must physically undergo the childbirth or the abortion, and while this may make her feelings about the matter stronger and somewhat more immediate than those of the man, it is still the husband and wife together who will be involved with the child as parents, and this longer view of things must be taken into account.

Coming to a decision jointly can help to make the marriage closer and more meaningful for both partners. It can also serve to lessen the burden of responsibility if the choice is for abortion by sharing it between the partners. Obviously, abortion is a rather extreme form of birth control, involving physical discomfort for the woman and possible negative psychological effects for both partners. Thus, it should not be chosen lightly. When an unplanned pregnancy occurs, the couple will naturally reconsider whether they want a child at this point in their lives, and in fact the majority of couples do decide that—once having conceived, they now want a child. But if it is clear that the addition of another child would have a negative effect on the family, that for whatever reason—financial, physical, or psychological—it would not be a good idea to introduce a child into the situation, an abortion may be the best possible alternative.

"There's always room for one more" may not be a very good guide to follow in such situations because sometimes there simply isn't room. The fact that a couple is married does not necessarily obligate them to carry through with each pregnancy. Approximately three out of every ten abortions are, in fact, performed on married women. A couple choosing abortion might remind themselves that in the future when conditions change they can conceive a child that is planned and wanted. Or, if they decide that they definitely want no more children, they should seriously consider sterilization.

Once the decision to have a child is made and the wife becomes pregnant, several new issues arise. Should the husband be involved in the pregnancy or should he be the sort of ingenuous supernumerary that we see in the sitcoms and soap operas? Well, when was the last time you enjoyed something you weren't involved in? Being a bystander isn't much fun, and this is as good a reason as any why a man might choose to involve himself wholeheartedly in the birth of his child.

Pregnancy cannot be physically shared. It can, however, be shared in other ways. One way is very practical: the couple can make a joint project of learning about prenatal care. They can visit the wife's obstetrician together and/or take a prepared childbirth course. Prepared childbirth (also called Natural Childbirth and the Lamaze Method) consists of a series of exercises in which a woman learns to diminish and control the pain of labor and delivery so that she is able to go through the birth process awake and conscious, without major anesthesia. The exercises used are designed for participation by the husband, who actually remains with the wife during her stay in the labor and delivery rooms. The knowledge he derives from the course allows him to become a functioning member of the delivery team.

Although only one in ten couples now have children by prepared childbirth, it is a method that can add immeasurably to the emotional satisfaction and pleasure of the experience. For the woman it means not only the chance to experience the extraordinary process of childbirth while fully conscious but also having a loving and trusted friend alongside her who has learned to anticipate and respond to the special needs she may have. For the man, it is something that may help him to feel a deep, meaningful attachment to his family, a sense of belonging. This is something I have personally found to be true. Seeing both of my children being born certainly represented peak experiences in my life.

But no matter how deeply involved a man is in his wife's pregnancy, there is always that most basic aspect of the process that can never be shared—namely, carrying and giving birth to the child. This can sometimes lead to problems.

Pregnancy not only affects a woman's body; it involves hormonal and emotional changes as well. While she is pregnant, a woman feels different from any way she has ever felt before. It is, in short, a "trip." And it is also something that may at times be difficult to share fully with a person who never has had and never will have the same experience. As a result, a husband may often feel left out. He may have the apparently childish but very normal feeling that his wife is not paying enough attention to him. This may cause him to withdraw emotionally and sexually from her. These feelings are actually very common and there is probably very little that can be done to prevent them. What can be prevented, however, is the tendency of many men to assume that their wives understand what is bothering them.

A moment's reflection will tell you that just as you find it hard to understand what she is going through, she may find it equally hard to understand your feelings. The answer is to communicate your feelings, fears, and hopes. It is your responsibility to share any doubts or negative feelings you are having with your wife, however silly or unmanly you may think they are. Sharing negative as well as positive feelings is another way of sharing the experience of pregnancy and making it more meaningful for both of you.

Pregnancy may also at times cause the relationship between a husband and wife to become distant by interfering with their sex life. This is entirely unnecessary. Contrary to popular belief, a growing fetus is one of the most effectively protected things in nature, so sexual intercourse can continue with no damage to it. In general, it is all right to have intercourse all through the pregnancy, including the last month, unless the woman experiences uterine bleeding, severe cramps, or pain. Sometimes, a doctor may advise a woman to avoid intercourse if she has a history of miscarriage. But except for those very rare cases where the obstetrician imposes restrictions, couples can have an active sex life during pregnancy. In fact, during the second trimester, increased pelvic vasocongestion in the woman might cause her to be even more responsive.

The type of positions you prefer will probably change, however. As the woman's belly gets larger, the male superior position may become increasingly uncomfortable for both partners. Some excellent substitutes might be the female superior, rear entry, or side-by-side positions. One of the best positions during pregnancy is one in which the woman sits back (pillows supporting her lower back), with her buttocks resting at the edge of the couch, chair, or bed and her feet on the floor. The man then kneels between her legs. The man may find that he must put pillows under his knees in order to bring their genitals to the same height so that he can enter her comfortably. But once entry has been achieved, this is one of the most comfortable possible positions since it not only alleviates pressure on the woman's belly but also allows the partners to touch, caress, and speak easily during intercourse. Some couples find that during pregnancy they prefer a slower, more gentle style of intercourse than previously, and this position lends itself beautifully to such a need. Each couple, though, should experiment in order to find the style they are most comfortable with.

Childbirth is a strenuous process for a woman, causing soreness in the vaginal area. In most cases, an episiotomy (incision to widen the vaginal opening) is performed, and this takes time to heal. Most physicians advise couples to refrain from intercourse for about six weeks after the woman has given birth. Not only might intercourse be painful during this period but there is also a serious risk of infection. This embargo on sexual intercourse may sometimes be responsible for causing a husband and wife to become distant from one another. In fact, the first pregnancy is the most common time for the husband to begin an extramarital affair.

It is probably this period immediately following birth—when intercourse is impossible and the woman is often very tired and is devoting most of her available energy to mothering the baby—that is the most trying of all. Rather than looking for sex outside his marriage, a more constructive course of action for a man to follow in this situation would be to speak to his wife about his need for affection and for a sexual outlet. This is a time for both husband and wife to lean on and derive support from their relationship, not allow it to begin fading away. The husband who cares about preserving the quality of his marriage should consider altering his sex life during this period in a way that will not endanger the marital relationship. He could use masturbation to achieve the sexual release he desires, and he could also ask his wife to manually stimulate or fellate him. Under the circumstances, a man might imagine that his wife has enough to concern her and does not want to be bothered by his sexual needs, but in most cases this is not true. By expressing his desire to participate in some sort of sexual relationship with his wife, a man can reassure her that she is important to him and that he continues to find her attractive.

Wendy and Phil, a couple who had been seeing me for a sexual problem, found this out when Wendy became pregnant. Phil, an enlisted man in the army, was a rather nonverbal, unassertive fellow who found it difficult to request specific kinds of sexual stimulation from Wendy. After their child was born and they had to temporarily stop having intercourse, Phil found it hard to ask Wendy to manually stimulate him to orgasm. Finally he did, but apparently his lack of self-assurance made him unpersuasive. "What's the difference between me doing it and you doing it?" was Wendy's reaction. Phil had to explain to her that it wasn't the same, that when she stimulated him he could look at her, touch her, feel close to her, and that this was very important to him. Phil's statement was significant for Wendy in helping her to feel that she was still attractive to him. There was also an increase in affectionate hugging, kissing, and caressing between them. As a result, their weathering of the difficult first few weeks of the baby's arrival was made easier.

Once he has gotten through the joys and difficulties of pregnancy and childbirth, there is no reason why a man can't continue to participate fully by learning to care for the child along with his wife. Why stop at being an occasional helper when you can be a fully involved partner in the business of baby care? Such an attitude is, of course, contrary to the traditional image of the American father. But in this case, as in so many others, it is the traditional images that are cheating us out of a great deal of the pleasure and emotional satisfactions that are available in life. It is perfectly natural for a man to feel warmth and affection toward a baby, particularly when it is his own. Let's face it, like most young things, babies are adorable. They are incredibly soft, they smell good (except when they need changing), and they do amusing and endearing things. W.C. Fields aside, it is a *human* response, not just a female one, to want to hold, cuddle, and play with a child. There is no logical reason why we should deny ourselves this pleasure just because of the traditional notion that a "real man" does not show feelings of love, warmth, and caring.

Learning to care for a child may involve a certain amount of time and effort, but the rewards gained by getting close to the child and feeling good about yourself as a father more than make up for the work involved. The best way to get involved is to make it clear to your wife that you want to participate and share the work of child care with her. She can help you learn what you need to know about diapering, feeding, bathing, and so forth. If neither of you knows very much about taking care of a baby, you could read up on the subject or take a course in child care together. The active involvement of the husband and wife in raising and interacting with the child is one of the best ways of creating a truly intimate family life. A further benefit is that when the husband shoulders his share of the burden of child care, the wife has more energy and attention left over to devote to him.

Surveys have shown that the birth of a child is one of the most difficult periods in marriage. The work involved, along with the extra financial and emotional demands, place a considerable strain on the marital relationship. In many cases a coolness, a sense of alienation creeps into the marriage. Men frequently begin extramarital affairs at this time, and in some cases the rifts that occur in the marital relationship eventually widen into divorce.

But none of this is necessary. The coming of a child is only a disaster when the couple is not ready for it. The best way they can prepare for its arrival is to go through all the necessary steps together—from decisions about family planning to taking turns at diapering and administering 2:00 A.M. feedings. Caring for a child is simply too much for one person to handle. In the past a woman might have received extensive help from her own mother and other female relatives. But since large, extended families rarely live under one roof anymore, such an arrangement is usually no longer possible. This change in family structure can be our gain. As men we now have a chance to participate and share in the wonder, excitement, and emotional thrill of birth. Guiding and sharing in the growth and development of another human being can be one of the most significant and emotionally rewarding tasks in your entire life. It's not the sort of opportunity that you get every day.

16
Sex, Your Children, and You

OBSTETRICIANS OFTEN REMARK on the fact that a newborn male baby will in most cases get his first erection before the doctor even has time to tie off the umbilical cord. For we humans have all the equipment necessary to experience sexual arousal from the day we are born, and probably before that. And it doesn't take very long for us to discover this for ourselves, either. Most children, both male and female, very quickly find that they can produce pleasurable sensations by touching their genitals.

During the child's early development, however, sexual sensations are not very clearly distinguished from other pleasurable feelings. Children often become sexually aroused by experiences that are not specifically sexual (and so do adults—probably more often than we admit). Nevertheless, an individual's sexual identity, feelings about his body, feelings about his genitals—components of his personality destined to play such a powerful and important role in later life—are in the process of formation during these early years. Children are not asexual, although this is still a common assumption with many people. Rather, they are learning to be sexual, and sexuality itself—the raw material—is there from the start.

A child learns to relate to his or her sexuality chiefly through example. The earliest and most formative examples are the parents themselves. Many of our sexual patterns, our sexual hang-ups, how we feel about our bodies, in fact, a good deal of our identity is connected with learning experiences, imprintings that occurred in childhood largely in parent-child interactions. This puts a great deal of responsibility on a parent. Most parents want the best for their children, and this should include a desire for them to have a healthy and rewarding sexual adjustment. But we cannot help them gain this adjustment unless we ourselves develop a positive attitude toward our own sexuality.

Many of us may feel that our sex education and early sex experiences were poor and generally negative. However, the father needs to be aware of these uncomfortable areas and be able to use his understanding to help his child deal with his own problems and difficulties. Thus, the effort that we put into exploring and developing our own sexual potential and improving the sexual relations between ourselves and our partners pays off in two ways. First, we reap the benefits ourselves in terms of pleasure and emotional satisfaction. Second, we become good role models for our children, able to set them on the road toward the attainment of fully aware and self-knowing adult sexuality.

Unfortunately, however, few of us have had sex educations that come up to these standards. It is fairly safe to say that the majority of today's adults grew up in homes where nudity was prohibited, masturbation brought severe reprimands, and discussion about sex was confined to a brief, uncomfortable five- or ten-minute talk between father and son or mother and daughter, probably in early adolescence. Often no real information was conveyed in this talk at all, just a vague admonition to "stay out of trouble." Whatever information the child received came from his peers, from sex magazines, pornographic movies and books, or from what he was able to puzzle out for himself.

As men, we probably have an added difficulty in achieving a healthy sexual identity—one that stems from the lack of warmth and communication between most boys and their fathers. Research indicates that both boys and girls report being much closer to their mothers than to their fathers. Women also report feeling closer to their children as well as enjoying them more than men do. Generally, boys and their fathers interact only within certain strictly defined contexts such as sports or camping trips. One of the greatest needs of a young boy is to have a sense of what it is like to be a man. It is difficult for him to develop this sense unless he can talk with his father about his feelings, discuss questions and doubts concerning his future, and ask frank questions about things like his own sexual development, the meaning of erections, VD, and attitudes toward women.

In fact, a clear identity as a male child will probably facilitate the boy's experimenting with traditionally "nonmasculine" activities such as playing house, enjoying taking care of babies, and experimenting with cooking. If the father feels comfortable engaging in child care activities as well as cooking and cleaning the house, this can provide an excellent and realistic model for the boy. And if the boy has a strong identity as a male, that will allow him individual choice and flexibility regarding his activities and interests. Thus, a secure and solid acceptance of his maleness is the foundation upon which a boy can understand and adapt to his growing awareness of sexuality.

Girls too need a close relationship with their father in order to grow into a full and healthy sense of their sexuality. One of the saddest things in our culture is the separation between father and daughter that begins to widen as the daughter enters adolescence, when she needs as much as ever to feel love, support, affection, and recognition of herself as a person from both her father and her mother. However, the father often avoids his daughter at this stage because he feels uncomfortable dealing with her as a developing young woman.

Thus, as males and as parents we have the responsibility of guiding and shaping the awakening sexuality of our children, but it takes a special effort on our part to meet that responsibility since we must first overcome the effects of our own inadequate sexual educations. Moreover, it is especially hard today because we live in a time of rapidly changing sexual mores. The puritanical equation of sex with sin and the age-old "double standard" are disappearing. This in itself is a very good thing, but it leaves parents in an uncomfortable and ambiguous position and makes it hard for them to provide sex guidelines that will be realistic and helpful to their children.

Parents often have the feeling that they may be too liberal in one situation and too restrictive in another. Since much of a parent's job is to set the limits of acceptable and unacceptable behavior for children, being able to tell what things have a positive or negative effect on a child's development is an especially urgent need. In this chapter, I will attempt to set forth some guidelines for making these decisions, with particular reference to the male parent. Of course, it must be remembered that sexual attitudes and values differ from family to family. It is possible, certainly, to be overly lax in setting guidelines about sex, just as it is possible to be overly restrictive. But between these two extremes there is a range of healthy and constructive parental attitudes. There are many different ways to raise a child to be comfortable with his or her sexuality. Nevertheless, certain basic guidelines seem to be applicable to most families.

Generally, men feel more inhibition about openly showing affection with their children than do women. Most fathers allow themselves to express affection with young infants, but beyond the kitchy-kitchy-koo stage, a father's hugs, kisses, and words of love become few and far between. It seems, in fact, that the typical father's ability to display affection diminishes in direct proportion to his children's growing consciousness of him as a person, almost as though he were afraid to be caught in the act. It is true, of course, that as a child grows older, it wants and needs less cuddling and holding. But a child never outgrows the need to feel that his parents love and care for him. And if a parent ceases to express his love either physically or verbally, the child will have no real way of knowing that the love exists.

Many children are aware that their fathers love them only because their mothers occasionally tell them so ("You know your father loves you very much"), usually to counteract evidence to the contrary such as a spanking or a gruff word. This coldness on the father's part is often justified as being an aspect of the traditional male role: it is the woman's place to be affectionate with the children, not the man's. But in effect, this lack of affection between a man and his children robs both of them of much of the enjoyment that is possible in the parent-child relationship. Moreover, it forces the child to live with the insecurity of never knowing for sure whether his father loves him, as well as creating a degree of coldness and distance between them.

But let's be fair to fathers. Most of them are not unaffectionate with their children because they are cold, unloving people. In most cases, mother is right when she assures the child of his father's love. Father does care. But he may be unable to show that he cares because of some irrational fears he has about himself and his body. Let's look into the nature of these fears.

As we have seen in previous chapters, there is a common tendency among men to think of physical affection only in terms of sexual intercourse. Showing love through touching, kissing, caressing, in ways that are not intended to lead to sexual arousal and intercourse, is a form of expression that most men are relatively uncomfortable with. One of the most encouraging developments among young people today is the acceptance by many young men of physical contact and even hugging of other males as a sign of friendly affection. But for the average man, unfortunately, physical contact with another human body is associated with only two contexts: sex and aggressive contact activities such as sports or fighting. The second of these contexts can be extended to include parent-child interactions, and perhaps this explains why the physical contact most fathers have with their children is in the form of roughhousing. Sexual intercourse, however, has no place in a parent-child relationship. In fact, there are very strong cultural taboos (not to mention legal ones) against sex between a parent and child. But if every time a man expresses physical affection he associates it with sex, then he will naturally have problems being affectionate with his children.

Many men do suffer from this problem. They fear the possibility of becoming sexually aroused through physical contact with their children and so end up avoiding contact altogether. This association in the mind of the average man between affection and sex manifests itself in different ways and in different situations, growing more and more inhibitory as the child matures. Most fathers stop acting affectionate with their sons after they reach a certain age for fear that such behavior might be construed as being homosexual, or that it might influence their sons to become homosexual. Similarly, they stop showing affection with their daughters for fear of appearing to be lecherous, "dirty old men."

One of the typical father's greatest fears is getting an erection while playing with or being affectionate with his child. He may believe that this would indicate something perverse or unnatural about him. But although an erection is usually a sign of sexual arousal, it does not have to be. And it is certainly not an indication in such a situation that he wants to have intercourse with his child. It can simply be a sign that he is experiencing physical pleasure which is not specifically sexual. Even if the man's worst fears come true and the child notices the erection and comments on it, it can be explained simply in just this way. There is no need to be embarrassed with the child or to feel that this is somehow shameful. In fact, responding in a natural, relaxed manner could be a way of conveying the lesson that the genitals are just a normal part of the human body, and nothing to be ashamed of.

Many men also feel self-conscious about being affectionate with their wives while the children are around. Again, the stereotyped, masculine, intercourse-directed view of physical affection is chiefly to blame. If a kiss or a hug is thought of as being a prelude to intercourse, then naturally a man will feel strange about letting his children see him and his wife behaving affectionately with one another. If, however, he thinks of physical affection as simply a normal way of showing love and caring which need not lead to greater sexual involvement, then he will be less likely to suffer from such inhibitions. Thus, learning to be comfortable about giving and receiving affectionate contact outside of the bedroom can be very important, not only for ourselves but for our children. Children need to see their parents being affectionate with each other as much as they need affection themselves. If affectionate behavior is a common occurrence between parents, the child learns that it is a normal part of life. These lessons will carry over into his own sexual relationships when he becomes an adult.

There should be limitations, however, to the kind of affection a couple display before their children. Certain writers have actually taken the extreme view that none of a couple's interactions ought to be kept private from their children, including intercourse. But it appears that such a total lack of restriction on sexual expression does a child more harm than good. Children need to learn that the sexual relationship between adults is an intimate and private thing. Teaching them that it is permissible to engage in erotic behavior when others are present is very poor preparation for the majority of situations they will encounter in later life. Moreover, specifically sexual behavior between parents makes most children uncomfortable. Many children whose parents pride themselves on being sexually liberated will tell you what a burden it is to have such a life-style imposed on them. With sex, just as with material luxuries, it is possible to go overboard in trying to give your kids the things you never had.

Instead of sharing their most intimate moments with their children, a couple would be much better off establishing rules of privacy that work both ways. In return for allowing their children a reasonable degree of privacy, parents can specify certain circumstances under which *they* are not to be disturbed.

One couple we know has three children—ages six, nine, and eleven—and has worked out a very satisfactory arrangement. After dinner, Harold and Susan often spend a few minutes over coffee having a quiet talk. During this time the children know that they are not to be disturbed, so they spend their time playing or doing homework, and if the telephone rings, they answer it and take messages.

A second aspect of the arrangement concerns the time that

Harold and Susan spend in their bedroom. When the door is open, the children know that they may come in freely. When it is closed and locked, however, they know that their parents are not to be disturbed except for emergencies. The children, naturally, have expressed curiosity about what goes on behind the locked bedroom door, and Harold and Susan have dealt with this curiosity quite straightforwardly. They have told the children that while they love and enjoy being with them, they also need time alone together. So they have explained that when the bedroom door is locked, they may be just lying around or making love or simply sharing a moment alone away from the hustle and bustle. The children seem to understand and accept this. As Harold and Susan have found, if a husband and wife are going to be effective parents, they need occasional time away from their children. It is good for children to be aware that their parents are husband and wife as well as being individuals with their own interests and needs.

Another important part of raising a sexually healthy child is for the parents to let the child explore and get to know and accept his or her own body. Parents should feel comfortable about allowing the young child to touch his genitals rather than slapping the child's hands and telling him that what he is doing is bad or unclean. As the child grows older, perhaps by age three or four, the parents may teach him that while these self-stimulation and self-exploration activities are healthy and acceptable, they should be indulged in private rather than in public. This should be done, however, in a way that lets the child know that his body is good and that it is okay to touch it, but that there is an appropriate time and place to do so.

Many of us were raised with the notion that if a child was allowed to touch his genitals "excessively," especially his penis, there would be terrible consequences. Since no one could adequately define "excessive," the tendency was to punish the child whenever he was seen touching himself at all. This treatment had extremely negative effects, since if the child is punished or not allowed to explore his own body, he can easily get the message that there is something bad or dirty about his genitals or his body as a whole, and in later life he might have a very hard time enjoying bodily and sexual feelings.

Not only is it normal for a child to touch and explore his body but it is also natural for children to engage in sex play among themselves. "Playing doctor" or "playing house" is a common and healthy activity for young children—an expression of normal curiosity and

part of their learning to relate to other people. This body exploration will probably take place between children of the same sex as well
as between children of the opposite sex and also among siblings, but
it is not a sign of developing promiscuity, incest, or latent homosexuality. Rather, it is a way of learning about other people, both male
and female. In terms of the parental role, the proper perspective
should be to think of the learning that is taking place and how it will
affect later adult sexuality. Thus, when the parent overreacts and
punishes the child for sexual exploration, the child is left with the
message that sexual or exploratory interaction with other people is
bad or disgusting. A better approach would be to accept the activity
and to interfere only when it appears to be forced or coercive or
when it becomes the dominant form of play over a period of time.
Even then, the parent should not stop sexual play by telling the
children that it is bad, but rather by suggesting another form of
activity. What this does is to give the child the message that sexual
play is an acceptable form among children and that it should not be a
source of anxiety to either the child or the parent.

Although it is traditional for information about sex to be conveyed
through talks between father and son or mother and daughter,
there is no reason why this same-sex rule should be rigidly adhered
to. While the same-sex parent or the parent who feels most comfortable with sexuality can and should sometimes speak individually
with the child, it makes a great deal of sense to have some discussions
of sex as a family. This adds to the feeling that sex is a normal and
good part of family life rather than something to be whispered about
in private. Sex education can begin early in the child's life and can
grow out of his own exploration of his body. Parents can aid the child
in his self-discovery by teaching him the proper names for his
genitals. The child should learn to be comfortable with words like
"penis" and "vulva," rather than euphemisms like "whatsit" or
"down there" or "my thing." As to the question of how much information about sex the child should be given, the best policy is to let the
child's own curiosity guide you. This allows the child to pace himself
in terms of what he wants to know or is ready to know, and if you
respond in a positive and open manner, the child gets the message
that sex is something that is okay to think and talk about, and that he
can feel free to ask again. Parents should not feel that because their
five-year-old asks where babies come from, they have to tell him
everything about sex, from VD to homosexuality. Rather, they

should try to give the child the information he is seeking in words that will make sense to him.

Perhaps the best form of sex education for children is a combination of formal teaching provided by school and religious groups combined with an informal approach coming from the parents. The parent might want to use one of the excellent books on sexuality that have been written for children. But instead of handing the book to the child, telling him to read it, and then asking if he has any questions, you might try another approach which allows the two of you to interact on a more personal level. First read the book on your own, then point out to your child some parts you found particularly interesting, or share with him a misconception that you had as a child. Rather than just a question-and-answer period, the interaction should be more of a sharing experience in which you impart not only information but feelings, attitudes, values, and experiences as well. If this pattern is established early, it makes later discussions about sex more comfortable as well as more frank and honest.

Discussions about sex should not be confined to parents and children of matching sexes; having three-way conversations with both the mother and the father included are equally important. Also family meetings including female children can further increase the range of the discussion. This can be a particularly valuable learning experience which will have a beneficial effect on later adult sexual communication.

Being the parent of an adolescent is quite a different thing from being the parent of a young child. Adolescence is a highly stressful period when an individual makes the transition from child to adult. The physical and psychological changes that occur are both rapid and profound; within the space of a very few years, the child must adjust to facing a whole different set of needs and expectations. Many societies, recognizing that this transition is both difficult and highly significant, mark the change with some sort of initiation ceremony or rite of passage. In our society, however, there is no single event that signals the transition from child to adult, and this lack of clarity about the status of the adolescent probably adds to the stress he experiences. As a parent, a man has a very definite role to play in attempting to ease the turmoil encountered by his adolescent son or daughter.

First, he must remember that an adolescent is in the process of becoming a self-directing and autonomous individual who is capable of making his own decisions and enjoys a degree of freedom nearly equal to that of an adult. A parent cannot hope to exert the same control over the actions of an adolescent as he did when the child was younger. He can establish certain rules, set guidelines for behavior, but he cannot expect to always be aware of the child's precise whereabouts or to supervise the child's activities as he may have done in earlier years.

An adolescent must be trusted to make the right decisions on his own. One of the most important lessons that he must learn is that actions have consequences and that he and only he can be held accountable for the things he does. Thus, a parent should neither play the role of the tyrant, expecting to maintain an iron control over his child's activities, nor should he feel overly responsible or guilty when his child makes mistakes. In either case, the parent would be performing a disservice to the child by impeding his own natural process of maturation.

At the same time, a parent must be aware that an adolescent is very much in need of support. An adolescent's first tentative entry into the world of adult freedom and responsibility may be exciting, but it is also quite confusing and frightening. The adolescent needs to be aware of the parents' values and views about such things as petting, dating relationships, contraception, premarital intercourse, and VD. And the parent should be aware that sexual behavior that is clearly inappropriate for a thirteen-year-old might be more acceptable for a seventeen-year-old. The parents also must make a distinction for themselves (as well as the adolescent) about the kind of behavior they will tolerate, even if they do not support it, and the behavior they will not tolerate. For example, some parents will accept their seventeen-year-old adolescent having intercourse, but will not accept having this intercourse take place in their home.

Once these guidelines have been established, the adolescent needs assurance that both his parents—mother *and* father—will support and accept him. According to the traditional pattern, it is usually the mother whom the child can count on to be lenient and accepting and to comfort him when he gets into trouble, while the father plays the role of the stern disciplinarian. But there is no reason why a man should be any less supportive as a parent than a woman. An adolescent child needs support from *both* parents, and there is no justification for a man to deprive his child of half of that support merely for the sake of fulfilling a socially dictated stereotype.

It seems odd that children, the living evidence of their parents' sexuality, should so often be raised in such a way that the knowledge of sexuality is kept from them for as long a time as possible. Sexuality is not something that is conferred on a person at maturity like a driver's license or the right to vote. It is with us from the time we are born, and, like any of our other natural faculties, needs to be molded and developed through learning experiences. For a parent to deny this sexual learning process is to deny an aspect of his child as a person.

17
Increasing Arousal and Potency

CONSISTENT FAILURE TO ACHIEVE or maintain an erection can be one of the most psychologically destructive and painful experiences a man can undergo. The name itself indicates how devastating the condition is felt to be: impotence, without potency, without strength. A man might be able to operate a jackhammer or supervise an office staff who jump at his every word, but if his penis does not become stiff when he wants it to, he may be considered a weakling, a sexual cripple. Worse yet, he may consider himself in this way. He may begin putting himself down, ignoring his own positive attributes and accomplishments, totally convinced that anyone suffering from erectile failure cannot be a real man or a successful person.

There is no reason why impotence should strike such terror in the male heart. Not that there is any easy or miracle cure for recurring potency problems—there isn't—although the great majority of men can learn to regain their erectile functioning. The point is that impotence is just not the sexual death sentence it is often thought to be. In fact, it is an extremely common condition. By age forty, 90 percent of men will have been impotent on at least one occasion. For the majority of men, it is a temporary state, a rare and atypical occurrence. For others, it may last longer, a few weeks or months, but eventually normal sexual functioning is restored. A few men may suffer with intermittent or severe impotence throughout their lifetime. In the great majority of these cases, however, impotence is primarily a psychological problem. There is nothing wrong with the sexual organs themselves; the trouble revolves around psychological feelings and attitudes. The reason the condition may sometimes be so severe is that, like any psychological problem, it can become self-perpetuating. Impotence can feed and grow on the performance anxiety that the condition itself produces.

But the anxiety responsible for perpetuating potency problems, however irrational, is nevertheless extremely real. It does little good to tell the man suffering from impotence that the problem is all in his mind. What he needs is help in feeling comfortable with himself sexually again. The first thing he needs to do is to review the information available on the subject. So let us begin by considering some of the realities of male sexual arousal and potency.

When we speak of potency problems, we mean either the inability to obtain an erection or the inability to keep an erection enabling the male to engage in intercourse. These problems are categorized as either primary impotence or secondary impotence—the latter by far the more common. A secondarily impotent male is one who has had at least one successful intercourse experience. Most men suffering from impotence have had successful intercourse a great many times, but they then begin having intermittent episodes in which they either cannot obtain an erection or more commonly achieve an erection and then lose it, most typically just prior to intromission. The primarily impotent male has never had a successful intercourse experience—a rarer condition but much more frequent than is commonly believed. He usually does masturbate to orgasm, however, and is often able to achieve orgasm through manual or oral stimulation. The man suffering from primary impotence tends to feel humiliated and embarrassed about his sexual problem and to see it as evidence of his inadequacy as a person. He does not realize that there is more to him and to his sexuality than just the state of his penis.

Arousal and erection are not the automatic result of any erotic stimulus. Rather, a man becomes aroused when he is feeling comfortable with himself and his partner and is enjoying the sensuousness and pleasure of their interaction. Feelings of sensuousness and comfort lead to sexual excitement and erection, and then to a desire for intercourse and orgasm. An erection is thus an involuntary occurrence. A man cannot force himself to get one. In fact, the more he wills himself to get an erection and focuses his attention on the state of his penis, the less likely his success. Erection is the end result of a chain of psychological and physiological pleasure events. If there are links in the chain that are missing, erection will probably not occur.

Often, when an erection fails to happen, the problem lies at the very beginning of the sexual response cycle. The man might be tired, depressed, frustrated, preoccupied, or just not very interested in sex at the moment. Since, by trying to have intercourse anyway—to oblige his partner or because he thinks it is expected of him—he is going against his own real needs and desires, it follows that he will not feel very comfortable in the situation. Nor will he be very receptive to sensuous and erotic stimuli. If he is unable to have or maintain an erection under these circumstances, his failure is altogether natural and understandable.

A slightly different situation often occurs when a man has had too much to drink—one of the most common causes of temporary impotence. Although an inebriated man may feel amorous and uninhibited, his physiological sexual functioning is impaired. Some men who experience impotence after drinking heavily may become very anxious about their ability to perform. This anxiety may lead to their being impotent on later occasions, even when they have not consumed any alcohol.

This is exactly what happened to a client of mine named Benjamin, a successful forty-two-year-old salesman for a boatbuilding concern. Benjamin had always been a fairly heavy drinker, but during one period in his life when there was an increase of pressure on the job, combined with trouble with his teen-age son, he began to consume more liquor than he was able to handle. On one occasion, Benjamin became quite drunk at a party and, when he and his wife arrived home, he tried to make love to her. He was unable to get an erection, and even though his wife understood it was because of the alcohol he had consumed, the episode began to worry and depress him. Later, when he attempted to have intercourse with her while cold sober, he initially achieved an erection but was unable to maintain it. This pattern continued. A few times he was able to maintain an erection and function successfully, but most of the time he could not. Eventually, he stopped attempting sex with his wife altogether.

Obviously, Benjamin's initial potency problem resulted from a combination of alcohol and personal and business pressures, but at the time he was unable to see it from this perspective. Meanwhile, the drinking got so bad that he was forced to admit that he was becoming an alcoholic. Finally, with the aid of Alcoholics Anonymous, he managed to give up drinking completely, but his potency problem remained.

It was at this point that Benjamin and his wife came to see me. At first he was quite negative and appeared to have all but given up hope of ever functioning normally again. Eventually, however, he began to see that impotence can be a self-fulfilling prophecy and that it is a condition which feeds on the anxiety of the sufferer. He and his wife began doing nongenital and genital pleasuring for the purpose of increasing arousal. Benjamin responded well to this treatment, and, in a matter of weeks, was functioning normally again.

The majority of men respond to an impotence experience just as Benjamin did. Generally, they ignore the importance of the initial, less obvious links in the chain of sexual arousal—namely, the feelings of comfort and receptivity that start things off. They make the erroneous assumption that erection should follow automatically whenever the opportunity for sex presents itself. It is an aspect of the myth of the male machine that a "real man" can have sex anytime, anyplace, and with any woman. The most sensible response a man can have to erectile failure is to interpret it as a sign that he does not really want to have sex at the moment—just as he would interpret the lack of an appetite as a sign that he should not order a full meal. He might simply tell his partner, "I guess I'm just not in the mood right now." Or he could request that she give him a body massage or stroke his inner thighs—something to relax him and make him more responsive. He might also offer to "do her" manually or orally.

But typically, men who experience impotence do not react in this way. Instead, their most common reaction is one of panic and desperation. Rather than trying to relax and spending more time with pleasuring activities or requesting his partner to use the kind of stimulation which is most sexually arousing for him, a man is more likely to avoid sharing his concerns with his partner or involving her. He may try to force himself into arousal, displaying a level of passion he does not feel. Often, if nothing seems to work, he will make futile attempts to achieve intromission with a nonerect penis. The sexual interaction usually ends on a note of frustration for both partners, with misunderstanding and resentment present on each side. The man will probably feel that he is a failure so that next time he will be putting even more pressure on himself to "redeem his manhood" with a good sexual performance. As a result, he may be even more inhibited by performance anxiety, and in this way a vicious circle may begin. What started as a normal occurrence is on its way to becoming a major tragedy.

In addition to the havoc it wreaks on the male ego, impotence can also be extremely detrimental to a relationship. Erectile problems can usually be traced to misunderstanding and lack of communication. When a man experiences impotence, it may be extremely difficult for him to explain to his partner what is happening to him. Indeed, he may not understand it very well himself. If he believes that it is a sign of masculinity to be able to perform flawlessly in every sexual encounter, then he will probably be filled with an overwhelming desire to cover up his failure or to find an excuse for it. Faced with this urgent need to find a scapegoat, he may try to pin the blame on his partner, letting her believe that his failure stems from the fact that he finds her unattractive or that she turns him off in some way. His partner may then retaliate by ridiculing him for his failure to perform, and in a very short time the relationship may become tense and hostile.

Another equally unproductive response to impotence is for a man to make a play for his partner's sympathy. Often the excuse he makes to explain his failure is basically accurate—overwork, tiredness, pressure on the job—only the attitude is wrong. If the woman responds as he wants her to, by showing pity and acting maternal, the situation becomes worse. For what the man has done is to substitute his partner's sympathy and concern for the sexual gratification he cannot obtain. Her pity, in effect, becomes a crutch, which makes it all the harder for him to function normally in the future. What he needs is not pity or sympathy or condescension, but rather a partner who is willing to see the potency problem as a couple problem and who will work with him at regaining the ability to respond to sexual stimulation.

While we are on the subject of the woman's role in male impotence, let us consider a thesis that has gained attention in recent years—namely, that male impotence is increasing as a result of the intimidating effect of the women's liberation movement. The idea is that as women become more sexually assertive and demanding, more unwilling to serve as passive "vessels of pleasure" for male gratification, the pressure on men to perform sexually becomes so great that they feel overwhelmed, and the result is erectile failure. First of all, it is important to point out that no conclusive study has been done which shows any great increase in impotence, although there does seem to be a moderate increase in secondary impotence. It may also be that impotence in men is becoming more visible because of a more tolerant, open attitude toward sexual matters in general. Thus, as in the case of homosexuality, it may appear that impotence is much more common now when actually it is simply more out in the open. But this still does not settle the question of whether the assertive attitudes and sexual awareness espoused by the women's movement have a negative effect on male potency. Ultimately, there may be no way of giving either a yes or no response to this question since the answer seems to depend so much on the reaction of the individual male and the interaction of the couple.

Certainly, it is a good thing for women to be sexually assertive, to expect pleasure from sex as males do. Studies have shown conclusively that the female capacity for sexual pleasure is at least as great as the male's, and there is no possible justification for denying women the opportunity to fulfill this capacity. Some men, of course, especially those who identify strongly with traditional ideas of male dominance, might be very threatened by the new female demands for equality in sex.

Part of the problem is that many men have not learned to expect that on some occasions the woman may be more sexually responsive and orgasmic than they are. The double standard has led them to believe that it is always the man who is the aggressor in sex and the one who enjoys it more, while women are supposed to be coy and restrained. When a woman is assertive, highly responsive, and multiorgasmic, these traditionalist men may feel very threatened and may react by becoming impotent. Other men who are more flexible may see the new sexual assertiveness among women as a positive development since it means that women will now feel motivated to become more responsive, more imaginative, more involved sex partners. These men will find that a woman's greater arousal acts as a turn-on for them. This attitude is certainly the more logical and productive one, and if more men adopted it, there would be little cause for concern with the negative effects of women's lib on male potency.

The most urgent question of any man who has a potency problem is what to do about it. Perhaps the first step might be to consult a urologist. Although impotence is psychological in origin in the vast majority of cases, it does sometimes have medical causes, and it might be a good idea to check these out initially. Some of the things a physician will check are external genitalia, testosterone level, alcohol intake, and general health problems. He will also check for diabetes, a condition that can contribute to sexual problems. However, contrary to an idea that is widespread even among people in the medical profession, men who are diabetic do not necessarily develop sexual problems. I myself am diabetic, and I find that if I maintain my diet and exercise program, the condition has no effect on my sexual functioning.

Chances are that the urologist will give you a clean bill of health, and this will give you a good start in tackling the problem since you will then be certain that the obstacles you face are psychological ones. However, even in those rare cases where the cause of impotence turns out to be organic rather than psychological, it is still possible to have orgasms and enjoy other aspects of sex without having an erection. There have also been breakthroughs recently that make it possible for such men to return to normal functioning. Prosthetic devices implanted in the penis are able to simulate a normal erection and thus allow a man with physiological impotence to enjoy intercourse.

Impotence is best thought of as a couple problem. Although it is the man who actually has the erectile problem, both the man and the woman are affected by it. Because of the man's impotence, the *couple's* sexual functioning becomes less satisfactory. Since successful sexual functioning is in the best interests of both the man and the woman, finding a solution to the problem is obviously a task for the couple. Besides, to think of it as the man's problem exclusively puts too much emphasis on the performance aspect of male sexuality. Such an attitude increases the psychological pressure experienced by the man and decreases his chances of breaking out of the vicious circle of anxiety-perpetuated failure he has fallen into.

Probably the best course of action to follow in trying to deal with a potency problem is for the man and his partner to seek professional help. A professional sex counselor can provide the objectivity and experience which are so important in helping a couple overcome sexual dysfunction. It is understandable, however, that many couples would be reluctant to go running to a sex therapist or psychotherapist at the first sign of a sexual problem, but rather would prefer to try to overcome it on their own. For such people, the following guidelines and exercises may be useful. If the potency problem is long-standing and persistent, however, professional assistance may be in order.

During normal sexual arousal in the male, physical and psychological stimulation results in the spongy erectile tissues of the penis filling with blood (vasocongestion), producing a firm erection. Either inadequate physical stimulation or, more often, interfering thoughts and feelings can block this naturally occurring process. The key to overcoming the dysfunction is to increase sexual stimulation and to replace any interfering feelings and thoughts with an acceptance and enjoyment of the experience. The way to do this is definitely not by trying harder. Potency is one area where you don't get "A" for effort. Trying to make yourself get an erection is, in fact, one of the most effective ways of breaking the chain of events that make up the normal sexual response.

When a man tries to make his penis erect by force of will, the result is a strained and anxious focusing of attention on the penis itself. Because it is not humanly possible to concentrate on two things at the same time, the attention he devotes to feelings of pleasure from the sexual interaction itself naturally diminishes. He becomes detached from the situation, an emotional spectator intent only upon detecting signs of arousal, yet nearly oblivious to the erotic stimuli which cause it. Obviously, such a response cannot be a very effective remedy for erective failure.

The best way a couple can deal with a potency problem is through a variation of the exercises for increasing sensual awareness presented in Chapter 9. The chief cause of impotence is performance anxiety and insecurity, so you might begin by having a quiet, intimate talk over a drink or coffee, followed by a relaxing, sensuous shower. Lather each other all over, including the genitals, then dry each other off. Go into the bedroom and get into a comfortable position for pleasuring with the woman as pleasurer and the man as pleasuree. The woman then begins to stimulate the man, starting on the chest or thighs and gradually working toward the genitals. The man should concentrate on accepting the feelings of pleasure he is experiencing rather than worrying about whether he is getting an erection. If the man is truly relaxed and the woman continues to pleasure him in a sensuous, nondemand way, a firm erection should eventually occur. At this point, pleasuring should cease and the couple should lie comfortably together until the erection subsides.

Be aware of your feelings at this moment. How does each of you feel as the penis returns to its flaccid state—anxious, worried, tense, angry, relieved? Gaining confidence that an erection will return after it has subsided is especially important. One of the chief psychological traps for a man with a potency problem is that as soon as he obtains an erection, he immediately feels that he has to use it. This is especially true of morning erections. When the erection dissipates before intercourse, as it usually does, the man becomes frustrated and depressed—two emotions that block sexual arousal. After the penis has become limp, begin pleasuring again until a second erection occurs. Again the man should focus on accepting and enjoying the feelings of sensuous pleasure rather than on getting an erection. Try to become totally receptive to stimulation. Let yourself respond to each touch. Let your body drink in each sensuous feeling. When an erection occurs, again lie quietly together until it subsides.

Now reverse positions, letting the man take the role of pleasurer and the woman that of pleasuree. The man should not think about getting an erection, but should concentrate on imparting feelings of pleasure to his partner. An erection may occur naturally. If it does, discontinue pleasuring and lie together until it subsides.

Continue doing this exercise until both of you have become comfortable about the man gaining and losing an erection. The point of the exercise is partially to help the man focus on erotic stimulation without being anxious about whether or not he is responding. But it is also to accustom both partners to his losing the erection when stimulation ceases. It is entirely normal for a man's penis to become alternately hard and soft during any extended pleasuring session. In fact, during a typical forty-five-minute pleasuring session before intercourse, the male's erection will wax and wane an average of three times. Interestingly, subsequent erections are usually firmer and the ensuing orgasm more pleasurable after this tantalizing buildup. There should be no cause for anxiety or alarm for either partner if the man's erection partially or entirely disappears. In fact, becoming anxious or concerned, or working harder to bring it back, will probably have a negative effect.

For the second exercise, the couple should assume the female-superior intercourse position. They will not actually be proceeding to intercourse during this exercise. Rather, the exercise will accustom both partners to having the penis close to and in contact with the vagina. After the man and woman have made themselves entirely comfortable, perhaps with pillows under the woman's thighs and one under the man's head, the woman should begin caressing and stimulating her partner. The man should feel free to request specific types of stimulation and should concentrate on accepting and enjoying the pleasurable sensations he is experiencing. If at any time the man starts becoming anxious or worried about the state of his penis, he should immediately tell his partner. Then, together, they can work on getting him reinvolved in the sexual interaction. He could do this by pleasuring her or through their mutual engagement in nongenital stimulation, or by a clear and direct request for a specific kind of sexual stimulation such as "rub the underside of my penis with just your fingertips."

When the man gets an erection, instead of letting it subside, the woman should take the penis in her hand and rub it around her vulval area. She may use the tip of the penis to stimulate her mons, labia, and clitoris, but should not try to insert it into her vagina. If the man begins to lose his erection or shows signs of becoming tense, she should not stop, but rather return to fondling and caressing the penis, the testicles, and the inner thighs, but moving it away from the vulval area. Both partners should remember that it is entirely normal for the penis to become alternately hard and soft as stimulation progresses. The exercise may end with the couple switching positions and the man pleasuring the woman, using the kind of stimulation that she enjoys most.

During the third exercise, just as an experiment, the couple can see how ineffective it is for the man to *try* to get an erection, compared with the technique that they have been using in the previous exercises. The couple should use any pleasuring position they want, with the woman stimulating the man until he gets an erection. Then she should let him try to maintain the erection by focusing his attention on it. Almost inevitably, the erection will be lost. Both partners should take note of their feelings at this time. The man should notice how he has suddenly become a spectator of his own reactions and how little pleasure or stimulation there is in this role. He is concerned with himself rather than being actively involved with the woman and the pleasurable, arousing situation. The woman should notice how anxious and *left out* she feels as her partner tries to maintain his erection without her participation.

After they have seen the pitfalls in trying to maintain an erection through willpower, the couple should move on to the positive part of the exercise. Taking the female-superior position again, the woman uses a variety of pleasuring techniques until the man gets an erection. She can then rub the tip of the penis around her vulval area as in the last exercise, but eventually, she can go on to insert the penis into the vagina. Intromission should be initiated and guided entirely by the woman. The man simply lies back and enjoys himself. The woman should try to insert the penis in a natural and easy way, and if she notices any tension or loss of erection on the part of the man she can return to the previous step and resume manual stimulation.

Both the man and the woman should be aware that a strong, firm erection is not necessary for intromission. With the woman's guidance and active participation, a semierect penis is relatively easy to insert into the vagina. It is a good idea for the woman to initiate the moment of intercourse and to guide the penis into her vagina. This takes the pressure off the man, and since she is the expert on her own sexuality, it is the most reasonable procedure.

When intromission has been achieved, the couple should initially confine themselves to slow, rhythmic, nondemand thrusting. There may be a tendency to thrust vigorously to try to prevent loss of the erection, but this should be avoided. The couple can proceed to orgasm if they wish, but the major concentration should be on the experiencing and acceptance of the pleasurable sensations of intercourse. Later, the couple can try other positions besides the female superior. They can experiment with "quickies," and they can take turns guiding intromission and setting the pace of the coital thrusting.

Always keep in mind that potency is natural and spontaneous for a man provided nothing blocks the chain of events that lead to arousal. To begin with, there must be comfort and receptivity. One of the most effective ways to eliminate these prerequisites and thus to make arousal impossible is for the man to give way to anxiety and to *try* to will an erection, thus becoming a spectator in the sexual interaction. It is crucial that he become actively involved.

Secondly, there must be adequate stimulation. Many men who are performance-oriented rather than pleasure-oriented have a great deal of trouble getting themselves to request specific kinds of stimulation. Faced with erectile failure, they are likely to remain silent, struggling with the problem themselves, rather than saying something like, "Honey, I really want to make love to you, but I guess I'm a little out of it right now. Could you run your fingertips along my thighs the way you did last Thursday?" A person can't have intercourse alone, and neither can he deal with the problem alone when things are not going as they should. Sex is an intimate form of communication. Impotence occurs when there is a breakdown in communications because one partner is tired, worried, preoccupied, or disturbed. The way to deal with impotency, or any sexual dysfunction, is to reestablish communication, not to destroy it further.

18
Learning Ejaculatory Control

PREMATURE, OR RAPID, ejaculation is, along with impotence, one of the two most common male sexual problems. It has been estimated that approximately one out of every four men is a rapid ejaculator. But while potency problems are usually seen as a sign of failure, an anxiety-provoking blow to the ego, rapid ejaculation is considered by a great many men to be no problem at all. This attitude is regrettable, for the man as well as the woman, but it is fairly easy to explain.

As we have already seen, most men learn to be rapid ejaculators during their early sexual experiences. Among adolescent boys, for example, masturbation tends to be a secretive, hidden activity, haunted by guilt and the fear of discovery. For this reason, most young boys who masturbate generally try to reach orgasm as quickly as possible. In fact, in the so-called circle jerk, when a group of adolescent boys masturbate in unison, the winner is considered the one who ejaculates first.

This push toward rapid performance usually carries over to the first intercourse experience. Typically, a young man's first inter-course might take place in the back of a car in a hurried, unplanned way, or on a sofa in the girl's house with the fear that her parents may return at any moment, or with a prostitute who puts a lot of pressure on the man to finish quickly so she can get on with business. Present in all these situations is not only sexual arousal but also a good deal of anxiety and an explicit demand to perform rapidly. The young man is usually solely concerned with proving himself sexually rather than being able to focus on the sensual aspects of the experience. And since he has learned to associate sexual prowess with rapid ejaculation rather than with giving and receiving pleasure, he is likely to reach orgasm rather quickly. First intercourse involves high expectations, high sexual excitement, high anxiety, and little skill. Thus, with all these factors, it is not at all surprising that in their first intercourse experiences the large majority of men are premature ejaculators. In fact, many men ejaculate before intromission. As a result of these early experiences, high arousal and high anxiety become closely associated. The outcome of this association is generally a pattern of rapid ejaculation.

Although many men learn to slow down somewhat as they become more comfortable and confident in their sexual functioning, premature ejaculation continues to be a problem for a considerable number. This may result at least partially from the fact that, until recently, rapid ejaculation was not recognized as being detrimental to the sexual fulfillment of the couple. When intercourse was seen primarily as a man's pleasure and a woman's duty, a man had little motivation to prolong the sex act. In fact, since it was believed that "nice" women did not enjoy sex under any circumstances, a man who could get the job done quickly was someone to be admired. If his wife found intercourse unpleasant or uncomfortable, she might even urge him to "get it over with." Surprisingly, much of this kind of thinking lingers to a pronounced degree even now, especially among men who are less aware of female sexual response and who are not accustomed to the idea that women can and should enjoy sexuality and intercourse. Men generally, and rapid ejaculators particularly, tend to be much too fast and too rough in their lovemaking. Their hurried style can be very unsatisfying to women who desire more affectionate, gentle, and sensitive pleasuring as well as more prolonged intercourse. But often problems arise when a woman decides to voice her dissatisfaction.

Arguments over rapid ejaculation can often create a great deal of tension between partners. The woman may feel that the man doesn't care about her as a person or about her sexual needs, and as a result, she may become frustrated and resentful. Instead of being a shared, positive experience, sex may then become a battleground. At this point the man might react in either of two ways, both destructive to the relationship. He might tell his partner that she is overly demanding and that they will have sex his way or not at all. This usually leaves the woman bitter and sexually frustrated, and many of the positive feelings the couple had for each other are destroyed.

Other men may react by telling themselves that they are sexual failures and becoming depressed. The man is then likely to avoid the source of his depression—namely, sexual activity with his partner. When he does have sex, he will try to withhold ejaculation by biting his tongue, fixing his mind on unpleasant, nonsexual thoughts, using special anesthetizing cream on the tip of the penis, wearing two condoms, or other distracting techniques to prevent him from becoming too sexually excited. When the man does ejaculate, he does not enjoy the experience because he is busy blaming himself for reaching orgasm too quickly. The eventual outcome of this approach commonly is that the man no longer enjoys sexual activity and sometimes develops a potency problem as well.

Even those men who recognize that rapid ejaculation can be a problem and that there is a need to do something about it may view the situation in a rather distorted and self-defeating light. Their attitude assumes that rapid ejaculation is detrimental only to the woman's enjoyment, and that any effort to prolong intercourse is undertaken exclusively for her sake. Many men believe that if only they had better ejaculatory control their partners would automatically become orgasmic during intercourse. Although this could be true for some couples, the majority of nonorgasmic women need more than just prolonged intercourse in order to reach climax. A recent survey indicates that the percentage of women who experience orgasm regularly during intercourse may be as little as one-third, and that those women who do achieve orgasm during intercourse use a variety of conscious techniques that they have found to work for them.

Contrary to popular opinion, orgasm in the female does not seem to occur automatically as a result of intercourse. Some women can enjoy sex and be orgasmic during sex play, but because of insufficient indirect clitoral stimulation, never learn to be orgasmic during intercourse. Other women find that being orgasmic through manual or oral stimulation is more satisfying, although they still enjoy the intercourse experience. This is not necessarily a sexual problem, provided both the man and woman understand and accept it as simply being a question of individual style and preference. Certainly, a woman who wished to learn to be orgasmic during intercourse would find it easier if her partner had good ejaculatory control. But a man who sets out to achieve better control simply for the woman's sake is missing the point.

The real reason for developing ejaculatory control is that there is much more to sex than orgasm. Not that there is anything wrong with the pleasure of orgasm, but why focus on it to the exclusion of other types of enjoyment? Most men are not aware of the degree of pleasure they can experience through nongenital and genital touching and how turned-on they can get by slow, tender, sensuous foreplay. They do not realize that not only can prolonged intercourse be very exciting for them, but that when they do ejaculate, the orgasm can be even more pleasurable after the long, tantalizing buildup.

In seeking to acquire better ejaculatory control, we would do best to keep our sights fixed on a happy medium rather than trying to pursue unrealistic goals. There is a tendency today for attitudes about rapid ejaculation to go to the opposite extreme from traditional expectations. Thus, while in the past it was considered acceptable for a man to ejaculate fairly soon after intromission, today any sexual encounter that does not last at least thirty minutes and result in multiple orgasms for the woman might be considered a failure. Obviously this is an overly doctrinaire attitude and one likely to give rise to as much frustration and performance anxiety as the view that condoned rapid ejaculation. However, it does point up the need to make clear just what does constitute premature ejaculation. In other words, how soon is too soon?

Obviously, there are degrees of rapid ejaculation and degrees of ejaculatory control. A man is clearly a premature ejaculator if he ejaculates before intromission, at intromission, or within seconds of intromission. But beyond this, it is very difficult to assign a definite time limit to mark the point at which ejaculation is premature. Research indicates that the average length of intercourse is two minutes. Can we say that ejaculation after only one minute is premature? Thirty seconds? Fifteen seconds? Masters and Johnson have attempted to define premature ejaculation in terms of percentages rather than amount of time. They state that if the woman is normally orgasmic during intercourse, premature ejaculation occurs if the man ejaculates before the woman's orgasm more than 50 percent of the time. Even this definition seems too arbitrary, however. What about the fellow who reaches orgasm before his partner only 40 percent of the time? Is he not also justified in seeking greater control? It may be that this whole attempt at defining premature ejaculation is on the wrong track and that the emphasis should not be on how soon is too soon, but on helping the couple gain greater enjoyment from intercourse.

The central point is that if you do ejaculate more rapidly than you or your partner would like, you are experiencing a very common problem, and you may find it helpful to try to learn better ejaculatory control. In fact, most men would feel more comfortable with intercourse if they understood what causes rapid ejaculation and felt that they had better control over their reactions. Thus, the most reasonable and practical way to look at ejaculatory control is as a learned skill which both the man and woman can be actively involved in acquiring and which will have a positive effect on the sexual enjoyment of both.

Basically, learning ejaculatory control consists of two steps. The first is to become more aware of the sensations just before the point of "ejaculatory inevitability." Male sexual arousal is a voluntary response up to this point, but afterwards the response becomes involuntary and a man will ejaculate no matter what he or his partner does. In fact, once you have reached this point, even if your mother-in-law were to surprise you by walking into the bedroom, you would still ejaculate. Men who do tune into their sensations just before the point of ejaculatory inevitability report a feeling of intense arousal, a sense of the penis being "full" and of wanting to push forward to release the ejaculation. Once the man is aware of these sensations, the second step is to develop the ability to prolong the pleasant sensations of arousal but without moving beyond the point of ejaculatory inevitability. This strategy is the opposite of the "common sense" approach of tuning out sexual arousal by focusing on distracting thoughts or biting on the corner of the pillow. It emphasizes instead tuning into penile sensations and learning to monitor them.

Men whose need to ejaculate rapidly is very strong may find it necessary to engage in a program of exercises designed to increase their ability to control the intensity of stimulation in order to prevent themselves from going beyond the point of ejaculatory inevitability. These exercises center around the "squeeze technique," a method of controlling a man's level of sexual excitement through a simple physical means. It has been discovered that if sufficient pressure is applied to the underside of a man's erect penis just below the glans, there will be a partial loss of the erection along with a complete loss of the urge to ejaculate. Although it is possible for a man to use this technique on himself, more effective and lasting results will usually be obtained if the woman learns to apply the squeeze and the couple employs it as part of a program of progressive exercises.

Using the squeeze technique is relatively simple, although it might take a few times before you feel comfortable with it. The woman encircles the penis with her hand, placing her thumb against the underside of the glans while her index finger rests just below the coronal ridge. She then applies pressure with the thumb until the man no longer has the urge to ejaculate. This usually takes between five and twenty seconds. The squeeze technique will not work unless the pressure is quite hard. There is no need to be afraid of causing pain or injury, however. When erect, the penis can stand considerable pressure without any discomfort being felt. Obviously, if any discomfort *is* felt, the man should immediately let his partner know.

During the first exercise, the man and woman should assume a comfortable position which allows the woman easy access to the man's genital region. She then manually stimulates him until he gets a firm erection. At this point she should use the squeeze technique, causing the erection to subside. After a few seconds, the woman resumes stimulation until the penis becomes erect again. She then uses the squeeze technique again. At this stage, the woman is applying the squeeze long before the point of ejaculatory inevitability simply to get the couple used to and comfortable with the procedure.

Once this has been accomplished, the couple can move on to the next step, which is for the man to employ some signal during manual stimulation to tell the woman that the point of ejaculatory inevitability is approaching. This signal can be a verbal one such as "now" or "okay," or he may simply motion with his hand. In any case, he should signal as soon as he feels the signs of approaching ejaculation, and the woman should use the squeeze technique without delay. The man should at no time try to fight down his urge to ejaculate by himself or attempt to detach himself from his feelings of arousal. He should accept and enjoy the stimulation given to him by his partner and rely on her to help him control his ejaculatory reflex by using the squeeze. They should continue to use these arousal and squeeze procedures for twenty to thirty minutes, or through at least three squeezes. When the man does finally ejaculate, even if it is earlier than he wants to, he should not be upset, but should simply relax and allow himself to enjoy the ejaculation.

This is true for all the exercises. If you make what you consider to be a "mistake" and ejaculate before your partner has a chance to apply the squeeze, don't feel as if you have failed or done something wrong. Nor should the woman try to use the squeeze if the man has already begun to ejaculate as it will no longer help and could prove uncomfortable; so just enjoy the ejaculation. In fact, the experience can be instructive as well as pleasurable since it can help you learn to discriminate the point of ejaculatory inevitability. Remember that the squeeze is not magic; it is a learning technique that helps you to focus more attentively on your own pattern of arousal and to break the connection between high arousal and high anxiety.

After the couple has finished practicing the squeeze, they can end their session with the man assuming the role of pleasurer and the woman that of pleasuree. The woman can then guide the man in using whatever form of stimulation she finds particularly arousing and satisfying.

When the couple has done this exercise long enough to feel thoroughly comfortable with it, they can move on to the next stage. This time, the woman assumes the female superior position, with her buttocks resting on the man's thighs. The woman then stimulates the man, but instead of just using her hands, she may also rub his penis against her vulva, although she should not insert the penis into the vagina. Again, as soon as the man feels the point of ejaculatory inevitability approaching, he immediately signals the woman and she applies the squeeze. The couple can experiment with various kinds of stimulation until they feel thoroughly comfortable with this stage of the exercises. For example, the woman might try rubbing the penis against her breasts and nipples, or they might use oral-genital stimulation.

The final stage involves using the squeeze technique with intercourse. Again, the female superior position is used. After intromission, the man lies quietly and focuses on the sensation of vaginal containment. After a while, the woman begins slow, rhythmic, nondemanding thrusting. As soon as the man feels the point of ejaculatory inevitability approaching, he signals, and the woman lifts herself off the penis and applies the squeeze technique. In this way, it should be possible to prolong intercourse for at least twenty minutes. As greater comfort and control are achieved, the couple can experiment with more rapid thrusting, always using the squeeze technique at the proper time to control ejaculation. Most men find that learning ejaculatory control is a gradual process and that it is more difficult with rapid thrusting, especially in the male superior position. It is probably a good idea to continue using the squeeze technique occasionally for at least six months, even after the initial problem has been overcome. In this way, you can gain even greater comfort and skill at prolonging intercourse.

Rapid ejaculation is actually one of the simplest sexual dysfunctions to deal with. The squeeze technique is, for most men, an easy and effective method for gaining ejaculatory control. However, men who have been rapid ejaculators for a long period of time often find it hard to believe that they can ever overcome their problem. One of my clients, Alex, a thirty-nine-year-old man in his second marriage, was a rapid ejaculator who had this attitude when he came to see me. His first wife had not complained about his premature ejaculation, so he never became fully aware of the problem during that marriage. Initially, his second wife said nothing, but her resentment kept building. It came out six months after they were married in a blistering attack in which she claimed that Alex was selfish, inconsiderate, and cared nothing about her as a person or about her sexual needs. Alex was stunned. His wife's accusations depressed him, and he felt put down and also angry at having these demands thrown at him. Most of all, he felt a sense of hopelessness; he realized that he had been a rapid ejaculator all his life and felt that now it was too late for him to change.

When his wife suggested that he try professional therapy, he refused, saying that he was not "crazy." Soon afterward, however, they heard about sex therapy for couples, and Alex felt that this would be less objectionable. The recommendation of an acquaintance brought them to me, and we began working on the problem. As treatment progressed, it became clear that Alex's initial anxiety was caused by his reluctance to tell a male therapist that he needed help in the sexual area. However, once he accepted the idea that learning ejaculatory control was like learning any other skill, and that he and his wife would approach the problem as a couple, he felt better about the therapy process and decided to cooperate. He soon found that learning ejaculatory control could be fun as well as beneficial. He and his wife found that the exercises were easy and effective, and Alex was amazed to discover that a problem that had been with him for so long could be overcome so simply.

Their case offers a good example of the value of using a therapist in such a situation rather than trying to do it on your own. A good professional can provide real help and guidance; he can help to keep the couple on track, monitor problems that arise with the exercises, and support them in dealing with anxiety or discouragement, which can interfere with progress.

So far, we have been speaking exclusively about men who have wives or partners who are willing to work with them to overcome their dysfunction. What about the single man who is a rapid ejaculator but does not have a regular partner?

Although it may take longer for him to learn ejaculatory control, it is possible for him to do something about the problem on his own. He can use the squeeze technique on himself while masturbating, stimulating himself up to the point of ejaculatory inevitability and then applying the squeeze. It may be more effective, however, to use the "stop-start" method instead. Here the man stimulates himself until he feels that he is approaching the point of ejaculatory inevitability, then stops the stimulation and allows his arousal to subside. He does this three or four times before finally ejaculating. This can be as effective as the squeeze in breaking the connection between high arousal and high anxiety; and in fact many couples prefer it because they find it more natural and comfortable. However, the single man should not be surprised or disappointed if the control he has achieved in masturbation does not have an immediate effect on his sexual interactions with partners. There are many more emotional factors in a couple situation, and these tend to complicate the task of putting a newly learned skill into practice.

It is also worth noting that the majority of men ejaculate rapidly in their first intercourse attempt. But a man (or the woman involved) who has this experience should not take it as a sign that he is selfish, or that he doesn't care for his partner, or that he is a sexual failure. Rather, he should understand that his control will get better if he and his partner continue to work at it. He might also try spending more time on tender and slow pleasuring, concentrating less on intercourse and orgasm. If he continues to ejaculate rapidly, he should not put himself down but rather enjoy the experience. And he needs to be aware that sex does not necessarily end with his ejaculation. He can continue to stimulate his partner and bring her to orgasm manually or orally. An orgasm brought about in this way can be just as enjoyable for the woman as one that occurs during intercourse, and there is no reason for the man to feel that he is any less masculine because he has given pleasure with his tongue or fingers rather than with his penis.

Learning ejaculatory control is much like learning any other new skill. You first have to decide that you want to learn it and keep your motivation high enough to go through the steps to achieve it. You must realize that it takes time and practice and that you should not become angry or discouraged if you do not notice an immediate improvement. Since it is something you learn as a couple, you need to work together, support each other, communicate clearly, and avoid falling into the trap of blaming each other for the occasional unsuccessful experience. In learning ejaculatory control you are not only learning a specific skill; you are also learning to communicate better and to widen the scope of your sexual interaction. You can use your increased ability to control ejaculation to make sexual activity more pleasurable for you as an individual and as a couple.

19
Overcoming
Ejaculatory Inhibition

EJACULATORY INHIBITION—the inability to ejaculate within the vagina—has the reputation of being a rather rare and exotic sexual disorder. Hence the subject is usually given short shrift. While it is true that ejaculatory inhibition *is* much less common than either impotence or premature ejaculation, it is actually a major problem for perhaps one man in two hundred, and many more men, perhaps one in twenty, are troubled by the problem in a less severe form. Exactly what percentage of men experience ejaculatory inhibition at some time in their lives is unknown, but certainly the problem is widespread enough to warrant some discussion of its characteristics, its causes, and its treatment.

A man who experiences ejaculatory inhibition is able to be aroused, develops and maintains an erection, but cannot reach orgasm. When this occurs at rare intervals, the effect is frustrating, baffling, and often anxiety-producing; but for most men the ability to ejaculate soon returns. Typically, a man with severe ejaculatory inhibition is able to reach orgasm during masturbation but not with a female partner, even though he may feel highly aroused. Some men only have this problem during intercourse, but others are unable to ejaculate even when their partner employs manual or oral stimulation. Oddly enough, although this condition can have acute psychological and, in many cases, physical effects, it is often not taken very seriously by either experts or by the general public. Let us examine why this might be so.

First, however, there is the matter of terminology. Since ejaculatory inhibition has not been studied as extensively as other sexual dysfunctions, there is less of a consensus about its basic characteristics. This uncertainty is reflected in the variety of terms that have been used by different writers to describe the condition. It has been called by several different titles in various clinical texts, including "ejaculatory incompetence," "retarded ejaculation," and "ejaculatory inability." Ejaculatory inhibition seems preferable to these terms, however, because it is the least value-laden and it most accurately describes the problem. The inability to ejaculate within the vagina nearly always stems from some type of inhibition—the inability to let go, to fully enjoy sexual arousal, and to allow it to culminate naturally in orgasm. Ejaculatory inhibition is not to be confused with retrograde ejaculation, a physiological condition in which orgasm does occur, but the semen goes into the bladder rather than being ejaculated from the penis.

The reason ejaculatory inhibition has received so little attention can be traced to two widespread and inaccurate assumptions. The first of these is that ejaculatory inhibition is a problem only when it occurs in its most severe form. The second is that the man with ejaculatory inhibition, because of his great "lasting power," is able to satisfy his partner to an extraordinary degree and therefore, while he may miss the pleasure of orgasm, at least he has the consolation of knowing that he is a superlative lover. We might call this the "blessing in disguise" hypothesis.

The trouble with the first assumption is that it tends to discount all the instances in which ejaculatory inhibition leads to or is associated with some other type of sexual problem. For example, in some cases of ejaculatory inhibition, the man may have an erection and begin intercourse, but even with continued coital thrusting and a high level of sexual arousal he is unable to reach climax. As he becomes more and more frustrated and more and more focused on the difficulty he is having ejaculating, his level of arousal often declines and eventually he loses his erection. "Ah ha," he says, "I must be impotent!" But because of the lack of attention paid to the problem of ejaculatory inhibition, he is likely to ignore it as the underlying cause of his erectile problem.

In other cases, a man suffering from partial ejaculatory inhibition might push himself so hard to reach orgasm and focus so narrowly on maintaining his level of arousal that, while he does manage to ejaculate, neither intercourse nor ejaculation holds much pleasure for him. His probable conclusion? Waning interest in sex. But again, because of his unfamiliarity with the fundamental problem of ejaculatory inhibition, he may not realize that it is related to his lack of sexual satisfaction. The common element in each of these variations is that the natural rhythm of moving from high sexual arousal to orgasm is inhibited, and, as a result, the man looks forward to and enjoys climax less. Rather than orgasm being the natural culmination of an enjoyable and arousing sexual experience, it becomes an anxiety-provoking goal that he fails to achieve.

The second assumption—the "blessing in disguise" hypothesis—represents the male glorification of performance over pleasure in its most extreme form. What it entirely overlooks is the fact that mutual pleasure is the key to true sexual satisfaction for a couple. Since ejaculatory inhibition rules out the possibility of pleasure for the man, it follows that there can be little real satisfaction for either partner. The first few times it happens the woman might be pleasantly surprised by her partner's intercourse; she may also find that she can be multiorgasmic with such prolonged penile stimulation. However, unless she is totally oblivious to her partner, she will soon become aware of his frustration. And if intercourse continues for over an hour with the man not ejaculating, the man will probably experience physical pain as a result of the continued high level of vasocongestion. This condition, commonly known as "blue balls," is not actually harmful but it can be acutely uncomfortable. The woman, too, may well find this prolonged intercourse physically uncomfortable.

The specific causes of ejaculatory inhibition are not well understood at this time and probably vary widely depending on the life experience of each individual. In general, they appear to be psychological rather than physical and usually stem either from some negative sexual experience or from inadequate sexual learning. However, it is also possible for there to be a physiological cause, particularly if the man is unable to ejaculate under any circumstances. In such cases, a urologist ought to be consulted to check out the possible medical cause for the dysfunction.

But except for those rare cases where the condition is medical in origin, the most typical cause is that the man has developed an irrational fear of ejaculating within the vagina or in a woman's presence, and the ejaculatory response has therefore become more and more inhibited. The major negative sexual attitude that many men with this problem have is the belief that there is something wrong, frightening, or immoral in really letting go, being uninhibited, and enjoying sexual pleasure with a woman. Other negative factors include the fear of being discovered while having sex, fear or misunderstanding of the vagina, a strict religious (and antisexual) upbringing, anxiety about ejaculation, an aversion to one's own semen, guilt over sexual pleasure, fear of loss of control, the fear of getting too close to someone, or a severely traumatic sexual incident in the past.

In married men, ejaculatory inhibition might also be connected with a tendency to think of marital sex as being routine and unexciting. If a man expects not to reach a very high degree of arousal while having sex with his wife, this may very well become a self-fulfilling expectation. The likelihood of this happening is especially great if the man has not learned how to make requests of his partner regarding the type of sexual stimulation that will most arouse him and help him to achieve climax. Eventually, his boredom and lack of involvement might make it difficult for him to reach orgasm at all. It is not unusual for a man with intermittent ejaculatory inhibition to develop secondary impotence and/or to begin avoiding sexual encounters with women.

Most men suffering from ejaculatory inhibition are excellent examples of the fact that in order to have a truly rewarding sex life a person must learn to please himself as well as pleasing his partner. Take Jack, a client of mine, a thirty-eight-year-old technical writer whose three children from two previous unsuccessful marriages lived with him. Jack seemed generally well adjusted, led an active, stimulating life, enjoyed being a single father, and reported that he had good relationships with women. But while he always experienced orgasm when he masturbated, Jack found that he was ejaculating less and less often in his sexual encounters with females. Typically, he consoled himself with the "blessing in disguise" theory that even if he was missing out on orgasm, at least he was a good lover, since his partners were nearly always orgasmic. During therapy, however, it emerged that Jack felt it to be unmanly for him to request certain kinds of stimulation from his partner. Instead, he focused most of his attention and energy on making sure that he was performing well, on making sure that his partner could have no cause to complain about his ability to satisfy her. As a result, he never got very turned on during sex. He never really let himself go and allowed himself to become an involved participant in the sexual experience. Jack had made himself into a kind of "sexual servant" who was not entitled to enjoy the experience himself. We worked on helping Jack learn to request specific kinds of stimulation from his partner. He found that it was particularly arousing for him when his partner moved her pelvis in a circular direction during intercourse and when she stroked and fondled his testicles. As he became more confident about making specific requests and as he gave himself permission to let go and enjoy the experience, Jack began to experience orgasm more and more regularly.

The major strategy in working with a man suffering from ejaculatory inhibition is to give him support and permission to enjoy sexual pleasuring, and to view ejaculation as a natural and positive culmination of sexual pleasure and arousal. Like almost every other sexual problem, the ideal is for the couple to see it as "their" problem rather than "his" problem and to work together in a supportive way to learn to be freer and more comfortable with sexual pleasure and orgasm. Treating ejaculatory inhibition is a gradual process in which the man allows himself to be more direct in requesting stimulation from his partner and in experiencing and savoring positive sexual feelings. As he gains confidence and allows himself to become more "selfish," he will usually be able to enjoy the feeling of growing arousal and allow it to culminate in orgasm.

During intercourse the man needs to allow himself to be actively involved with his partner, continuing to touch and be touched, and to attend to and enjoy all the sensations involved in the intercourse rather than trying to force an orgasm. He must learn to be aware of his sexual feelings and needs and to trust himself and his partner enough to let go sexually.

While gaining the ability to ejaculate intravaginally is obviously the ultimate aim of a man wishing to overcome ejaculatory inhibition, it is generally more effective to lead up to this goal gradually. An important and positive first step is for the man just to be comfortable reaching an orgasm and ejaculating with his partner present. Thus, letting go and lowering inhibitions by allowing yourself to ejaculate in front of your partner as a response to her manual or oral stimulation is not only normal but also a very positive step in learning to overcome ejaculatory inhibition. After you are comfortable with this, subsequent steps include relearning that sexual arousal usually culminates in orgasm and sexual satisfaction for the male, and continuing on a regular schedule to ejaculate when your partner uses manual or oral stimulation. The next step would be to begin ejaculating closer and closer to the woman's vagina in order to reduce anxiety and inhibitions related to the vagina. As the man continues to feel less inhibited and more comfortable with regular ejaculations near the vagina, the couple can begin using intercourse as a major stimulation to ejaculation. The man should be aware of and request the type of intercourse stimulation that is most arousing and can bring him to climax. For example, the woman's rapid and demanding coital thrusting might be arousing for one man, while another might prefer the woman be passive while he moves in short, rapid strokes. Often the couple will use manual or oral stimulation until the man is very aroused and then will begin intercourse. During intercourse the man should enjoy and attend to all his feelings and sensations as well as the responses and feelings of his partner rather than focusing only on his penis. The couple must work together to reduce anxiety and inhibitions so that the man learns to feel comfortable when he ejaculates intravaginally. Remember, this is a joint effort with the male and female working *together* toward a mutually satisfying sexual interaction in which arousal naturally culminates in orgasm for the male.

Rather than trying to follow such a program on their own, many couples will want to consult a professional sex therapist or psychotherapist to help them learn or relearn these freer, less inhibited attitudes, feelings, and behaviors. If the man does not have a regular sex partner to help him, he might be particularly interested in consulting a therapist not only to help him understand ejaculatory inhibition but also to develop an individual program that will aid in reducing his anxiety and making him feel less inhibited sexually.

As is true with other sex problems, the man suffering from ejaculatory inhibition needs to understand his sexual behavior, accept it without feeling less masculine or putting himself down, and with the help and cooperation of his partner and/or a professional therapist work toward greater comfort and more enjoyable sexual functioning. It is also important to note that, just as with impotence or rapid ejaculation, a man might experience ejaculatory inhibition as a once-in-a-while thing without this being a sign that there is anything basically wrong with his sexual functioning. Any situation or feeling that interferes with free-flowing sexuality could occasionally prevent the male from ejaculating. For instance, if he is tired, if he has drunk too much, if he is depressed, if he is angry with his partner, if the sexual activity is unexpectedly interrupted by a phone call or children's demands, he might feel no need or desire to ejaculate.

Nor should the problem of ejaculatory inhibition be confused with the normally occurring decrease of ejaculatory frequency in older men. As a man reaches fifty and beyond, it is not at all unusual for him to be having and enjoying intercourse, but to feel no need to carry each encounter through to ejaculation. For instance, an older man who has intercourse five times a month may feel the need to ejaculate on only three or four of those occasions. Many older men do not understand that this is a healthy and normal part of aging, and instead feel that "they're over the hill" sexually, or they have developed a sexual dysfunction. (I will deal with this in more detail in Chapter 22, "Sex and the Aging Male.")

The important point that men in general need to keep in mind about ejaculatory inhibition is that it is neither a catastrophe marking the end of one's sexual life nor something to be shrugged off or disregarded. It is a definite sexual dysfunction which, like other dysfunctions, is worth your taking the trouble to seek professional help. In most cases, ejaculatory inhibition responds readily to treatment; thus, if you are one of the men troubled by this problem, there is really no excuse for you to avoid doing something about it.

20
Sex in
the Middle Years

"IT'S CHEMISTRY"—an intriguing way to describe the feelings of sexual attraction that are kindled spontaneously between a particular man and woman. Comparing love with a chemical reaction stresses the heat and power of the forces that are set loose when a man and woman who are "right for each other" get together. The chemistry metaphor has one unfortunate connotation however. Chemical reactions involve a release of energy, but once the energy is released, the resulting compound settles down again to an unexciting, static existence. And usually the stronger the reaction, the sooner it is over.

Regrettably, there is a tendency in our society to make the same assumption about sexual relationships. If they're good, they flare up at once into white-hot incandescence, burn brightly for a few months, perhaps a year or two at most, then sink into a dim glow, and finally go out altogether. But if this is true, then where does it leave marriage? Judging by the pictures presented to us by the media, marital sex in the middle years is considered a dull, routine affair, certainly nothing to look forward to. Youth is where it's at as far as love and sex are concerned. Not only does popular opinion assume that the "chemistry" between a man and woman disappears as their relationship endures; there is also a common belief that as men and women grow older, their sexual interest and ability diminish accordingly. Thus, couples entering their middle years apparently have two things working against them: the tendency for the "chemistry" that began their attraction in the first place to run its course and lapse into inactivity, and second, the certainty that they themselves will cool down and lose interest in sex generally.

Fortunately, these opinions, although held by a great many people, are demonstrably false. The relationship between a man and a woman is far more complex than what occurs between two re-agents in a test tube. Unlike a simple chemical reaction, the feelings that occur between two people are renewable. A couple can keep adding more to the process—new emotions, new experiences—enough to keep it going indefinitely. Moreover, while it is true that with age there is a slight and gradual slowing down of all physical functions, the change is by no means enough to impair sexual enjoyment. And what is lost in terms of speed and frequency of sexual arousal can be more than made up for by greater control, experience, and depth of feeling.

For many couples in the middle years, sex becomes just what the social myths predict for it—a routine, unchanging, and less frequent act. The original chemistry, unrenewed and unattended, just stops working, and the marriage settles into mediocrity and boredom. All that holds the couple together is habit and joint responsibilities, and often these frail bonds are strained to their capacity. As soon as some extra stress appears—perhaps in the form of an economic setback, a problem with children, or an extramarital affair—maintaining the empty relationship suddenly seems pointless, and the couple opts for divorce.

If it isn't necessary for a couple's sexual relationship to fizzle in the middle years, why is it that so many of them do? The blame, it seems to me, can be traced chiefly to the expectations and assumptions that each partner (and especially the man) brings to the marriage. One of the most pernicious notions about marital sexuality and one that is highly detrimental to sexual satisfaction is that the most enjoyable part of sex is the "chase and conquest," and that everything after that is more or less downhill.

Certainly there is a special kind of excitement in pursuing a woman, in being charming and getting positive signals in return, in gaining greater intimacy with her, and in enjoying the first touch, the first kiss, the first time in bed together. But when the relation-ship becomes a long-standing one and especially when it is for-malized by marriage, there is a tendency for these experiences to become far more routine and to lose the excitement they had at first.

This development probably can be attributed at least in part to our expectation that the "magic" *will* evaporate and that it is useless to try to do anything to prevent it. Indeed, novelty never entirely disappears from a relationship, or from any experience in life. Your partner is always undiscovered territory; people can never know one another completely and are usually changing, so there is always something new to find out. You may have had intercourse with your wife hundreds, even thousands of times, and yet each particular time can be a new experience with the possibility of new feelings and sensations.

But the thrill that came so effortlessly in the beginning of the relationship may take some effort to recapture later on. Our minds and senses have to be awakened periodically through the introduction of variety. Some men may feel that such an effort is useless, that if excitement and pleasure do not come of their own accord, they will not come at all, and that any attempt to revivify a stale relationship is a wasted effort. But this is a very unproductive attitude. A couple must learn to take responsibility for their relationship, to actively prevent it from falling into disrepair. I've been married eleven years, and I find that when I put time and energy into my marital and sexual relationship, it pays great dividends, and I am amazed at all the new things I discover about both Emily and myself. Generally speaking, sexual relationships become boring because partners begin taking each other for granted, confine themselves to doing and saying and thinking the same things. "A foolish consistency," Emerson said, "is the hobgoblin of little minds." This same "foolish consistency," it seems, can be the hobgoblin of little sex lives as well.

The tendency for relationships to get stuck in a rut can manifest itself in many ways. One of the most common involves the question of which partner should initiate sexual interaction. In most relationships it is the man who almost always begins sexual activity, and this may cause difficulty for middle-aged couples. Even though the woman often becomes more responsive and interested in sexual activity as she enters her thirties, she typically does not express this by directly initiating sexual intercourse. She may have learned that "nice" women never assert their desire for sex, but always wait to be approached. In their youth such an attitude may not have seriously restricted a couple's sexual activity, but with the coming of middle age, other factors enter that may complicate matters.

For example, a man who is convinced that interest in sex must diminish with age may interpret his wife's unassertive behavior as a confirmation of that idea. Her passivity may directly influence his interest as well, since there is a definite tendency for our own level of arousal to be affected by the interest and responsiveness of our partner. In addition, a man who is in the habit of initiating sexual activity is often misled by the signals given to him by his own body. As a young man, he may have waited to initiate sex until he felt aroused himself. But as he grows older, it becomes less common for him to experience spontaneous erections. This does not mean that he is no longer interested in sex—merely that he now may require more direct stimulation in order to get an erection. If his wife feels free to express her own sexual feelings, then there is usually no problem. Their mutual interest in sex will continue to make them both sexually active and responsive. A surprising number of men, however, interpret the cessation of spontaneous erections—a phenomenon that may occur as early as the mid-thirties—as a sign that their sex life is pretty much over. And when the woman, by her unwillingness to initiate, gives the impression that her interest is waning too, the result may be a drastic reduction in the couple's sexual activity.

The sexual slump of the middle years can be the result of outside forces as well. One of the main factors is the presence of children—who are justly renowned for interrupting their parents' sexual activity by crying, asking for a drink of water, or stumbling into their parents' bedroom, rubbing their eyes and inquiring about the "funny noise." Moreover, caring for a young child places demands on the parents' physical and psychological energy which may detract from sexual activity.

Many couples manage to find ways to deal with these difficulties. For example, they may plan their sex lives around those times when the children are most soundly asleep or being taken care of by relatives or neighbors. But many couples whose sex lives survive these early difficulties succumb to the knottier problems posed later on when the children are older. As children stay awake longer and are more aware of what is going on around them, parents often become extremely self-conscious about sex, convinced that their children will be psychologically damaged if they happen to catch their parents having intercourse or even suspect that intercourse might be taking place. Often a husband and wife become so concerned with maintaining their "parental image" that they forget that they are also sexually active people with feelings toward one another. Sexual activity, when it occurs at all, is relegated to late evening, when both partners are often tired, and is generally as brief and restrained as possible so as not to arouse the children's attention.

Pleasuring, experimentation, tenderness are often kept to a minimum—hardly the best conditions for a satisfying sex life.

Coordinating an active sex life with the demands of a family is not
easy. It can be done, however, and perhaps the most important
factor in maintaining a pleasurable and active sex life in the middle
years of marriage is having an attitude that encourages enhance-
ment of sexuality. Couples should not feel that their status as parents
requires them to become less sexual, that they are doing their children a favor by concentrating less on their own sexual gratification.
In fact, quite the opposite is usually the case. Children who see their
parents being affectionate with each other and who are aware that
they have a positive sexual relationship are more likely to have a
healthy attitude toward marital sexuality when they become adults.
Children should learn that sex is a private and intimate experience
and that it is not appropriate to make it a matter for public display.
Affectionate behavior may be shared by all members of the family,
but when a couple's activity becomes overtly erotic, the time for
privacy has arrived.

Nevertheless, couples should not be unduly anxious about keeping their sex lives hidden from their children. If anything, knowing
for a fact that his parents are sexual people is beneficial for a child.
One of the most satisfactory ways of handling this is to explain to the
child that couples need private time together—to be affectionate, to
have intercourse, or just to talk. A lock on the bedroom door is an
effective method of enforcing such a rule. Children can be in-
structed that when the door is closed or locked, their parents are not
to be disturbed, unless there is a pressing problem demanding their
attention. There should be no negative psychological effects if this is
done lovingly and reassuringly. On the contrary, the chief message
conveyed will be that sex is a positive and healthy part of marriage—
an excellent model for the child's own development.

Being frank and straightforward with children about sex can have
a positive effect even when the effort is long delayed. This was
proved by two of my clients, Saul and Martha. They had been
married for twenty-seven years, and for the last fifteen years had
had serious sexual difficulties revolving around Saul's intermittent
potency problem. During the past two years Saul had been totally
impotent, and this was the reason that they finally sought professional help. One of the unfortunate side effects of Saul and Martha's
discomfort over sex was that they had all but neglected the sex

education of their children, a son of twenty-five and a daughter of twenty-one. The most they had been able to manage was some vague advice to "save sex for a good relationship." As a result, their children felt, even as adults, an extreme reluctance to discuss any sexual topic with their parents. The sex therapy that Saul and Martha underwent was extremely successful, probably due in large part to the fact that they really cared about each other and about revitalizing their sexual relationship. Not only did Saul overcome his specific dysfunction, but as a couple they developed a better understanding of each other's sexuality as well as the ability to communicate their thoughts and feelings. This new comfortable attitude about sex extended to their relationship with their children, whom they eventually informed about their experiences with sex therapy. Almost immediately, both children gratefully dropped their defenses and began sharing their own sexual concerns with their parents. They no longer felt that their parents judged them or looked down on them for engaging in sexual activity or that they would make their parents uncomfortable by talking about sex, and they were able to find positive reinforcement for their own sex lives in the example of their parents' loving and committed relationship.

Another factor that often affects the relationship of couples in the middle years negatively is the tendency for the partners—particularly the man—to become so deeply involved in work and other outside activities that there is very little energy or interest left over for the marriage. It goes without saying, of course, that it is very important for a man (and woman) to be actively involved in a career, in hobbies, in community activities, and in individual and couple friendships. People need freedom to grow and develop and to pursue the goals they have set for themselves, and the middle years in particular are a time when a person makes his mark in the world. Competition is keen and it is reasonable to expect a man to take advantage of whatever opportunities for growth and advancement come his way. Only a person who is happy and fulfilled as an individual is able to find real satisfaction in a relationship with a partner.

Many men, however, overinvest themselves in outside activities while stinting on their marriages and family lives. The situation is paradoxical because in most cases the ostensible reason (or rationalization) for a man trying to better himself in the business world is to be a good provider, to make a better, fuller, and more enjoyable life for himself and his family. But by becoming wrapped up in his work, he may end up providing his family with material goods while denying them to himself. What is equally important, he cheats himself out of the intimacy and support that his wife and family are capable of giving him. Seeing him continually preoccupied with his work, his wife and children are bound to become less warm and caring in their dealings with him. This is unfortunate for the man because it is often during the stress and strain of the middle years that he most needs the solace and emotional reinforcement of a warm, intimate relationship with his wife and children.

What can a man entering the middle years do to prevent the zest and enjoyment from going out of his sex life? Obviously, the first and most important thing is to abandon the assumption that his age automatically entails a drop in sexual activity. Such an assumption almost always becomes a self-fulfilling prophecy. The man's interest in sex declines because he expects it to. Men who have no such expectations, on the other hand, often remain sexually active throughout the middle years and beyond. The so-called male menopause, although rumored to occur sometime during the forties, fifties, or sixties, is, in the vast majority of cases, a mere chimera. The average man entering middle age encounters no abrupt hormonal changes akin to those experienced by women, but rather a very gradual slowdown of physical functions.

It is also worth noting that there are certain principles or values that are found among married couples who remain sexually active throughout their middle years: (1) spontaneity, (2) experimentation, (3) communication, and (4) affection. You would do well to consider these values and the ways they might be adopted in your relationship. Let us look at each of them in turn.

Spontaneity. Any activity that becomes routine, standardized, and predictable eventually loses its appeal. Dull sex may still produce some pleasurable physical sensations, but it isn't usually something to look forward to because it doesn't go very far toward satisfying deeper emotional needs. Obviously, not every sexual encounter can be a totally novel experience. Nor should it be, since the most enjoyable sex is usually a combination of the old and the new. Still, allowing yourself to act on your spontaneous impulses and introduce new, unexpected elements into your sexual relationship is an important part of keeping the enjoyment in your marriage. Spontaneity can take many forms. You might, for example, decide to initiate a sexual encounter right after breakfast on a Saturday morning while the kids are out playing or busy with other activities.

Or you might make specific arrangements to have a friend or neighbor take care of your children for two hours so that you can have a sexual get-together. An unexpected gift of flowers is always a good way to perk up a relationship, but it might be even more effective if they contained a card that said something like "Tonight, at 11:00." Many men find it hard to act in ways that are unexpected or out of character. They are afraid of being rejected or laughed at. But most women are extremely receptive to their spouse's efforts to add romance and excitement to the relationship. Spontaneity is nearly always worth the slight ego-risk involved.

Experimentation. There are many ways to experiment in sex. You might simply introduce a slight variation in your favorite intercourse position. For instance, if you most often use the male-superior position, try varying it by having your partner put her legs over your shoulders. Even something as seemingly insignificant as your partner's placing a pillow under her buttocks may introduce a definite change in the intercourse experience, produce new sensations, and make sex suddenly seem innovative and exciting. If you want to go further with experimentation, you might consider setting aside a whole evening when you would use a special bath oil, read a sophisticated sex manual together, and try different pleasuring, intercourse, and afterglow techniques. Or you might experiment with having sex in unaccustomed places. One of the characteristics of sex in young, unmarried couples is that it is often carried out in odd and inconvenient locations such as a public park, the back seat of a car, or a deserted hallway. While sex under these conditions is rarely a relaxed and leisurely experience, the sense of danger involved often adds a special kind of excitement. Thus, one of the things that a middle-aged couple might do is to plan to have sex in an unfamiliar situation in order to recapture that excitement.

Or you might go to the other extreme and have a romantic, nostalgic evening to celebrate your years together. This might include a candlelight dinner and champagne, followed by a warm, intimate get-together on the sofa with the family album on your laps. Another good idea is to go off together for a weekend—just the two of you, without the children or work worries. Or you might experiment by making changes in the setting where you generally make love. For example, if you usually have sex in the dark, try it with the light on. If you are accustomed to having sex in the nude, try it partially clothed. There is no need to become a sexual "gourmet" or a sexual acrobat if that isn't what you want. But at least give yourself the chance to find out what variations you enjoy so that you can add them to your repertoire.

Communication. Lack of communication is one of the most common complaints of couples who feel that their marriage has become stale and unstimulating. The fact that it is expressed far more frequently by women than by men reflects the average man's feeling that he does not need to discuss his intimate feelings—that, in fact, it is unmasculine to do so. Many men tend to consider their relationship with their partner from an inappropriately utilitarian viewpoint, assuming that it is satisfactory as long as things are running smoothly, as if marriage were primarily an arrangement for promoting efficiency. But of course there is far more to marriage than this. A successful marriage should be a cooperative partnership not only in a utilitarian sense but also, and preeminently, as a sharing of feeling, intimacy, and pleasure. Marriage should enrich the lives of both partners, not just help them to run smoothly, and if this goal is to be met, communication on a deep, personal level is essential.

How much you talk is not nearly as important as what you talk about. Research has shown that merely increasing the quantity of communication will not necessarily improve the marital relationship. Too often, husband and wife only discuss practical matters and stay away from the topic of themselves. The focus of communications should be more on the couple, their relationship as husband and wife, their feelings, and their sexual interaction. There is a special skill involved in intimate communication, the object of which is to keep the discussion moving forward in a manner that allows both partners to express themselves fully. First, each partner needs to be as direct, specific, and clear as possible in stating his feelings. These are "I" communications because they always begin with phrases like "I feel," "I think," and "I want." They serve as a starting point since, before discussion can proceed, it must be clear what each person's position is. It should be remembered, however, that "I" communications are not demands. It is not "I want this or else," but rather "I want this. What do you want?"

Second, each partner must be open to the other's feelings and requests in order to encourage continued communication. Even if a particular "I" statement appears to be upsetting or threatening, there is no point in becoming defensive and either shutting up or counterattacking. Such a reaction usually serves to subvert the communication process. Far better to suggest an alternative which you think may be a possible compromise. Couples also need to learn to express negative feelings because otherwise frustration and anger often result and cause avoidance of sex or the use of sex as a battleground for other problems.

It is important to remember that, however skilled a couple may become at the art of communication, there will never be a time when all problems and disagreements disappear from the relationship. It is simply not in the nature of human interaction for two people to be in harmonious agreement about every aspect of their lives. Therefore, you as a couple need to cultivate the ability to accept one another when there are still issues between you that remain unsettled.

Communication skills and principles are equally relevant in terms of the sexual relationship. Partners must learn to make specific requests for particular kinds of sexual stimulation. And, if you feel unwilling to comply with a particular request, you should be able to respond in a flexible, understanding way that does not place a damper on the sexual interaction itself. For example, if your partner wants you to give her a full body massage and you don't feel like it, rather than saying no, you could offer to give her a back rub.

One of the major impediments to open communication about sex is that couples often lack a sexual vocabulary that they feel comfortable with and are therefore unable to express themselves clearly. It is immaterial what terms a couple chooses to use to describe the parts of the body. They may prefer the "polite" terms (penis, make love) or colloquialisms (prick, screw), or they may want to make up a set of words of their own. What is essential is that they have some means of making their requests specific and clear.

In some cases, however, verbal communication, no matter how explicit, must be supplemented with nonverbal ones. Couples would find it valuable to develop ways of showing each other what kind of stimulation they want through touch. By gently guiding your partner's hand, you can show her not only just where you want to be stimulated but also how hard or soft, fast or slow. Nonverbal communication should be supportive and caring rather than abrupt and demanding. Ideally, it should be combined with verbal communication in order to achieve optimum clarity and expressiveness.

Affection. People who see a couple behaving very affectionately often make the comment, "They must be newlyweds." It is unfortunate that such displays of affection are not generally associated with the middle years of marriage because that is when affection is most needed. Too often, middle-aged couples get out of the habit of holding hands, kissing, hugging, giving each other backrubs, and generally participating in nondemand affectionate behavior. When touching does occur, it is usually in the context of intercourse, and since sensuality and affection outside the bedroom are important in enhancing a couple's sexual feelings for each other, the result of this decrease in affectionate touching is that sexual encounters may grow less and less frequent. One way to make touching a positive part of your relationship is to engage periodically in sessions of sexually arousing pleasuring that do not culminate in intercourse. The couple who behave sensually and affectionately in a variety of situations will usually find that the frequency and satisfaction of their sexual interactions will increase.

Too many couples enter their middle years with the expectation that their sex lives must decline, in both frequency and enjoyment. This expectation often ends up being self-fulfilling, and the "chemistry" that existed at the start of the relationship simply stops working. But contrary to this all too common pattern, there is no reason why the sex lives of people in their middle years should not actually get better. The added years together can give a couple a chance to develop a greater sense of comfort and intimacy in their sexual relations. If they make the commitment to work at their relationship, instead of letting it stagnate, they will be able to introduce greater spontaneity and variety, more effective communication, and more warmth and affection. A sexual relationship that possesses these characteristics will continue to be exciting and gratifying throughout the middle years and well beyond.

21
Single Again

SOME WRITERS have suggested recently that the laws governing marriage should be changed to conform to those which apply in business situations. Instead of marrying for an unspecified period, prospective partners would agree on the number of years they promised to stay together. Thus, couples who were not completely sure of their compatibility but still wanted to try living as legally bound partners could sign a contract for just one year. Others who were more sure might sign a five-year contract. When the specified period was over, partners would then have the choice of renewing the agreement or of going their separate ways.

Such arrangements may indeed become popular with some couples in the future. But at present it is still safe to say that most of us marry with the expectation, or at least the hope, that the relationship will be a source of intimacy and security for a lifetime. How many of us are lucky enough to achieve this goal, however, is another matter. The fact is that a substantial proportion of today's marriages fail to live up to the "happily ever after" expectations with which they begin. Out of every ten couples choosing wedlock today, about three end their relationship with divorce. Others are separated when one of the partners dies. Although there are more widows in our society than widowers, the number of men who lose their wives through death is considerable. What widowers and divorced men have in common is that after becoming used to being married and relating to one special partner over a period of years, they are suddenly "bachelors" again. Indeed many of the emotional reactions a man typically experiences following the death of a spouse are also experienced by a divorced man, though of course the intensity of the emotions is usually somewhat lower. In either case, the transition can be a difficult one, and it takes a lot of energy and effort to readjust psychologically, socially, and sexually to the new state.

The death of an intimate companion is often a severe trauma for the survivor, and it is normal and healthy to experience a variety of negative and not always controllable responses. In cases where the death of the wife is sudden, the husband's first—and natural— reaction will often be to reject the situation as unreal, to feel that it can't be happening. Whether we realize it or not, a partner fills a very large space in our lives. To have that presence removed without warning leaves a gulf we are incapable of comprehending at first. Often it takes a while before the widower feels that he is part of the world again.

The next reaction is usually one of immense grief and depression. As the widower begins to take in the dimensions of his loss, the feelings of sadness seem overwhelming. He may find himself at times crying uncontrollably, experiencing a breakdown of self-control for which he would be wrong to blame himself. Painful, often maudlin feelings and regrets may obsess him at this time. He may think about things he and his wife had planned to do together and now will never have the chance for. He may feel guilty for not being more attentive or generous, for not buying her gifts she always desired or taking her places she always wanted to go. He may even feel guilty simply because he is the survivor and can continue to live and enjoy things while the wife is deprived of these opportunities. Surprisingly, anger is not an uncommon reaction at this time. Many widowers feel furious at their wives for abandoning them, for leaving them alone—an irrational but natural feeling that the widowed man should try to accept. Feeling angry with a dead spouse does not mean that you hated her; it is simply a sign of how important she was to you and how hard it is for you to reconcile yourself to her loss.

Marriage involves not only emotional ties but practical considerations as well, and many of the negative feelings a widowed man experiences are connected with his sense of being overwhelmed with the responsibilities that are suddenly his alone. This is especially true if there are young children to take care of. It is quite common for a widowed husband to feel that it is unfair that he must suddenly do all the things he and his wife once shared, such as caring for the children's physical and emotional needs or running the household on a day-to-day basis. There may be a temptation for the grief-stricken man to shut these responsibilities out by drinking heavily or by simply ignoring them. But it is important for him to begin to take things in hand at this point, to recognize the problems that exist and face them head-on rather than trying to avoid them. It is not that he is no longer entitled to his grief as soon as practical matters intrude, but rather that in the midst of grief he must deal with his present reality and begin to look toward the future and the rebuilding of his life.

Often the widowed man will find it impossible to take the full responsibility for home and family upon himself. In this case, it would probably be a good idea for him to find some female friend or relative whom he feels close to and comfortable with to help him manage things. Having someone who is familiar with the running of a household will make it much easier for the widower to begin living on his own. Above all, he should not reject such help when offered on the grounds that he would prefer to be self-sufficient. It is not a sign of weakness to accept help while trying to adjust to the death or divorce of a spouse. Rather it is an indication of your commitment to creating a new life in the future.

It may also be very helpful if the widowed man has someone with whom he can share his strong and complex feelings of guilt, sadness, and anger. A friend, relative, minister, or family doctor may often be able to fulfill such an empathetic, supportive role. But if the widower has no one to whom he can turn, the best option may be to seek a professional counselor or psychologist who can help him to talk about, understand, and integrate his feelings. This is a normal need and professional help is one alternative. But whether he goes to a professional or nonprofessional, there is no doubt that a newly widowed man needs *somebody* who can be a caring and supportive listener. Feelings produced by the death of a spouse—or by divorce, for that matter—if they are not allowed to come out, nearly always prove highly disturbing, and may prevent a man from successfully making the transition to a single life.

If your wife is dying of a long, drawn-out disease like cancer, making the adjustment to the fact that her days are numbered is certainly one of the most painful and difficult tasks imaginable. Yet, there are several very good reasons why both partners should try to honestly face what is happening and prepare for it. For one thing, it is unfair to the dying spouse for the survivor to pretend that everything is all right, to try to keep up a false front. A dying person needs closeness and support to help her adjust to what is happening. Attempting to maintain the pretense that all is well, that she will eventually recover, has the effect of isolating her in an envelope of unreality, of denying her the chance of expressing her true thoughts and feelings. Secondly, by being dishonest to the dying spouse, however good his intentions, the survivor actually makes it harder on himself. Not only must he bear the strain of keeping up a pretense but he makes it impossible for himself to go through the natural psychological process of confronting death with the dying person. Thus, when death finally occurs, he is unprepared for the devastating effects of the loss.

What happens to sex during the wife's extended period of illness? Of course, the husband continues to experience his normal sexual desires, and the first point to be made is that feeling the need for sex when his wife is terminally ill is not something a man should be dismayed or guilty about. The sex urge is a basic and natural part of being alive, and it is liable to assert itself whatever the circumstances. The question is, what is the best way for a man to integrate his need for sex with his responsibilities toward his dying spouse?

Generally speaking, sexual relations between husband and wife should continue for as long as possible. If the wife's illness makes it impossible for her to engage in intercourse, the couple can continue to experience enjoyable sexual interactions through the use of other pleasuring techniques, from stroking and massaging to the use of manual or oral stimulation to orgasm. There is nothing "perverse" or offensive about continuing sexual relations when one spouse is dying. Indeed, usually a primary need of dying people is not to be rejected, ignored, or denied, but to feel that they are cared about and worthwhile. One of the chief ways of affirming someone's worth is through tenderness, of which sex is an important expression.

Sometimes sexual relations with the dying spouse may be limited or inappropriate, and in the latter stages of illnesses, sex may be impossible altogether. In such instances, masturbation can serve as an excellent sexual outlet for the man. He should not feel childish or selfish for engaging in masturbation at this time, but look upon it as a sensible way for him to satisfy his very human needs within the confines of the situation. Another possibility, of course, is for the husband to seek sexual relations outside the marriage, and some couples may, in these circumstances, decide that it is all right for the husband to become sexually involved with other women. Careful thought should be given to the matter, however, before going through with such a step. If you do have sex with other women, you will have to give further serious consideration to the question of whether to discuss these contacts with your wife. Since sexual relations often lead to feelings of emotional closeness with the partner, the husband might find that a sexual liaison with another woman would interfere with the closeness he wants to have with his spouse during her last months or years. Ultimately, it is a matter of weighing the alternatives involved—something each man must decide for himself according to his own value system.

Once the death of the spouse has occurred, the widower must face a somewhat different set of sexual problems. Although he has lost his usual sex partner, he probably has not lost his sexual interest. Again, it is very important that the widower be aware that his sexual needs are quite normal and can still be a source of pleasure to him. He shouldn't be embarrassed or ashamed of having sexual feelings after his wife has died, but should view his continuing interest in sex as something positive, an indication of his will to survive and to continue leading an active and fulfilling life.

However, he may have to go through a period of exploration and experimentation in order to determine the best way, given his present needs and feelings, of expressing himself sexually. While some men will find that they are at a point in their lives where sex is not very important to them, many more will wish to find a way of integrating some sort of sexual activity into their lives. The widower should be aware of the options available to him. For many widowers, masturbation is a helpful and enjoyable way to relieve sexual tensions when no partner is available. As has already been noted, masturbation is not abnormal or harmful, at this or at any other time; and it may be very beneficial and appropriate in situations where the widowed man is not ready to start any sort of relationship with a partner. The widower should also be able, without feeling guilty, to think about and try out a variety of sexual and life patterns until he finds one that suits his own needs and values. For example, he might seek out another partner for marriage; he might want a stable partner for sex and companionship but without marriage; or he might wish to have a variety of brief, less intense sexual relationships. Frequenting massage parlors or prostitutes may also be a valid sexual choice for the widowed or divorced man, although the need for intimacy and affection is less likely to be satisfied in this way.

One major problem that widowers frequently encounter is the feeling that if they become sexually involved with another woman they are being unfaithful to their dead wives. What the widower needs to realize is that it will not bring back his spouse if he deprives himself of all sexual satisfaction; it will merely make his own life even more unhappy and difficult. He owes it to himself to gain as much happiness as he can after the death of his spouse—most wives who really care for their husbands would almost certainly not want it any other way—and sexual activity can be an important source of happiness. The fact that he has sex with other women does not mean that he did not love his wife; it simply means that he is a healthy male who must continue with his life despite his loss.

If he does find a new sex partner, however, the widower is likely to find that he is a little out of practice sexually. Sex is a natural physiological response, but making love is a skill. Just as you do not play tennis or piano very well after several months or years away from it, when you resume sexual activity with a partner after a period of abstinence you will probably feel awkward and need practice to regain your skill as a lover. Anxiety, guilt, and other negative feelings may also intrude in these early experiences, causing such problems as impotence, premature ejaculation, or ejaculatory inhibition. These difficulties are not unusual under the circumstances, and the main thing for the man to remember is not to be discouraged by them. Through practice, he can become comfortable as a sexual partner again, and normal sexual functioning can return. If the sexual problems continue, though, he might want to consult a sex therapist.

As he forms new sexual attachments, the widower should also avoid making comparisons between his new partner or partners and his former wife. Interactions with a new partner, both sexual and otherwise, are likely to be very different from those with the lost spouse, and comparisons between them are not apt to do anyone very much good. Idealizing the dead wife can put pressure on the new partner and may cause her to feel discouraged and unloved. On the other hand, if the widower sees the new partner as superior, it may lead to feelings of guilt on his part. A happier course seems to be for the man to refrain as far as possible from making comparisons, but rather to try to see the new sex partner as a unique individual, capable of bringing her own sort of enjoyment, happiness, and sexual companionship.

Although being separated from a wife through divorce seems quite different from losing her through death, the two processes are experientially similar in many ways. Like the widower, the divorced man must learn to deal with the loss of an accustomed companion and sexual partner. No matter how poor the relations between the couple were, divorce usually leaves an emotional gap that can be a source of pain and grief for a time. Research studies indicate that it takes approximately one to two years to reintegrate one's life after a divorce. Also, like the widower, the divorced man must consider the various options available to him now that his marriage is dissolved and think through or experiment with different alternatives for the future.

A divorced man may also experience considerable depression, except that it is apt to be based more on a sense of failure rather than just on a feeling of loss. Many divorced men feel that they are failures in the eyes of family, friends, and society in general—that they have not lived up to the husband-father roles they undertook when they married. Rather than dwell on this sense of failure, however, it is far more productive to view a divorce as an unfortunate but necessary step and one that can ultimately be a valuable learning experience. If there is no possibility of partners achieving happiness within their marriage, then divorce is a logical and psychologically healthy alternative. But the lessons that a person can learn from such an experience, about both his own character and the nature of marital interaction, can be significant to him in dealing with future relationships.

The divorced man with children also has to deal with his role as father, as well as the complexities of child-support payments and visitation rights. This is a complex subject that needs full treatment, but I would like to offer at least some basic guidelines here. Sometimes children feel that they somehow caused the divorce—that if they had behaved differently the marriage might have been saved. You need to make it clear to the children that the problem lay not with them or with your role as parent, but rather with the relationship between yourself and your wife. It is important to stress to them that they do not have to take sides, and that although the marriage is coming to an end, you are still their father and you care about them and their development. Often there is a good deal of anger and bitterness between spouses, and they use the children as their battleground. This is destructive not only for the children but also for you in your ability to develop a new single life.

It can be very hard for a man who has lost his partner, whether through death or divorce, to have the courage to try to establish a new relationship. Particularly when the loss of the spouse involved a great deal of pain, the newly single man might find that he is unwilling to become intimate with another woman and thereby make himself vulnerable to further hurt. Still, many men find that the dangers of investing in a new relationship are outweighed by the joy and satisfaction that new closeness can bring. In fact, about five out of six divorced men do remarry, usually within a few years of the breakup. What happens all too frequently, however, is that the man picks a new marriage partner who is similar in significant ways to the first wife, and with whom the tensions and difficulties of the original marriage are repeated.

The fact that the divorce rate for second marriages is significantly higher than it is for first ones indicates that this pattern may be quite widespread. Instead of falling into this trap, the divorced man should make every effort to use the unsuccessful marriage as an opportunity to learn what elements must be present to make a marital relationship work for him. In addition, the divorced man who wishes to remarry should take the time to seek out a truly compatible partner rather than just rushing into marriage again to escape the loneliness of being a bachelor. When a man uses divorce in this way, as a positive opportunity for learning, his second marriage is very often a much more intimate and satisfying one than his first.

Jim, a student of mine, was a divorced man of twenty-eight who had been through an unsuccessful first marriage of five years' duration. Although the divorce was a bitter, drawn-out one, Jim continued to function well through the turmoil, completing his master's degree in business administration and functioning effectively in his profession. During the waiting period for the divorce, Jim had a series of affairs lasting a few months each. When the divorce became final, he decided that he had had enough of these short, primarily sexual contacts and wanted a more intimate, lasting relationship, though not necessarily one that involved marriage.

After two unsuccessful tries, he did establish a close relationship with a divorced woman with one young child. They lived together for two and a half years but finally decided to split up. Then Jim met another woman at work and began to date her. She was also divorced and had two children, and although their relationship soon became a deep and intimate one, Jim continued to live alone, having learned the dangers of establishing commitments without first being clear about just what was involved. Eventually Jim and this woman did decide to live together and later to marry, but not before thoroughly discussing their feelings and expectations about their relationship. They agreed that Jim would adopt the two children and that in a year they would have a child of their own. They also discussed their sexual relations, career plans, and living arrangements, making sure in each case that the mistakes that had been made in their first marriages would not be repeated in the new relationship. This planning paid off, and their marriage has proved to be a very solid and satisfying one.

Before establishing a new and successful relationship, however, a divorced man must first be able to meet possible partners socially, and our society does not always make it easy for him to do this. There is a tendency for married people to have married friends, and a newly divorced man may find that most of the social occasions open to him are centered around couple activities. Some married couples, unaware of the loneliness a divorced man experiences may feel a little awkward about including him in their activities. Rather than expecting others to read his mind, the man who finds himself single again should take responsibility for letting his friends know his needs and feelings. They may feel uncomfortable discussing social activities and women with him, or unsure about whether and how to bring up the subject of his divorce, and it is often up to him to put them at ease by being honest and straightforward. He must make certain things clear, such as whether or not he objects to being invited along with his ex-wife or her friends, whether he appreciates his friends' efforts to "match him up" with unmarried women, and whether he objects to being the only single person at couple get-togethers.

Certainly the widowed or divorced man faces problems that are unique to his special circumstances. I have attempted to deal with some of the most important ones in terms of male sexuality. Being widowed or divorced is a setback, an experience that causes pain, anguish, depression, and self-doubt. However rationally we deal with an experience of this kind, we cannot hope to escape entirely from its negative effects. However, by keeping in mind our basic worth as men and as human beings, by remaining positive about ourselves and affirming our right to happiness and fulfillment, we can profit from the breakup of a marriage by looking upon it as a valuable learning experience, a chance to try again and to do better next time. By affirming our sexuality and using our sexual feelings and experiences in a positive way, we can affirm ourselves as people.

22
Sex and the Aging Male

How DIFFICULT IS IT for you to picture your parents making love? What about your grandparents? How would you feel about seeing a picture of a nude seventy-year-old woman as the centerfold of *Playboy* or *Penthouse*? Or how about a nude man in his seventies as the centerfold of *Playgirl*? Are you turned off by these images? If you are, it is probably because you share the tendency, common in our society, to deny sexuality to older people. Where sex is concerned, you are a youth chauvinist.

We may have had a so-called sexual revolution, but the changes it brought in our sexual attitudes do not extend to all of us. Yes, sex has become freer, more open, but only for that segment of the population between adolescence and middle age. For those above or below these chronological boundaries, sexuality is still not supposed to exist. It is commonly assumed that neither children nor old people are capable of sexual feelings or entitled to any sort of sexual gratification. Children are expected to be innocent, pure, unaffected by sex. This may partially explain why many adults become so upset when children engage in self-stimulation or play sexual games like "doctor" and "nurse." At the other end of the age scale, old people are considered to be "over the hill" sexually, and are expected to lapse uncomplainingly into a peaceful, nonerotic state, free of all sexual thoughts or arousal.

In fact, we are all sexual creatures from the day we are born to the day we die. Infants are capable of becoming sexually aroused and having erections. Men and women in their seventies, eighties, and beyond can and do experience sexual excitement, are able to have intercourse, and can be orgasmic. In Chapter 16, "Sex, Your Children, and You," we saw how important it is for parents to acknowledge the sexuality of their children, to allow them to explore and enjoy their bodies, and to provide them with a positive, unambiguous sex education. Here we will take a look at the role of sex in the life of the older man. What we will see is that, while a man's sexual responses change in certain ways as he gets older, the aging man in good health is still quite capable of effective sexual functioning, of being an involved sex partner, and of being able to enjoy a variety of sexual activities, including intercourse. As a man grows older, he will find that sex is different from his younger days, but not necessarily less enjoyable.

But if the older man is still capable of functioning sexually, why is it that so many men give up on sex as they enter their fifties and sixties? The answer may have something to do with cultural conditioning. Our society simply has not included sexuality as part of the "role" which elderly people are supposed to assume. This is not true of some other cultures, where it is considered quite natural for older people to show an open interest in sex and to lead active and fulfilling sex lives. Yet our society has long associated sexuality primarily with the adolescent and young adults and often tends to see sexual enjoyment as inappropriate for anyone beyond the childbearing years. Only rarely is the sexual activity of older persons presented in a sensitive, accepting manner by the media. More often, older men who openly express interest in sex are assumed to be "dirty old men" or even "perverts." Faced with such opposition, it is understandable that a large number of older men simply give up and content themselves with being nonsexual for the remainder of their lives.

Unfortunately, physicians, the very people whom older men often rely on for information about aging, sometimes share this false idea that sex should end when a man enters old age. But after all, they are only reflecting our society's preconceptions; also, many older doctors were trained during a time when there were no sexuality courses in medical schools, and thus they may be unfamiliar with recent scientific findings about sex. It is not uncommon to find older men discouraged from pursuing an active sex life or being told that they must accept the loss of sexual desire and functioning as a part of the aging process. Some doctors, along with many laymen, seem to think that sexual dysfunction is a natural part of the aging process. But this is simply not true!

Feeling unsure about their right to sexual feelings, many older people block sexual thoughts from their minds because they feel that such ideas are wrong or unnatural. As a result of such self-imposed mental censorship, many older men actually do become nonsexual. Others, while remaining in touch with their sexual feelings, may become convinced that they are no longer capable of acting upon them. If a man believes or fears that he cannot get an erection, his negative feelings may actually prevent him from getting one. This experience of impotence will then serve to reinforce his original belief, that he is no longer a sexual person, and, as a result, he will eventually resign himself to a life without sexual activity.

But there is no real reason why an older man should have to make such a sacrifice. Sexual functioning does not cease naturally with aging. Studies show that all men, no matter what their age and whether or not they are active sexually, continue to have regular erections during sleep. And if a man can get an erection in his sleep, he should also be able to get one with a partner; and if he can get an erection with a partner, he should be able to have and enjoy intercourse. In fact, there is no more reason for a man to lose his ability to have sex than for him to lose the ability to perform any other natural physical function. To use an analogy, a man of seventy may not be able to run as fast as he could when he was twenty, but if he has kept himself in good condition he will be able to jog a few miles or at least take a brisk daily walk. Similarly, a man who has remained sexually active into old age will not respond as rapidly to sexual stimulation or ejaculate as frequently, but he will still be able to enjoy sex on a regular basis. The important thing is for a man to realize that sexual pleasure is something he can and should have as he grows older. Sex is a part of life. As long as he is alive, a man has a right to be sexual.

One major reason why many older men become discouraged with sex is that they are not well prepared for the changes in sexual functioning that gradually come upon them as a result of aging. If he doesn't understand them, an aging man is liable to interpret these changes as a sign that he is losing his sexual ability. Consequently, he may become uneasy about his capacity to satisfy his sexual partner and either avoid sex altogether or become so anxious about performing well that sex is no longer enjoyable for him. But there is no reason why this should happen. If men can educate themselves so that they expect their sexual functioning to change in certain ways as they age, they should be able to derive as much enjoyment from sex as ever—perhaps even more.

One change that commonly occurs with aging is a decrease in the need and desire for ejaculation. This, like most sexual changes, usually begins between the ages of fifty and sixty, although there is a great deal of variation from one individual to another. Older men often find that they do not feel like ejaculating each time they have intercourse, even though they may be quite aroused and enjoy the intercourse experience. If a man does not feel the need for orgasm on a particular occasion, he should not try to force the ejaculation, but rather just enjoy the sensations of intercourse. Vasocongestion of the testicles during sexual arousal is not as pronounced in older men, so there should be no problem with "blue balls" as a result of not ejaculating.

This decrease in the urge for orgasm is a natural change and is not to be confused with ejaculatory inhibition. The aging man should accept this change and not try to force himself to ejaculate when he has no genuine need or desire. When ejaculation does occur, there are again differences. The older man will generally find that his ejaculation might last a shorter time than before, that his penis might contract fewer times, that semen might come out less forcefully, and that less semen might be ejaculated. Instead of ejaculation being a two-step process, consisting of the point of ejaculatory inevitability followed by the ejaculation itself, it will occur more and more as a single-stage process—that is, he will not experience the feeling of inevitability before ejaculating. Thus, sex becomes less ejaculation-oriented, but not necessarily less pleasure-oriented.

One as yet unanswered question is whether the man can actually experience an orgasm physiologically without ejaculating. What is known is that many men report that even though they did not ejaculate, they enjoyed the sexual or intercourse experience; and some even report experiencing an intensity of pleasure that they consider to be an orgasm, although it is not accompanied by ejaculation.

Another difference is that once an older man has ejaculated, he usually finds that his penis becomes flaccid much faster than it did in earlier years. This often causes older men to fear that they are losing their sexual powers and that they may not be able to achieve an erection next time. This fear may also be connected with the fact that the older man experiences a longer refractory period. That is, following ejaculation, he will not be able to achieve another erection for a period varying from several hours to a full day, while as a young man he may have been able to get a second erection in an hour or less. Such anxiety is unjustified, however. The fact that a man's sexual responses are slowing down doesn't mean that they are about to stop altogether. If he is willing to accept the new sexual pace that age imposes on him, he will find that sex can be as fully satisfying as it was before.

One definite advantage of the older man's less urgent need to ejaculate is that he far exceeds the younger man in ejaculatory control. This greater control can be utilized to delay ejaculation so that he and his partner can enjoy intercourse to the fullest. As sex becomes less ejaculation-oriented, the older man is often able to relax and become receptive to the myriad, subtle, whole-body sensations of lovemaking. In the sense that his ability to both give and receive pleasure is increased, a man may actually become a better lover as he grows older.

Along with the lessened need for ejaculation, the whole process of sexual arousal tends to be slower as a man ages. For example, while a younger man may require only seconds of stimulation before getting an erection, an older man may need several minutes or more. In addition, older men usually need more direct stimulation of the penis before becoming aroused. A young man may get an erection just from thinking about intercourse, or from seeing his partner's nude body. With older men this is much rarer, and it is usually necessary for the partner to use the stroking or rubbing motions the man finds most arousing. Once achieved, the erection of an older man is often not as full as in earlier days, but all that matters is for it to be hard enough to allow penetration. Even if the penis is not completely erect, a partner can help guide it into the vagina, and after several thrusts the strength of the erection will often increase anyway.

A woman's sexual responses change as she grows older, just as a man's do. For women, however, menopause serves as a clear milestone of physical change, whereas changes in a man's body are usually more gradual and less obvious. In addition to stopping menstruation, the aging woman generally finds that her vagina becomes somewhat smaller in size and that the vaginal walls become thinner and less elastic; the breasts and the clitoris also decrease in size. Despite these changes, a woman's body continues to be responsive to sexual stimulation. Like her male counterpart, the aging woman's response pattern is generally much the same as it was when she was younger, but somewhat slower.

For instance, it will take the older woman longer to become lubricated when she is sexually excited, and the amount of lubrication will not be as great as when she was younger. Because of this, many older couples find it helpful to use a sterile lubricating jelly such as Aller-cream or K-Y Jelly, both available without a prescription. Saliva can also serve as an excellent and perfectly safe lubricant. One common fear that aging couples have is that menopause will put an end to a woman's sexual desire. Hysterectomy (the surgical removal of the uterus) is also frequently thought of as being the death knell of a woman's sexuality. Neither of these beliefs is valid. In fact, a woman may feel freer and more sexual after she has lost her ability to reproduce since she no longer has to worry about the danger of an unwanted pregnancy.

It is apparent then that aging brings with it certain definite changes in the sexual functioning of both men and women. These changes, however, are not indications that a person's sex life is over, but rather that it is entering a new phase, taking on a new style. Sex between older people tends to be slower and gentler than in earlier years. An older man concentrates on experiencing and giving pleasure rather than turning in a good performance. He needs to be able to communicate with his partner and feel comfortable requesting specific types of stimulation, especially direct penile stimulation.

It helps if he can learn to appreciate other aspects of sex besides orgasm—open himself to the limitless possibilities of increased sensual awareness and pleasuring. In short, an older man must learn most of the principles that have been presented throughout this book if he is to continue leading an active sex life. He must learn, if he has not already done so, to be a lover rather than a stud. As he grows older, the changes in his body will help him make this adjustment, provided he accepts them. But if he fights the course of nature, he is bound to lose. Being a sexual man of seventy is different from being a sexual man of twenty. But the essence of sexuality—pleasure and sharing—is still central.

Aging itself is not an illness, but rather a natural physiological process. The more a man takes care of himself, eats well, exercises regularly, and stays in good general health, the better his body will adjust to aging and the better his sexual functioning will probably be. One mistake that many aging men make is to assume that frequent sexual contacts will wear them out or use up their sexual abilities. Older men who find that they are unable to get an erection or ejaculate on a particular occasion often decide to avoid sex for a month or two and give themselves a rest. This is definitely the wrong approach. They do not need a rest from sex. What they do need is to have sex on a regular basis. The idea that a man only has a certain number of ejaculations and that when they are used up his sex life is over is totally false. In fact, the more regular his sexual expression, the easier it is to continue functioning sexually.

By continuing to be affectionate and sensual in his relationship with his partner, by having intercourse and ejaculating regularly, an older man keeps up the self-confidence he needs to lead an active sex life.

Of course, not all older men are in good physical health, and it is well known that certain diseases, for instance, certain forms of cancer and chronic kidney dysfunction, can interfere with satisfactory sexual functioning. In fact, almost any kind of illness will tend to inhibit sexual activity, but it does not have to end it. Too often, men who have had prostate conditions, heart trouble, stroke, lung disease, diabetes, and other illnesses assume that they can no longer be sexually active. If you do have an illness, you should try to gain as full an understanding of it as possible, including its effect on your sexuality. Consult your physician, accompanied by your wife if possible, and explain that sex is an important part of your life together and that you would like to know what changes you will have to make in your sexual activities, if any. Remember, however, that some physicians have little training in sexuality and may not be very comfortable or competent discussing your sexual problems.

If you are not satisfied with the advice that your general physician gives you, the next step should be to go to a urologist. He should be able to explain clearly how your sexual functioning may be affected by your illness or by any medication you may be taking for it. If you do have an illness that places limitations on your sex life, then it is best for you to discuss these problems openly with your partner and physician. Both of you need to vent your feelings and to work together at planning your sexual activities. Even in cases where intercourse may be very limited (as in some forms of chronic diabetes), there may be other ways in which a couple can continue to provide pleasurable, sensual, and sexual experiences for each other, including oral and manual stimulation, hugging, massage—in fact, any enjoyable physical interaction.

Often, when a disease limits a man's ability to have erections, his ability to have orgasms remains unimpaired. Thus, it may still be quite pleasurable for him to continue affectionate and sexual interactions. Too many couples are willing to give up sex entirely when illness or some other physical incapacity strikes. As a culture, we are too used to thinking of sex as something just for the young, the strong, and the healthy. In fact, sexual pleasure is one of the basic constants of life. It is available to both the young and the old, the healthy and the not so healthy. A person should not give up on sex or try to convince someone else that his or her sexual days are over. Sexuality, physical affection, intimacy, communications help to make life enjoyable. A person is entitled to be sexual, whatever his age or physical condition.

In a small number of men, a decrease in testosterone level occurs between the ages of fifty-five and sixty-five that affects their ability to function sexually. These men can derive a great deal of benefit from seeing a physician and receiving testosterone replacement therapy. This is somewhat similar to the hormone replacement therapy often prescribed for women when they go through menopause.

Older couples who have sexual dysfunction problems often use their age as an excuse to avoid seeking treatment. This is an unjustified fear since therapists report a success rate of about 70 percent with couples in their fifties, sixties, and seventies. Success in sex therapy depends on the couple's commitment to each other and their desire to enjoy satisfactory sexual functioning, not on how old they are.

Karl and Trudy, for example, were in their mid-seventies when they came to me for sex therapy. Karl had owned a small chemical plant and had been actively involved in running the business until just a few years before. However, he had decided that he wanted to spend the rest of his life enjoying hobbies and activities that he had never had time for while he was working. So he sold the business and retired. The transition from active businessman to perpetual vacationer was a difficult one for Karl, and the lack of self-respect that he began to feel manifested itself as a potency problem. Karl and Trudy had resigned themselves to a life without sexual interaction until Trudy happened to confide the problem to their minister and he suggested that they consult a sex therapist. Once they accepted the idea that it was not normal for sexual functioning to stop in old age, Karl and Trudy began to make rapid progress. We used the same nondemand pleasuring exercises employed by younger couples, and their response was very positive. After a few sessions they were making love more frequently and with more pleasure than they had for the past twenty years.

So far I have been dealing only with the older married man. What about the man who is either widowed or divorced and goes through old age without a marital partner? While many of these men may find other partners, a good number face the problem of feeling sexual urges yet having no one to interact with sexually. One valid outlet in such cases is masturbation. Our culture tends to view masturbation as appropriate, if at all, mainly for boys and young men, but it can be an important means of sexual expression for the older man as well. And no one should feel guilty about using masturbation as a sexual outlet. Many older men (including well-functioning married men) do, in fact, masturbate, and this activity is just as normal and healthy for them as it is for any young man.

It is also quite common for older single men to remarry. Because women, on the average, have a greater life expectancy than men, the number of women in proportion to men increases steadily according to age. Therefore, an older man who wishes to remarry generally finds no shortage of available partners. Those who do remarry, however, often make the mistake of seeing their second marriage as a replacement for the old one. In establishing a new personal and sexual relationship, it is important to view it as something new and unique, rather than comparing it with the first marriage. Since it is a new relationship, you will need to be aware of the preferences and feelings of the new partner, and be able to communicate your own needs and desires. Don't assume that the things that worked in the last relationship will work in this one. You will need to explore, be spontaneous, and communicate so that you can establish a satisfying sexual relationship.

The attempt to set an age limit to sexuality is both unrealistic and unjust. We never outgrow sex, nor does a healthy man or woman ever entirely lose his or her ability to function sexually. Even where physical disability is present, the need for sexual expression remains, and this need should be acknowledged and acted upon. The couple who remains together and is able to function sexually in old age is extremely fortunate. They should not feel self-conscious about their continuing desire for each other, but rather feel proud of keeping their relationship so vital and take advantage of it to the fullest. If they understand and accept the unique characteristics of sex in the later years, they may be surprised to find their sexual relationship becoming more enjoyable, sensitive, and tender than it was in their earlier years.

EPILOGUE

WE LIVE IN A TIME of rapidly changing values. Many of the ideas and attitudes that were taken for granted as recently as ten years ago are no longer valid today. Attitudes toward sexuality are among those that have undergone the greatest change. Men used to be very certain of their place in the world. They occupied the most important positions; they were the decision-makers, the leaders. Even in the domestic realm, the man was supreme. "Every man a king in his own household," went the slogan. And this extended to sexual relationships as well. Men were considered the ones who had a greater need for sex, who had a greater knowledge of sex, and who enjoyed sex more. They initiated sexual encounters when it pleased them to do so, and the woman was expected to follow their lead. Even the sexual position that enjoyed the greatest popularity—the male superior—stressed the dominance of men over women.

Now all this has changed. There are holdouts, of course—both men and women who cling to the double standard, who want the old male-centered domestic monarchy to endure. But clearly these traditionalists are fighting a losing battle. Sexual equality is obviously one of the guiding principles of today's world and will continue to be in the future. In business, politics, interpersonal relations, and in sex, women are demanding the autonomy that has for so long been denied them. Eventually, sexual equality will be an accomplished fact.

As men, I think we ought to rejoice that such a change has finally come about. The double standard was never really in our interests anyway. It tended to stress what was different in the sexual responses of men and women rather than what was similar. There *are* differences, of course, but none so drastic as those the double standard would have us believe in. Under the double standard, we were led to believe that a man's only interest in sex was intercourse and orgasm—"getting your rocks off." Everything else was just frills. Women, on the other hand, were supposed to care primarily about gentle caresses, kisses on the neck, "moonlight and flowers." It was as if men and women were two entirely different species—each with its own mating habits.

Today, however, with the decline of the double standard and the increase in scientific research into human sexual behavior and response, it is becoming increasingly clear that men and women have very similar sexual and emotional needs. Men are finding that gentleness, sensual awareness, and intimacy greatly enhance their sexual response. Women are finding that their need for direct genital stimulation, their capacity for orgasm, and just plain lust are as great as men's. Some men find the idea of a woman who is as sexually active and responsive as themselves somewhat threatening. A far better attitude, however, would be to celebrate the fact that men and women, after so many years of alienation, have, so to speak, finally found each other. Having discovered that their sexual needs and desires are so similar, they can now collaborate on finding the best ways of fulfilling them.

I hope that this book will represent a step toward bringing about that collaboration. While many recent publications have been devoted to awakening women to the aspects of *their* sexuality which have for too long been ignored, there has been a paucity of similar works directed at men. My aim has been both to provide accurate information on male sexuality and to influence men to become more sensually aware, more responsible for their own sexuality, more able to communicate with their partners about sexual matters, more conscious of the part that sex plays throughout their lives, and more able to integrate their sexuality with their personal and emotional lives. Such changes may seem like a lot to ask for, and yet, in a sense, they are not since there are few areas in which there are such powerful incentives for change.

It is in a man's best interests—any man's—to make the transition from sexual machine to sexual person. By doing so, he can increase not only his sexual pleasure but also his general level of satisfaction with himself, his spouse, his family, with life in general. It is time we realize what a positive element our sexuality can be and how we can use it to make our existence a much more rewarding experience.

APPENDIX:
How to Find a Therapist

As I STATED at the outset, this book is not meant to be a therapy book. Many men are reluctant to consult a professional counselor or therapist, feeling that to do so is a sign of some kind of "craziness," inadequacy, or weakness. But I believe that it is actually a sign of psychological strength in that you are able to accept the fact that there is a problem and to make a commitment to change and growth.

The mental health field is confusing to many people. There are many approaches to counseling and therapy, and a number of different types of professionals in the field. In sorting this out, your first concern should be to find someone who is professionally competent in your problem area. Psychotherapy encompasses various techniques, and it is offered by several different groups of professionals, including psychologists, psychiatrists, sex therapists, social workers, marriage counselors, and pastoral counselors. But of less importance than the particular label of the practitioner is his competency in your special area of need.

In obtaining a referral for a therapist, one of the best resources is to call a local professional organization (psychological association, mental health association, or mental health clinic). Another method is to ask for a referral from a family physician, minister, or even friends who might have some information on the therapist's areas of competence.

Many people have health insurance which provides coverage for mental health services, and thus can afford the services of a private practitioner. Those who do not have either the financial resources or the insurance could consider a city, county, or state mental health clinic or perhaps a university or medical school mental health outpatient clinic—all of which usually provide services on a sliding-fee scale (that is, the fee is based on your ability to pay).

In choosing a specific therapist, be assertive enough to ask about their credentials and areas of expertise, as well as fees. A competent professional therapist will usually be open to discussing this with you. Be especially diligent in discussing credentials (university degrees, licensing) with people who call themselves personal counselors, marriage therapists, or sex counselors, since there are some poorly qualified persons (and some out-and-out quacks) working in any field, and a practitioner who has not been educated in a formal degree program is more likely to be deficient.

If you have a problem that deals principally with marriage or family issues, you could write the American Association of Marriage and Family Counselors, 225 Yale Avenue, Claremont, California 91711, for a list of certified marriage and family counselors in your area. If you have a specific behavior problem such as phobia, lack of assertion, overeating, alcoholism, or sexual anxiety you could write the Behavior Therapy and Research Society, c/o Eastern Pennsylvania Psychiatric Institute, Henry Avenue, Philadelphia, Pennsylvania 19129 for a list of certified behavior therapists in your area. If you are specifically interested in sex therapy, you could write the American Association of Sex Educators, Counselors, and Therapists at 5010 Wisconsin, N.W., Washington, D.C. 20016 for a list of certified sex therapists in your area.

Do not hesitate to talk to two or three therapists before deciding on a specific one with whom to work. You need to be aware of your degree of comfort with the therapist, of whether you feel you can relate to him, and whether his assessment of the problem and approach to treatment make sense to you. However, once you begin therapy, give it a chance to be helpful. There are few "miracle cures," and change requires your commitment and is a gradual and often difficult process. It is not like going to a medical doctor, who might prescribe pills and tell you exactly what to do. The role of the therapist is as a facilitator and consultant rather than one who decides upon a change for you. Psychotherapy requires effort, but it can be well worth it in terms of changed attitudes, feelings, and behavior and making your life more functional and pleasurable.

SUGGESTED READING

THE SEXUAL REVOLUTION of the past decade has brought with it a deluge of books on virtually every aspect of sex. Some of them are quite good, but unfortunately many more have poor information and reflect a performance-oriented view of sexuality. The following are, in my opinion, some of the best of the recent books published for the general reader.

Andry, Andrew, and Steven Schiepp. *How Babies are Made*. New York: Time-Life, 1968. A fine book for children under five describing conception, basic sexual anatomy, and birth. Done very simply and directly.

Barbach, Lonnie. *For Yourself: The Fulfillment of Female Sexuality*. Garden City, N.Y.: Doubleday and Co., 1975. An excellent book on female sexuality that focuses on the development of the preorgasmic women's group approach. The role of masturbation is highlighted, as well as the importance of the woman feeling responsible for her own sexual response.

Belliveau, Fred, and Lin Richter. *Understanding Human Sexual Inadequacy*. New York: Bantam Books, 1970. In my view, the best book for the lay public describing the research and clinical work of Masters and Johnson —very readable and very descriptive.

Boston Women's Health Collective. *Our Bodies, Ourselves*. New York: Simon and Schuster, 1975. The second edition of this book provides a view of many aspects of female sexuality. The major emphasis is on self-knowledge and self-help approaches for women.

Biller, Henry, and Dennis Meredith. *Father Power*. New York: Anchor Press, 1975. A fairly good and readable book that describes various components of the male's role as a father. There is a special emphasis on the influence the father can exert on the child's academic achievement and sense of competence.

Butler, Robert N., and Myrna I. Lewis. *Sex after Sixty: A Guide for Men and Women for Their Later Years*. New York: Harper and Row, 1975. This book provides a real breakthrough in the area of sex and aging. An exceptional book, covering a range of issues—not only sexual but also in regard to relationships and practical matters. There is a particularly well-thought-out chapter on the person without a partner.

Comfort, Alex. *The Joy of Sex*. New York: Crown, 1973. A sophisticated book reviewing a range of advanced sexual techniques and using very attractive illustrations. A fine book for liberated, experimenting couples, it is probably not as valuable for couples who first need to achieve a basic sense of comfort with their sexuality.

Demarest, Robert J., and John J. Sciarra. *Conception, Birth and Contraception: A Visual Presentation*. New York: McGraw-Hill, 1976. Beautiful and explicit illustrations showing the basic processes. This book should give you a greater understanding of and comfort with this aspect of female functioning and sexuality.

Downing, George. *The Massage Book*. New York: Random House, 1972. A very specific, detailed book on the art of massage, with both a theoretical and a practical emphasis.

Ellis, Albert. *Sex and the Liberated Man*. New York: Lyle-Stuart, 1976. A book written chiefly for the single male, with heavy emphasis on enjoying one's sexuality and not being caught in guilt traps.

Gordon, Sol. *Let's Make Sex a Household Word*. New York: John Day, 1975. A rather liberal and liberated book for parents which emphasizes an open view of sexuality in a family. The role of the parents as primary sex educators of their children is the central theme.

———. *The Sexual Adolescent*. Belmont: Buxburg Press, 1973. A very liberal book written for parents with the goal of helping them to understand and accept their adolescent's emerging sexuality. Emphasizes the positive role of masturbation, and discusses use of contraception and dealing with VD.

Guttmacher, Alan. *Pregnancy, Birth, and Family Planning*. New York: Viking Press, 1973. A basic source book for information on the complex field of contraception and family planning.

Heiman, Julia, Leslie LoPiccolo, and Joseph LoPiccolo. *Becoming Orgasmic: A Sexual Growth Program for Women*. Englewood Cliffs, N. J.: Prentice-Hall, 1976. This is probably the best book on female sexuality. There is special emphasis on developing sexual awareness via use of masturbation, and three excellent chapters deal with the role of the male partner.

Hite, Shere. *The Hite Report*. New York: McMillan, 1976. Although this is not a particularly good scientific study, it does provide a lot of information concerning emerging views of female sexuality. The 3,000 women covered in Ms. Hite's survey provide a frank and open discussion, and their comments regarding masturbation, clitoral stimulation, and orgasmic response are of particular interest.

Hunt, Morton, *Sexual Behavior in the 1970's*. New York: Playboy Press, 1974. A limited and somewhat biased sample, but it does report very interesting changes in the way Americans view premarital, marital, and extramarital sex. The author also reports on other topics such as homosexuality, oral sex, and anal sex.

Komarovsky, Mirra. *Dilemmas of Masculinity: A Study of College Youth*. New York: W. W. Norton, 1976. A thought-provoking look at the views of college males regarding masculinity, women, and sex. Special emphasis on the changing roles and attitudes of young males.

Krantzler, Mel. *Creative Divorce: A New Opportunity for Personal Growth*. New York: M. Evans, 1973. This is a fine book for males who are coping with a divorce. Very specifically, the author outlines the common traps that males who consider themselves "failures" fall into.

Lieberman, E. James, and Ellen Peck. *Sex and Birth Control: A Guide for the Young*. New York: Thomas Y. Crowell, 1973. A very clear and readable book for high school and college-age readers, this explores in detail the responsible use of birth control.

McCarthy, Barry, Mary Ryan, and Fred Johnson. *Sexual Awareness: A Practical Approach*. San Francisco: Boyd and Fraser, 1975. A specific behavioral book emphasizing concepts and techniques for developing a pleasurable, sexually functional relationship. The exercises described in *What You Still Don't Know about Male Sexuality* are presented in more detail in this book.

McCary, James L. *Freedom and Growth in Marriage*. New York: John Wiley, 1975. Basically a textbook, but one of the best books written on marriage. Presents a positive view of marriage and incorporates a host of specific ideas and suggestions.

————. *Human Sexuality*. Second Edition. New York: D. Van Nostrand, 1973. This textbook, used in college courses in human sexuality, provides a comprehensive overview of all aspects of human sexual behavior.

————. *Sexual Myths and Fallacies*. New York: Van Nostrand, 1971. A very readable book describing the most common as well as some rather unusual sex myths. A quick way to check your sexual knowledge.

Masters, William, and Virginia Johnson. *The Pleasure Bond*. Boston: Little, Brown, 1974. The only book by these eminent sex researchers that is oriented to the lay public. Discusses sexual commitment and communication. The first and last chapters are particularly good.

Money, John, and P. Tucker. *Sexual Signatures: On Being a Man or a Woman*. Boston: Little, Brown, 1972. A book for the general reader that summarizes a great deal of technical research on the most important variables in understanding gender development.

Pomeroy, Wardell. *Boys and Sex*. New York: Delacorte Press, 1968. This classic is still probably the best book for understanding the development of male sexuality during childhood. Highly recommended for parents of boys. There is a companion book called *Girls and Sex*.

Scheingold, L., and Nathaniel Wagner. *Sound Sex and the Aging Heart*. New York: Human Sciences Press, 1974. Sex does not have to end because of a heart condition. This book describes in detail how to cope with a heart condition, and some options for couples for continued sexual functioning. Excellent chapters on heart functioning and effects of aging.

Steinmann, Ann, and D. Fox. *The Male Dilemma*. New York: Aronson, 1974. This book examines the effects of sex roles on males and females. It is perhaps the most thoughtful and helpful of the books on changing male roles and attitudes.

Tripp, C. A. *The Homosexual Matrix*. New York: McGraw-Hill, 1975. A comprehensive and complex book about the multitude of homosexual roles and relationships. Especially interesting insights on homosexuality as a social phenomenon.

Weinberg, M., and C. Williams. *Male Homosexuals: Their Problems and Adaptations*. London: Oxford University, 1974. A scholarly but readable book that sets forth the view that homosexuals should accept themselves with pride and dignity. Describes various strategies homosexuals use to cope with societal prejudices.

INDEX